Y0-CKO-310

978.8
Hen

105564

Henderson.
Colorado.

The Library
Nazareth College of Rochester, N. Y.

DISCARDED

COLORADO: SHORT STUDIES OF ITS PAST AND PRESENT

BY

JUNIUS HENDERSON
E. B. RENAUD
COLIN B. GOODYKOONTZ
JOE MILLS
JAMES F. WILLARD
H. M. BARRETT
IRENE PETTIT MCKEEHAN

WITH INTRODUCTION BY
GEORGE NORLIN

AMS PRESS
NEW YORK

Reprinted from the edition of 1927, Boulder
First AMS EDITION published 1969
Manufactured in the United States of America

Library of Congress Catalogue Card Number: 73-100508

AMS PRESS, INC.
New York, N.Y. 10003

Table of Contents

Chapter		Page
	Introduction	ix
1.	The Prehistoric Peoples of Colorado	1
2.	The Indians of Colorado	23
3.	The Exploration and Settlement of Colorado	42
4.	Early Range Days	91
5.	The Gold Rush and After	101
6.	Education in Colorado	122
7.	Colorado in Literature	141

INTRODUCTION

The Semi-centennial publications of the University represent a departure from custom in that, while they are the result of careful research, they are addressed, not to technical scholars, but to the general public, and primarily to the people of Colorado.

They are, therefore, appropriately dedicated to the citizens of this State, in the desire that they may be of value to those whom it is the duty of the University to serve and that they may stand also as a token to them of a sense of gratitude in the University to a commonwealth which in the course of a half-century has built up with generous foresight in the shadow of these "delectable mountains" an institution where scholars are privileged to share in and contribute to the intellectual life.

The first three volumes of this series deal with the physical endowments of our State—its material setting. It is the purpose of this volume to touch upon the human side of its history—its spiritual quality. It does not pretend to be in this respect complete. Certain aspects of the development of our civilization have had to be neglected for the time being. But although this volume is modest in its scope and execution, it is hoped that it has not failed to suggest that the human story of Colorado has had thus far a distinctive character.

Mystery veils, and will forever veil, the prehistoric people who long ago abandoned their dwellings in our cañon walls for what life or death we know not. Veiled from us hardly less is the soul of the nomad tribes who within the memory of men still living roamed our plains or encamped in our mountain parks; even more than the cliff-dwellers, whose monuments we still have and cherish, they have vanished from the scene and become phantoms of romance. When we come to the explorations and settlements of our own race, we are on more realistic ground. We possess at least bare chronicles of what took place; but for this period, not less than for the undocumented past, the inner truth of what happened calls upon the creative imagination. The settlement of this western country is one of the great epic adventures of man. Every caravan which dragged its way across the plains to the fulfillment or the frustration of its hopes lacked only its Homer to become an *Iliad* or an *Odyssey*. Not alone the lust for riches to be found in mine or land lured the early settlers on, but the longing for adventure in the splendid setting of these mountains. Walt Whitman, when he dwelt for a time among us, voiced a sense of kinship beteeen his own adventuring temperament and the

> "Spirit that formed this scene,
> These tumbled rock-piles grim and red,
> These reckless heaven-ambitious peaks,
> These gorges, turbulent-clear streams, this naked freshness."

Something of this feeling, now more now less, though for the most part inarticulate, has set this State apart, both for the earlier and the later comers to this region, as a refuge from the dead levels of existence—a land of romance.

GEORGE NORLIN.

Chapter 1

THE PREHISTORIC PEOPLES OF COLORADO

Junius Henderson

Long before the dawn of the Christian Era the inhabitants of Southwestern Colorado and adjacent territory had developed an unique culture far removed from a state of savagery. Centuries before Columbus landed upon American soil that ancient culture had reached its zenith, and, so far as Colorado is concerned, probably had passed away. When the early, intrepid Spanish explorers reached New Mexico and Colorado in their wanderings, the great cliff dwellings of the Mesa Verde region had been abandoned and were fast falling into ruin. When Europeans first examined the extensive and ancient ruins of the Southwestern States, and the varied and highly decorated pottery and other articles of human manufacture were revealed by the excavator's pick and shovel, four questions were at once asked, which even to this day, after many years of exploration, excavation and study, remain only partially and vaguely answered, namely: Who? When? Whence? Whither?

While these problems are vast and very complex, they are not altogether insoluble, and considerable progress has been made in their elucidation. A widespread and rapidly growing public interest in the subject indicates the desirability of their early solution. The days of haphazard, uncontrolled, unscientific excavation of these archeological storehouses, for the mere purpose of collecting pottery and other artifacts, has passed. Such work should be conducted only under the direction of trained archeologists, capable of making important observations and fully aware of the complexity of the problems to be solved. There are literally thousands of prehistoric dwelling sites in that region yet to be explored, and better methods of investigation are constantly being devised, the outgrowth of experience. Hence if larger funds can be obtained for the financing of such exploration, there is reason for a strong hope that some or all of these questions may ultimately be answered with a considerable degree of certainty.

The Environment

The influence of the environment upon the development of the ancient cultures of the Southwest is quite obvious. It is a region of scant rainfall, not favorable to the support of a large population without a great amount of labor expended in the production of food. Native plants and animals could afford but meager sustenance for small groups of people. Agriculture was imperative for larger communities, and was necessarily carried on under discouraging circumstances.

The prehistoric inhabitants of the Southwest, including Southwestern Colorado, Southern Utah, New Mexico and Arizona, possessed hardy varieties of maize, or corn, as it is better known to modern Americans. They had also squashes, gourds, beans, and, in the warmer areas, cotton. In the valleys the seepage water made it possible to raise these crops in many places without irrigation. In other places reservoirs and canals for irrigation purposes were constructed. Even on the tops of some mesas fair crops could be grown in favorable seasons. The primitive farmer did not raise crops for the market, in order to obtain money with which to buy other needful things, pay taxes and build homes. There were no large manufacturing cities or non-productive populations to be supplied. Each community had but to feed itself. Under the drive of necessity the people became adept at so cropping their discouraging land as to get the best results with the primitive means at their disposal. There is evidence that they held surplus crops of favorable seasons in storage for less productive years. At an early period the need for the storage of grain led to the construction of pits in caverns under overhanging cliffs, where they were protected from adverse weather. These Basket Makers' storage pits may have suggested the pit dwellings, which long preceded the pueblos and cliff houses.

The occupants of the prehistoric cliff houses, pueblos and pre-pueblo structures of Southwestern Colorado and adjacent territory were essentially agriculturists. Indeed, the very foundation and inspiration of their cultures was the possession of maize. Game was probably at all times too scarce to afford more than a very small proportion of the food required. Permanent habitations of agriculturists were not favorable to the development of a race of hunters. A large population must, in order to live by hunting, be nomadic. The region is far from the former range of great herds of bison. Deer and other animals were not sufficiently abundant to greatly influence the food habits of the people. The large ancient refuse heaps exhibit a comparative scarcity of the bones of large mammals. Leather objects are not at all abundant and are mostly from the skins of smaller animals, though buckskin thongs and fragments are not absent. Rabbits were probably about as abundant as now, but more difficult to get with primitive weapons, though doubtless the people possessed considerable skill in the use of traps and bows and arrows. Even these animals would soon have become scarce if large numbers of people had been dependent upon them for food. Probably the chief source of a meat supply was wild turkeys, though there is evidence that they may have domesticated these birds and they certainly kept some of them in captivity. They had no other domestic animals except the dog, which may have been used to some extent for food, as it certainly was by many other American aborigines. They had no horses, cattle, or sheep until these were introduced by the Spaniards. Some fishes may have been obtained in the few perennial streams, but they must have been quite negligible as a source of food for large communities. Furthermore, some of the prehistoric people may have had scruples against the use of fishes for food, growing out of their mythology, as some groups of Southwestern Indians are said to have at present.

This brief account of the environment suggests the chief reason the cultural development of the people took a direction so different from that followed by the development of the Indians of the Great Plains. The plains Indians were to a great extent dependent upon the large herds of bison, which they followed to and fro in migration. They indulged in long hunting expeditions. They cured the meat of the bison for a supply of food to last between hunts. Bison skins provided garments and tepees for shelter from storms and cold weather. Little need for them to engage extensively in agriculture; little encouragement for them to construct permanent houses; no necessity for conserving water. Their need was for easily transported shelters and equipment. Physical labor was not their idea of a happy existence. Hunting was sport. Their life was not conducive to the development of the potter's art. Pottery was heavy and inconvenient to carry about and not much needed by them. The constant use of weapons encouraged warlike proclivities, rather than the arts of peace.

The cultural differences between the Indians of the plains and the inhabitants of the ancient structures of Southwestern Colorado is environmental, not psychological. The agricultural life forced upon the latter by their environment led them far from warlike emotions. There are indications that in the Pre-Pueblo period of the Southwest the people had little to fear from enemies. Their building sites were not chosen and their structures were not built with a view to ease of defense. Later, the depredations of marauding nomadic tribes drove the farmers to the cliff caverns and the edges of the mesas for protection, and led gradually to the evolution of the more easily-defended cliff house and pueblo types of construction.

Pottery, too, one of the most important and distinctive elements of the various Southwestern cultures, was a direct product of the environment. Furthermore, it represents the highest development of technique, not exceeded even by the manufacture of beads and other purely ornamental objects, though the latter, having no utilitarian purpose, may possibly be considered higher in the scale of aesthetic development.

Water was scarce. Vessels which would hold water were needed in quantity for carrying it from the springs and storing it, and for culinary purposes. Fixed habitations enabled them to make and use a great variety of pots, bowls, jars and other earthenware, such as could not well have been carried about by wandering tribes with only the most primitive means of transportation. The fact that the vessels were not merely for temporary use, but could be kept and used for many years, encouraged the development of decorative art, which in the course of centuries reached a high plane.

So far as known, Colorado and Utah constitute the northern limit of the portion of America occupied by ruins of great buildings of stone and adobe, though southward they extend through Mexico and Central America and into South America to Peru.

Culture Areas

Archeologically the Southwestern United States may be divided into rather distinct areas. These are not arbitrary, though the cultures of various areas overlap to some extent at their margins and their study is more or less complicated by ancient migrations and interchange of pottery. On the whole the fact of these natural divisions is well established.

The San Juan Area

One of the most important of the major divisions is the San Juan area, in the region of the "Four Corners," the only place in the United States where four states meet at a common point—Colorado, Utah, Arizona, and New Mexico. It includes the streams, mostly of intermittent flow, which drain into the San Juan River. It appears to have been, as Kidder has aptly expressed it, "the breeding ground for many of the basic traits of Southwestern culture."

This plateau, gashed by numerous canyons and dry washes and not well watered, furnished a difficult environment, if climatic and other conditions were the same in prehistoric times as now. Nevertheless the ancient inhabitants there attained the highest achievements of their history. The river itself is a perennial stream, but most of its tributaries carry little or no running water except in the spring run-off or after violent summer rains. There are, however, many springs, in the neighborhood of which ancient ruins are usually found, though many others are far from any known source of water.

The Mesa Verde District

The larger cultural areas are subdivided into smaller districts, each having its own cultural elements, partly related to, but exhibiting definite deviations from the general types of the larger area. The Mesa Verde subdivision of the San Juan area is one of the most striking, interesting, distinct and best-known archeological districts in the southwestern part of the United States. Examples of pottery of Mesa Verde types are more generally distributed in public museums and private collections than any other types of prehistoric American pottery.

Mesa Verde is situated in Montezuma County, Southwestern Colorado. Here a large area, including some of the finest examples of cliff houses, has been set aside by the national government as Mesa Verde National Park. The Mesa Verde cultural district, however, extends in all directions far beyond the confines of the mesa itself. Its pottery is found as far south as the Chaco Canyon, New Mexico, in some portions of Pueblo Bonito. Vessels found in the great ruin at Aztec, New Mexico, and the Broomfield ruin, in the same state, indicate that they were occupied by people belonging to the Mesa Verde group after their abandonment by the original Chaco inhabitants. This may have been coincident with a southward migration at the time of the final abandonment of the Mesa Verde region, though, if so, it remains to be demonstrated.

Characteristic features of pure Mesa Verde construction are block-stone masonry, perhaps chiefly due to the character of the available building material, and the use of square, rectangular and D-shaped towers. The character of these towers, the loop-holes that pierce their walls and the strategic positions they occupy, have led to the designation "watch towers," which likely correctly expresses their purpose. Though some of the large ruins of the district are pueblos situated on the level uplands and along the rims of canyons, the great majority are cliff houses occupying great caverns in the canyon walls.

A very characteristic element in the pottery of the district is the flat-bottomed, decorated, black-on-white mug, with nearly straight sides converging slightly toward the top, and with a broad, flat handle extending from just below the rim nearly to the base, reminding one of a rather squat German beer stein. Examples of this type are numerous in collections. A great many other forms of black-on-white ware and many very fine corrugated jars are found in the ruins.

Perhaps on Mesa Verde this culture reached its highest development. There are the finest and best-known examples of cliff houses, including Cliff Palace and Spruce Tree House. Many excellent photographs of the former and some of the latter have been published in the technical literature of archeology, as well as in popular magazines.

Government roads have recently made Mesa Verde accessible

to the public and it is annually visited by rapidly increasing numbers of tourists. The widespread and growing interest in the subject warrants increased expenditures in the effort to solve all the various problems and make known the facts as definitely as possible.

The Montezuma Valley

The general cultural elements of this district are similar to those of Mesa Verde, but much less work has been done there and the region is not so well known.

The La Plata-Mancos Divide

Morris' report, based upon two seasons' excavations conducted by him under the joint auspices of the University of Colorado and the American Museum of Natural History, has made known some of the important facts of this district, which lies north of east from Mesa Verde. Many ruins occupying the tops of mesas are very different from the pueblos and cliff houses, not only in construction, but also in the character of the pottery they yield. They were one-storied buildings, composed of aggregates of small rooms, partly below the surface of the ground. Some of the pits were plastered. Others were lined with stone slabs set on edge, strongly suggestive of derivation from the stone-lined storage pits of an earlier period in other parts of the southwest. The walls above ground were composed of rows of poles set upright and plastered with a heavy coat of mud. Owing to their flimsy construction and ravages of the weather for many centuries, only small remnants of the walls are found in the excavations.

The pottery from these dwelling sites is very diversified, but quite inferior to that of the cliff houses, from which it differs in color, form and texture. The decorations of the painted ware are crudely conceived and executed, and the true corrugated ware of later types is absent. There are excellent reasons for the conclusion that these pit-slab-pole-and-mud structures antedate the cliff houses and pueblos of the San Juan area. Indeed, it is not improbable that they antedate even the Pre-Pueblo period, and should be considered a late phase of the Post-Basket Maker period.

The Pagosa-Piedra District

The archeology of this district, situated east of Mesa Verde, has been in part made known by the reports of Jeancon and Roberts, based upon excavations under their direction for the Colorado State Museum and Denver University. They recognize six types of house construction, probably representing as many stages in the development of the culture of the district, as follows:

1. Pit houses, semi-subterranean, plastered.
2. Pit houses with cobblestone walls.
3. Pit houses with cobblestone walls and horizontal slabs above the cobblestones.
4. Single-room structures above ground, cobblestones for foundations, horizontal stone slabs for remainder of walls.
5. Small structures of from three to eight rooms, otherwise like No. 4.
6. Large pueblos.

With the development of construction from the more ancient pit houses of type No. 1, through successive stages to the large pueblos, they trace also the development of pottery from very crude ware to quite elaborate types, though ceramic art here at its very best did not equal that of Mesa Verde. The whole prehistoric culture seems to have been a purely local development, not introduced from other regions.

Other Districts in Colorado

Aside from the Southwestern part of the State, but little is known of the archeology of Colorado. Probably nomadic hunting tribes wandered over the state before even the Basket Maker period, and continued this desultory occupation throughout subsequent time down to the middle of the nineteenth century. Tribes living under such conditions and establishing no permanent habitations could leave very little evidence of their history. Stone implements of various kinds are generally distributed over the whole region, though more abundant at some localities than others, but it cannot be determined what, if any, proportion of them may be prehistoric.

Mr. H. N. McConnell, of Boulder, has placed in the University of Colorado Museum quite a number of fragments of pottery found by him at White Rock, in Boulder County. Dr. A. V. Kidder has examined and identified them as belonging to the Nebraska earth-lodge culture.

There are very persistent rumors of ancient dwellings in Northwestern Colorado, which should be carefully investigated.

ARCHEOLOGICAL CHRONOLOGY OF THE SOUTHWEST

The most important recent advance in Southwestern archeology is the definite establishment of chronological sequence of cultures of the region, especially in the types of pottery and architecture. While there was abundant evidence in support of the hypothesis that certain crude pottery is older than the finer ware and represents the beginning of ceramic art in the Southwest, definite proof was long lacking. Such proof has now been in a large measure obtained, though there are still some gaps in the sequence to be filled. Many sites are now known to have been occupied successively by people representing different stages of cultural evolution. This has been demonstrated by digging deep beneath the later ruins and through to the bottoms of great rubbish heaps, carefully studying each stratum and keeping separate the objects obtained therefrom. It was thus found that the walls of one type of building, associated with certain types of pottery and other artifacts, were superimposed upon ruins of an earlier period, associated with pottery of different aspect, and in some cases this earlier type upon a still older type. In the refuse heaps of sites which have been long and repeatedly occupied, the successive occupancies are well established by difference in the pottery at different levels. By comparing the records at different sites it is found that the different kinds of pottery, sandals and other manufactured articles represent widespread stages in development. The principal stages have been differentiated thus, beginning with the earliest yet definitely recognized:

Basket Maker.
Post-Basket Maker.
Pre-Pueblo.
Pueblo.
Historical.

Various substages are also recognized, but space does not permit their discussion in this article.

The Basket Maker Period

The first people to leave recognizable evidence of their former existence in the Southwest, so far as now known, were the Basket Makers. Their dwelling-sites have been reported from limited areas in New Mexico, Utah, Arizona and Colorado. This culture perhaps reached its highest development in the San Juan area. It is not known to have extended into the Rio Grande Valley.

Basket Maker remains have been found directly beneath remains of the Pueblo period, leaving do doubt that it is older. Such remains have not yet been found definitely beneath remains of the Post-Basket Maker period, but other evidence amounts almost to proof that it had priority.

As no house ruins assignable to this period are known, it is highly probable that these people lived in temporary habitations constructed of perishable material, possibly resembling the modern hogans of the Southwest. This accords with the theoretical natural course of the evolution of architecture. They did, however, construct pits for the storage of grain, usually slab-lined, situated in caverns in the cliffs. The pits were used also as graves, perhaps secondarily. Besides "mummies", or desiccated bodies wrapped in fur-string blankets, the graves yield many other articles that differ from the most nearly allied objects of other cultures.

The Basket Makers possessed the atl-atl, or throwing stick, an ingenious contrivance for extending the reach of the arm and thus adding to the force with which the darts, four or five feet long, could be thrown. They did not possess the bow and arrow, a very significant fact in the consideration of their relation to the later Pueblo culture. Had the two cultures coexisted, it is inconceivable that the Basket Makers would have failed to adopt so useful a weapon as the bow and arrow, to replace the primitive atl-atl.

The Basket Makers made fur-string cloth, used extensively for burial robes, not feather-string cloth, such as is found in the Pueblo and Cliff Dweller ruins. This is another significant fact. Was it because the wild turkey had not yet arrived in the region, or merely that the Basket Makers had not learned to strip the webs from the shafts of large turkey feathers and use them for wrapping the heavy cord before weaving it into robes? A narrow strip of rabbit skin is a more simple form of wrapper, more easily obtained and applied to the cord; hence would naturally have been the first to be used

Without a loom, the Basket Makers acquired great skill in the manufacture of large twined-woven bags and sandals, the latter with square, fringed toes, unlike those of any later period. They had but one variety of maize, while several varieties are found in the pueblos and cliff dwellings. Their pottery is scarcely worthy of the name, consisting of the crudest sort of unbaked clay vessels.

The distinctive element which has given to this culture its name is the abundance, excellence and variety of *coiled* baskets. As pottery-making advanced during subsequent periods, basket-making rapidly declined.

The cranial problem in the Southwest is an exceedingly interesting one, whose solution would go far toward solving some other problems. Complications have arisen in the past by failure to keep separate the skulls obtained from different levels in the excavations, just as pottery and other things were mingled before it was realized that different levels might represent different cultural stages. The Basket Makers had long skulls (dolichocephalic), which were undeformed. The Post-Basket Makers' skulls were also undeformed. The skulls of the Pueblos and Cliff Dwellers, on the other hand, were shorter in proportion to their width (brachycephalic), and were deformed posteriorily, the result of carrying the infants on hard cradle-boards before the skulls had thickened and become firm. Whether this should be interpreted to mean that the later inhabitants were of a different race is not altogether certain, as it is not known just how much effect the deformation has had upon the general shape of the skull, but it is hard to believe that the radical difference is due entirely to artificial deformation as a result of the introduction of the hard cradle-board. From the evidence at hand it seems likely that after the Post-Basket Maker period there was an invasion of people from another region, who brought with them the bow and arrow and some other elements of a different culture in its primitive stages. This may account for the difference in skulls.

Some fine examples of Basket Maker material may be seen

in the University of Colorado Museum, but they are from Canyon del Muerto, Arizona, not from Colorado.

THE POST-BASKET MAKER PERIOD

Remains of this culture have been found definitely beneath the Pre-Pueblo culture of Arizona, therefore representing an earlier stage. It has not yet been observed actually superimposed upon Basket Maker material, but from other evidences there is scarcely a doubt that it is earlier and developed from the Basket Maker culture. It is characterized by the presence of pit-houses, crude pottery, much better than the rude vessels of the Basket Makers, and excellent twined-woven sandals with unfringed toes. These people did not possess feather-string cloth, cotton or the bow and arrow, but did possess fur-string cloth and their skulls were undeformed, in all these respects resembling the Basket Makers and differing from the people of the Pre-Pueblo and Pueblo periods. The pit houses may have evolved from the storage cists of the preceding period.

This period was a long one, apparently marked by a steady evolution of the arts. So far as positively known, this culture was confined to Arizona, but in view of the distribution of the preceding and succeeding cultures and their relationships, this does not seem at all likely, and there is excellent reason for the belief that it extended into Colorado.

During two seasons Dr. Earl H. Morris excavated sites in the LaPlata-Mancos divide district, for the University of Colorado Museum and the American Museum of Natural History, obtaining much pottery and other material apparently representing a late phase of the Post-Basket Maker culture. Furthermore, Nordenskiold reported from the Step House, on Mesa Verde, a sandal with concave toe, unfringed, of characteristic Post-Basket Maker type. Dr. Kidder has suggested also that the "earth lodges" of Mesa Verde may belong to this period. This is a very interesting and promising subject, and further investigation may produce important results.

THE PRE-PUEBLO PERIOD

The Pre-Pueblo period witnessed the introduction of cotton and the bow and arrow into the Southwest, and a great advance in agriculture, architecture and ceramic art. Rudimentary subterranean kivas made their appearance. Turkeys were apparently domesticated, if not introduced, and their feathers furnished material for the manufacture of feather-string robes, similar in general appearance to the fur-string robes of the preceding periods.

The houses of this period were mostly one-story structures, consisting usually of a row of rooms built of slabs of stone laid horizontally. Larger communities constructed loose aggregates of such houses, not compact pueblos, but probably representing a stage in the evolution of the true pueblo type. Dwelling sites were evidently chosen with reference to surface drainage, and general convenience, rather than for the purpose of defense. These early dwellings were long overlooked and have not even yet received the investigation they deserve, as attention has been so largely focused upon the great structures of later date.

The pottery of this period is clearly related to that of the Pueblo period, but less highly specialized. The black cooking-vessels exhibit flat, broad coils or bands on the upper parts or necks, but there was no true corrugated ware. The black-on-white ollas, bowls and small jars bear rather elaborate decorations, but not usually so well executed as those of the pueblos and cliff houses.

The Pueblo (and Cliff House) Period

This is the "Great Period" in Southwestern archeology. No sharp break separates it from the Pre-Pueblo period on the one hand or the Historical period on the other. It was a time of comparatively rapid evolution of cultural elements theretofore initiated. It was marked particularly by concentration of population, resulting in large communities, fewer in number. Buildings became more compact, better suited for defense, and were placed on sites more easily and effectively defended. Though it has been denied by some competent archeologists, there is considerable weighty evidence in support of the general belief that the concentration of population, as well as the change in the character of building sites and in architectural forms, were the results of increasing pressure from war-like, nomadic tribes who had learned that the stores of grain maintained by the agricultural communities were highly desirable in time of scarcity of other food.

There was no Cliff House period apart from the Pueblo period. Both types of structures were used at the same time. However, the pueblo construction has continued in New Mexico and Arizona to the present time, while the cliff house type has been long abandoned. Indeed, the cliff house is but a pueblo set in a cavern, the rocky walls of the cavern serving as rear wall and to some extent as side walls of the house. Nevertheless, the general practice is to reserve the term pueblo for the purpose of designating structures built in the open. It is not even definitely known whether the general type originated in the cliff caverns and was afterwards adopted for the open mesas and valleys, or vice versa. It has been argued from the compactness of the pueblo type that it originated in caverns, where limited space compelled compact construction.

The pueblos and cliff houses were two-or-more-storied buildings, composed of compact groups of small rooms arranged in terraced form. The first story extended several feet beyond the borders of the one next above, thus providing a broad shelf which could be reached from the outside only by means of ladders. There were no entrances to the rooms of the ground floor through the outside walls. They were entered through the roof. This was an ideal arrangement for defense, and its inconvenience otherwise strongly suggests that defense was its sole purpose. The defending force assembled on the shelf had a great advantage over an attacting force seeking to scale the walls. That advantage was greatly enhanced, in case of pueblos placed, as was customary, at "rim-rock", by the walls of the mesas, which prevented approach from the valley side. In case of cliff houses the advantage was still greater, as the walls of the caverns effectually prevented approach from the rear and in many cases from either side, while it was difficult or impossible to scale the canyon wall from the front, in order to reach the cavern, in the face of vigorous resistance. Many of the caverns could only be reached by means of ladders, yucca ropes or such rude steps and hand-holds as could be pecked in the rocky walls by the use of stone implements, the only tools the cliff dwellers possessed for that purpose.

Each pueblo and cliff house was a communal building or village, housing many families. Indeed, the term pueblo is a Spanish word meaning town or village, not house. Some pueblos in the Southwest included several hundred rooms and perhaps housed not far from one thousand people. Because of lack of space the cliff houses were not so large as the largest pueblos, yet they also were sometimes fair-sized villages. There were ninety-five ground-floor rooms in Cliff Palace, besides twenty-three kivas. How many rooms were contained in the upper stories cannot now be determined. Spruce Tree House was 216 feet long, 89 feet in width in the widest portion, three stories high in some portions, and is said to have included 114 rooms and eight kivas. Fewkes estimated its population at 350.

The Pueblo and Cliff House culture reached its highest development at Mesa Verde. Among the very finest examples of cliff house construction are Cliff Palace and Spruce Tree House. This culture developed in the region surrounding the "Four Corners". It was not brought in from elsewhere.

Ceramic art reached its apex for the region during this period. The ruins, refuse heaps and cemeteries yield many large, beautiful coiled-ware jars and black-on-white decorated ware in great variety as to shape, size and decorative designs. The designs are chiefly geometric figures. The pottery is not so varied in color as that from one or two other localities in the Southwest, but is not inferior in other respects, and is superior to that from most localities.

The popular belief that the corrugated ware of this period was made by moulding it in baskets has no foundation in fact. It was made by coiling thin strips of clay round and round, pressing the strips together as they were coiled, thus building up and shaping the vessel. The true corrugated ware is a late development, not having appeared until this period, instead of being the primitive type, as some have supposed.

The Historical Period

There is little evidence of the occupancy of permanent sites in Southwestern Colorado after the arrival of the Spanish in the sixteenth century. Doubtless nomadic Indians continued to wander over the region, but left practically no evidence of their wanderings. While that region was being abandoned, the Rio Grande Valley culture in New Mexico was developing and spreading, continuing to the present time, greatly modified by new elements derived from contact with Europeans.

Who Were the Prehistoric Peoples?

The people who built and occupied the cliff houses and prehistoric pueblos of Southwestern Colorado, as well as the Pre-Pueblos, Post-Basket Makers and Basket Makers, were American Indians. They were at least in part ancestors of Indians now living in Arizona and New Mexico. There is a great deal of very definite evidence in support of this conclusion, which is generally accepted by archeologists, and none in support of the popular supposition that these peoples were Aztecs, or belonged to a distinct, superior, vanished race, or were the "lost tribes of Israel".

This, however, does not fully answer the question. The race of American Indians is divided into a large number of linguistic families, each consisting of a group of "tribes" speaking dialects which are closely related but not the same, with the exception of a few small linguistic families having but one dialect. Not much progress has yet been made in placing the prehistoric peoples in their proper linguistic families, much less in determining whether they used dialects now in use by any living groups. However, there are some suggestive facts worth following up, and with further investigation a solution or partial solution of this difficult problem may not be altogether hopeless.

It is quite likely that various dialectal groups were represented, and not at all unlikely that they belonged to more than one linguistic family. Especially does the difference in skulls suggest that the Pre-Pueblos and Pueblos were of different stock from the Basket Makers and Post-Basket Makers. There is no certainty even that the cliff dwellers and the people who inhabited the prehistoric pueblos all spoke the same language. The pueblo-dwelling peoples of the present day in New Mexico and Arizona do not all have a common language.

Where two or more ruins of the same type of construction yield pottery and other articles of just the same sort, there is considerable probability that the inhabitants were closely related. Indeed, it is likely that in some instances two such ruins were actually occupied by the same group of people at different times. It is known that within the Historic period pueblos have been abandoned and villages established elsewhere.

On the other hand, when we come to deal with distinct cultures, represented by different types of construction and different sorts of pottery and other manufactured articles, the probability of close relationship is much lessened, if not completely eliminated.

Whence Came the Prehistoric Peoples?

From the foregoing discussion it is clear that very little may be said in answer to this question. There is no worth-while evidence upon which to base a conclusion. It is not improbable that various groups came from different directions. Vague myths of the modern Indians of the region as to the direction from which their ancestors came are not reliable, and prove nothing at all as to the direction from which the ancient invasions came.

Maize originated far to the southward, probably on the tablelands of Mexico or Central America, but that does not at all indicate that the original home of the inhabitants of Southwestern United States was in Mexico or Central America. On the other hand, their failure to bring with them other important elements of the southern cultures discredits that idea. Maize was generally distributed over the eastern parts of the United States, west to the Mississippi Valley long before the coming of the white race. It almost certainly has been passed along from tribe to tribe, its migration having occupied a long period, instead of having been brought all that distance by people who formerly lived beyond the limits of the United States. The Basket Makers had one variety of this valuable grain, at the very beginning of the development of Southwestern cultures. The Cliff Dwellers had several varieties. If it could be ascertained just where these varieties originated, it would possibly be one step forward in the solution of the origin of the prehistoric peoples of the Southwest.

When Were the Prehistoric Structures Built and Occupied?

Sufficient progress has been made to permit one or two definite statements concerning this subject, though much yet remains to be done in the establishment of a complete chronology. When the Spanish reached the Southwest (A. D. 1540) many pueblos, and so far as known all the cliff houses, had been abandoned, though some of the largest pueblos in New Mexico and Arizona were still occupied, and some of them still are. In excavating sites which have been occupied since the Spanish invasion numerous articles introduced by the Spaniards are found. On the other hand, such articles are not found in the prehistoric ruins of Southwestern Colorado. It is scarcely presumable that had the great ruins of Mesa Verde and surrounding region been then occupied the inhabitants would have failed to obtain the much-coveted metal objects—buttons, buckles, bells, crosses, axes and other things such as are found at the sites which have been occupied during and since the arrival of the Spanish.

Furthermore, the failure of the Spanish chroniclers, whose detailed observations afford such an insight into conditions of Southwestern culture of their period, to describe such a remarkable culture as that of the Cliff Dwellers, is very strong presumptive evidence that they knew nothing of such people. The Spanish explorers were, above all, inquisitive people. One finds it difficult to believe that if the cliff houses were then occupied they would have failed to learn of it from roving Indians and to visit them and record the fact. They were quite in the habit of investigating such rumors and reporting their discoveries.

Early Spanish travelers over the old trail from New Mexico through Mancos and Cortez, Colorado, to Utah, according to Fewkes, mention roving Indians, but apparently knew nothing of pueblos or cliff houses in the Mesa Verde district or in Montezuma Valley, where ruins are abundant.

The lack of dependable traditions of the present Indians of the Southwest and their immediate ancestors, concerning the people who inhabited the cliff houses and associated pueblos, must also be considered. Such traditions as exist are vague and unconvincing, seldom confirmed and often contradicted by archeological evidence (Kidder). Had the structures not been long abandoned, one would expect very definite, consistent and convincing traditions, handed down from generation to generation.

It seems quite certain, then, that the abandonment of the Colorado ruins dates back at least three or four centuries, with good reason for the belief that five or six may have to be allowed. This is the general opinion of the best informed students of the subject.

On the question of when the pueblo culture began and how long it lasted the evidence is not so definite, but by no means wanting. There are many hundreds of ruins of both pueblo and cliff house types scattered over seven thousand square miles of territory in Southwestern Colorado, a region extending from the Pagaso-Piedra district on the east to the Utah border on the west, and from the New Mexico boundary northward to within sixty miles of Grand Junction (Jeancon).

It is unthinkable that these people constructed so many large and small buildings with their rude implements and spread them over so large a territory in anything less than many centuries. Even single structures of the many-roomed type, such as Spruce Tree House, Cliff Palace and the large pueblos, show that they reached their final dimensions gradually by accretion as growth of population required more room. The magnitude of the refuse heaps about some of the ruins also show long occupancy. Furthermore, the development of such a culture must have required a very long period. It is believed that the culture of this period was indigenous in the San Juan drainage area. There is very little evidence of outside influence. While the open-country pueblo phase reached its highest expression perhaps in the Chaco Canyon district of New Mexico, the cliff house phase reached its highest development in the Mesa Verde district of Colorado.

Another interval must be added to cover the time that elapsed between the culmination of this culture and the complete evacuation of the region. The abandonment was not a sudden affair. It was probably a comparatively slow process, covering many years, likely a century or more.

In view of all the known facts and circumstances, it seems fairly conservative to place the beginning of the Pueblo period back about two thousand years. That estimate meets the approval of some of those best qualified to express an opinion on the subject, and probably the estimates of few or none now engaged in that field of research would differ very widely from that result. It is admittedly, in the nature of the case, only an estimate, though by no means a mere guess.

However, the discussion of that period does not even closely approach the boundary of the subject. Other peoples inhabited the region long before the day of the Cliff Dweller. Before the concentration of population and the construction of the great communal houses, occurred the Pre-Pueblo period, during which pottery making and architecture were developing and almost innumerable small houses were constructed, scattered over a large area. This must have required several centuries. Then back of that were the Post-Basket Maker and Basket Maker periods, during which the arts and industries were advancing from a very primitive stage to a rather high degree of evolution. These two must have occupied several centuries.

Taking all the evidence into consideration, it is not at all extravagant to estimate that the beginning of the Basket Maker period was 3,000 years ago or more. In all probability primitive people lived in the region long before they began to manufacture articles recognizable as their handiwork, which could have been preserved as evidence of their former existence. The stone axes, hammerheads, arrow points and spear points of the various periods are not distinctive enough to throw much, if any, light upon the subject.

What Became of the Prehistoric Peoples?

This is probably the most-discussed problem of Southwestern archeology. Various theories have been advanced to account for the apparently total disappearance of the Pueblos and Cliff Dwellers from Southwestern Colorado—the abandonment of communal houses which at one time probably housed thousands of people. Earthquakes, floods and other cataclysmic episodes, pestilence and war, resulting in the wholesale destruction of the people, have all been suggested as the cause of their disappearance. There is, however, no evidence of a general, widespread catastrophy or epidemic. On the other hand, the evidence is entirely consistent with the idea of general decrease in numbers, through death from various causes and migration in small groups.

It is easy to suppose that the people representing the earlier cultures were simply absorbed by the increasing numbers of the later groups. After the concentration of population in large communal houses, with no knowledge of hygiene or sanitation, in a region where water was scarce, living conditions must have become very unsanitary. This may have resulted in repeated local epidemics. It is also likely that there were periods of prolonged drouth and consequent famine, weakening the people and reducing their power of resistance. It is not improbable that there was a slight change in climate toward adverse conditions, which, with a population that taxed the productive capacity of the country to its utmost, would have been disastrous.

There are botanical, zoological, geological and archeological reasons for the belief that the Southwest has for untold thousands of years been semi-arid, so that in unfavorable seasons but little grain could have been grown. In a region where rainfall is barely sufficient for crops in ordinary seasons, and not sufficient during seasons of minimum precipitation, even a slight decrease in the average annual rainfall would be serious, compelling the abandonment of all but the best-watered fields, resulting in more and more frequent famines. There is a widespread belief, based chiefly upon archeological evidence, supported by some botanical evidence, that there has been progressive desiccation in that region. If true, this would account in a large measure for the abandonment of the region, but not altogether, because the country is still able to support a small population as well as other regions to the southward which have been occupied down to the present time. The arguments against such a change in climate have been based upon theories of climate change which are not tenable, because of their failure to conform to geological and climatological facts.

It is quite possible that increasing depredations of hostile Indians continually drained the various communities of their most robust men, the warriors, thus reducing the power of the villages. To this may have been added strife between the various agricultural communities over the possession of springs and tillable lands, causing further gradual decrease in the population.

The theory of a general, widespread migration to another region is highly improbable. So large a population, with so highly-developed a culture, could hardly have migrated in a body, or in the same direction in small bodies, or even in various directions, without leaving abundant evidence of their movements and final destination. There is evidence that some remnants of the people from the Mesa Verde district did migrate southward and occupied Pueblo Bonito and the buildings now in ruins at Aztec and Broomfield, New Mexico, after their abandonment by the original inhabitants, but the reoccupation was for but a short time and by only small groups of people. Tewa, Hopi and Zuni are said to have traditions of migration of their ancestors from the northward. The Tewa legends include a temporary stay at Mesa

Verde, and the modern Tewa have place names for that district. However, the cultures of these three groups do not strongly suggest derivation from Southwestern Colorado. It is, nevertheless, highly probable that a slight percentage of Colorado blood does flow in the veins of some of the Pueblo Indians now living in New Mexico.

Turning now to the great ruins at Pecos, New Mexico, we find some very suggestive and significant historic facts. This ancient site was occupied for many centuries, including three centuries of historic occupancy from the arrival of the Spaniards in about 1540 down to 1838. In 1620 the community is said to have included about 2,000 inhabitants. The decline began prior to 1700, when hostile Comanches became troublesome. By 1750 the population had been reduced to 1,000. About this time the remnant was nearly destroyed in battle. In 1788 a smallpox epidemic left only 180 survivors. Mountain fever increased in severity and the population continued to dwindle. In 1805 there were only 104 left and in 1830 only from 50 to 100. In 1838 the 17 survivors accepted an invitation to move to Jemez, thus abandoning a site which, three centuries before, had been occupied by a large and flourishing people.

This bit of history may in a general way represent the history of the abandonment of the pueblos and cliff houses of Southwestern Colorado. Adversities of various sorts, famine, pestilence and war, may have slowly reduced the population at the various sites, until the small remnants perhaps became discouraged and moved to more prosperous sites in New Mexico, there being soon absorbed, leaving in their traditions very little trace of their former history or migrations.

Chapter 2
THE INDIANS OF COLORADO
E. B. Renaud

The crest of the Rocky Mountains naturally divides Colorado into two clear-cut sections. The eastern portion of the State is an integral part of the Great Plains. The western half is covered by the mountains prolonged by high plateaus with the characteristic mesas and cañons, so named by the Spanish explorers. This geographical division coincides fairly well with the distribution of those Indian tribes which used to roam over this vast territory.

The Various Tribes

The central and western districts of Colorado were peopled mostly by the *Utes*. They constitute an important contingent of the Shoshonean linguistic stock, which comprises the other tribes of eastern Utah, the Bannock and the Shoshoni of Idaho and Wyoming, in the North, and the Comanche to the southeast. They were also in frequent contact, along the Colorado-New Mexico border, with the Jicarilla Apache, a southern branch of the Athapascan stock.

The Utes are of medium stature, their average being 1.661 meters or 65.4 inches, which classifies them as the shortest Colorado Indians. They were warlike and notably unfriendly to the whites up to a recent date. For that reason, relatively very little is known with certainty concerning their culture, or their social and political organization. A census, even approximately correct, has always been difficult. Of the original 10,000 or so, about 2,200 Utes still remain, 94% of them being full-blooded. This is the highest percentage among the Indians of this State, and is undoubtedly due to their hostility to the whites.

The eastern portion of Colorado was peopled by a greater variety of tribes, belonging to three important linguistic stocks—Algonkian, Siouan, Kiowan. These picturesque Indians are better known on account of the conspicuous part they took in American history during the incessant Indian Wars of the nineteenth century and the place they occupy in art and literature as a subject of inspiration for descriptions and for accounts of adventures. As they had been met by many explorers and travelers at different times, we have some notions of their history and migrations. Besides, in more recent years, the ethnologist has been able to study what is left of their material and social culture. We feel, then, more at ease in speaking of them and in describing their mode of living.

The most typical of the Colorado Indians are probably the Arapaho and the Cheyenne. Strange to say, they reached this part of the country at a relatively recent date. Altho characteristic representatives of the Plains culture, these Indians used to be farmers cultivating corn somewhere beyond the Missouri river in Minnesota.

The *Arapaho* tribe is called Inunaina in their own language, that is to say, "our people". Their present name probably came from the Pawnee words Tirapihu or Larapihu, meaning trader, on account of their proclivity to barter and trade. Leaving their lodges and corn fields of northern Minnesota, they crossed the Missouri and moved in a general southwestern direction in company with the Cheyenne, both tribes having been driven away by the pressure of the Sioux. Reaching the foot of the Rockies, the northern branch of the Arapaho established themselves about the head of the North Platte. The southern group continued migrating southward toward the Arkansas, and came into conflict with the Kiowa and the Comanche. About 1840 they made peace with these tribes and the Sioux, but never ceased their hostilities with their other enemies: Ute and Shoshoni, west and North; the Pawnee, east. Unless driven to war on the whites, due to circumstances such as their alliance with the Cheyenne, the Arapaho were more friendly disposed toward the Americans than were the other neighboring tribes.

As a consequence of the Treaty of Medicine Lodge in 1867 the Southern Arapaho and their old friends, the Southern Cheyenne, were placed upon their reservation in Oklahoma, but later, in 1892, they became citizens when their land was opened to the whites. Not until 1876, the Northern Arapaho having finally made peace with their traditional enemy the Shoshoni, were both tribes located on their present reservation of Wind River, in Wyoming.

The Arapaho people number over 1,400 individuals with the high percentage of 92.4 full-bloods. They have been described as good-looking and tall men. Their average stature is given as 1.728

meters or slightly more than 68 inches. They were among the tallest Indians of the plains, coming only after Crow and Cheyenne, were brave in battle but kind in peace and possessed several other good traits of character. They were very religious and addicted to many ceremonial observances, their greatest annual and tribal ceremony being the Sun Dance. They took an active part in the propagation of the so-called Ghost Dance about 1890. They distinguished themselves, among other things, from Sioux and Cheyenne, by their custom of burying the dead, which was not a common practice among the Western Indians. For the rest their culture resembles a great deal that of the other tribes of the plains.

The *Cheyenne* Indians owe their present name to the Sioux, who called them Shai-ena or "people of alien speech". But their own name is Dzitsiistas, which, freely translated, means "people alike", or "our people", the same as many tribes call themselves. Their first recorded contact with the whites was in 1667, when they met the French, and later, in 1680, when they went to La Salle's fort in Illinois to invite his men to come and trap for fur in their country. This shows that originally they were friendly, altho later, when hard pressed in Colorado by the Americans, they became the most aggressive Indians and the hardest to reduce to submission.

Before 1700 they were agriculturists in Minnesota, the same as the Arapaho, and like them were forced across the Missouri by the advancing Sioux. Henceforth they became nomadic hunters. Lewis and Clark met them in the Black Hills in 1804. Their enemies, the Mandan and the Hidatsa, two Siouan tribes, fought them constantly. Then the Cheyenne drifted farther South, establishing themselves on the upper branches of the Platte, and later they reached the Arkansas. In that region, with their allies the Arapaho, they came into repeated collision with the Kiowa and the Comanche, who claimed that part of the country as their rightful hunting ground, but they finally made peace in 1853. Warfare was again prevalent between 1860 and 1878, against the Sioux in the north and the Kiowa and the Comanche in the south. That unfortunate position between two sets of enemies developed a strongly bellicose spirit among the Cheyenne and made them the best warriors in the West: brave, daring, in fact feared and admired even by their best opponents. American officers more than once spoke highly of the splendid appearance and the audacity of the Cheyenne. It is said that no tribe lost more men in battles with the whites.

They had been decimated by cholera in 1849. The Sand Creek Massacre in 1864 was another hard blow, to which Custer added the defeat of Washita four years later. They took a leading part in the outbreak of 1874-75. The following year the Northern Cheyenne were the allies of the Sioux in the Sitting Bull War and participated actively in the Custer Massacre. Only after the defeat inflicted on them by Mackenzie did they surrender. Many of the same Northern Cheyenne were killed after escaping from Fort Reno and Fort Robinson. Those who were left were finally placed on a reservation in Montana, altho the Southern Cheyenne had been sent to Oklahoma in 1867. In 1901-2 they were granted citizenship and their land allotted.

At present the Cheyenne number altogether about 1300, including only 87% full bloods. They are the tallest of the plains Indians, their average height being 1.745 meters or 68.7 inches. They are considered by many as the most virile and handsome Western Indians, proud and brave to the extreme. The standard of morality of their women is unusually high, altho polygamy is followed as is common among all these tribes.

The *Kiowa* constitute a distinct linguistic stock, different from all their neighbors. They call themselves Ka-i-gwu, hence the present corruption, which was formerly pronounced Ke-owa. Contrary to the Cheyenne and the Arapaho, they were truly Western Indians, but like these two tribes they were not inhabitants of the plains until a few centuries back. According to well authenticated traditions they formerly lived in the mountains of Montana, near the headwaters of the Missouri and the Columbia rivers. For reasons not clearly known they moved toward the plains, where they were the friends of the Crow. Then, becoming buffalo hunters, they moved southward under the pressure of the Cheyenne and the Sioux. The various stages of their migration are marked by their camping first in the Black Hills, then near the Platte river and later by the Arkansas. This brought them into collision with the Comanche in the South. In 1790 they made peace and together fought the advancing Arapaho and Cheyenne. The

Kiowa were among the most hostile and turbulent tribes of the plains.

In 1867, by virtue of the Treaty of Medicine Lodge, in Kansas, they, together with the Arapaho, the Cheyenne and the Comanche, reluctantly consented to go to live on the reservation of the then Indian Territory, now Oklahoma. The outbreak of 1874 saw them on the war path with their fellow rebels above named, but when vanquished by Mackenzie they paid dearly. Many leaders and their followers were exiled to Florida; the rest have remained since then quietly on the reservation. In 1901 their land was opened and they became citizens. They also practiced the Sun Dance, and they have a nearly anthropomorphic stone image as their principal tribal fetish. They were divided into six bands, the men grouped in a military order, with six classes or degrees. They never reached 2,000 in the course of the nineteenth century and are now slightly over 1,100, of which 72.6% are full-bloods. Their average stature is 67.2 inches, shorter than both Arapaho and Cheyenne, but taller than the Comanche, who measure only 66.06 inches.

MATERIAL CULTURE

The keystone of the whole culture complex of the Indians of the plains is the fact that the extension of the prairie and the area over which the buffalo roamed very nearly coincided. This led to the development of a highly characterized culture based entirely on the buffalo, the chase of it for food and the utilization of its skin, bones, fat, sinew, and hair for all the principal needs of these Indians. It could very well be called the bison culture; and the Cheyenne, the Arapaho, the Kiowa and the Sioux are products of this environment and typical of the plains specialization. This splendid American animal, the bison or buffalo, is, then, the central figure of the whole cultural complex and the main explanation of all its special features. To consider the relations of the plains Indians to the buffalo naturally results in describing the mode of living of our Colorado Indians, their principal occupations, and the material, social, religious, and artistic aspects of their culture.

Food is the primary and constant need of man. Hence the quest for suitable food, in sufficient quantity, will govern all other activities and will furnish the basic understanding for the culture of primitive peoples. Our Indians, depending so extensively on the bison as their staple food and source of material to satisfy many important needs, were made nomadic hunters, for the buffalo migrated northward in summer and southward in late Fall and Winter. Thus, from Canada to Texas and through Colorado —centrally located on the plains—there were constant seasonal migrations of game and hunters. After the horse was introduced by the whites, the chase was easier and swifter, and the acquisition of fire arms still more increased the facility of obtaining abundant food. Unhappily it accelerated also the destruction of the main food supply, led to the demoralization of the Indians, and caused wars and massacres until the placing of the tribes on the reservations gave subsistence to these Indians and peace to the settlers.

The general method of *hunting* the buffalo in summer was by means of cooperative and well organized expeditions. Scouts were sent to locate a herd and keep it within sight while others reported to camp. In the old time bands on foot under leaders then took their respective positions and on signals would surround the animals but for a narrow passage. When on horseback the hunters would whirl round and round the herd and kill all they could with arrows, spears or guns. In winter, especially in the north, they drove the buffaloes into inclosures. In the more rugged country they pushed the herd into a defile or more often stampeded them on a mesa, driving them over the cliff. Still another method described by early travelers consisted in setting fire, late in the season, to the dry grass around a herd and then killing all the frightened animals as they tried to escape the flames. Of course, with fast horses it was sufficient to race along the flanks of a herd and shoot down the buffaloes, especially after fire arms had been introduced.

The *hunting implements* of the plains Indians were principally bows and arrows. There were two styles more often found in the Colorado region: the plain wooden bow and the sinew-backed bow, a more advanced type, the latter commonly in use among Shoshoni and other plateau tribes. The arrows were carried in a quiver made of rawhide or of skin with the hair on the outside. An effective weapon when thrown by a strong man on a swift horse was the lance, sometimes decorated with feathers. The point of this spear was made of stone, preferably flint or obsidian, held in place by means of sinew, the same as for the arrow. Buffaloes wounded in the chase or caught in inclosures were killed with a stone-headed club or maul. This consisted of a good sized river boulder, oval shaped, kept tightly in the grip of a surrounding handle by means of rawhide which covered the handle and most of the stone and which was sewed with green sinew. This is the most effective method of hafting devised by these Indians.

After obtaining food, the next problem for nomadic peoples is the *preservation* of the surplus and its transportation, as buffalo could not be hunted every day and there was often a great deal of meat to preserve for future use. The most general method consisted in drying in the sun thin slices of the flesh—or better yet, after a short boiling, in placing steaks, thinly cut, on racks to dry, out of the reach of the dogs. The same was done for fat. After that, meat and fat could be stored and carried easily in skin bags. But the important invention of the Indians of the West was the *pemmican*, a preparation so practical that explorers, trappers and soldiers often used it when necessary. It consisted essentially of dried meat of buffalo or even elk, pounded. Sometimes wild cherries were gathered, crushed, pit and all, and dried in the sun, being thus reduced to a sticky paste. It was mixed later with the pulverized meat, in melted fat and marrow. This excessively rich food was easily transportable in the flat and rectangular bag of rawhide called parfleche and would keep in eatable condition for several years. It answered perfectly the need of nomads and hunters.

According to places and seasons the menu of the Colorado Indians was completed by adding the flesh of antelope, deer or elk, bear, rabbit, or other small game. Hunting was of course exclusively the business of the men. The women, however, contributed the vegetable element of the diet by gathering wild berries, nuts, seeds, and roots. On the whole, the Indians of this part of the country were well fed, even if agriculture and gardening were practically unknown to them.

How did the Cheyenne, Arapaho and the others do their *cooking?* There are three principal methods used by primitive peoples before the whites brought them metal kettles: broiling, baking, and boiling. The meat to be broiled was held at the end of a stick or impaled on a stick planted in the ground, and if it were big supported by other sticks or poles. This is a common method extensively used by hunters. Meat and roots also were baked in a hole, from which hot ashes and embers had been removed, and which had been lined with leaves or bark; the food was left covered up till it was judged fit to eat. Finally, boiling could have been resorted to but only by means of "indirect firing", so to speak, as the plains Indians in general had no pottery. They took a fresh paunch, hung it upon short sticks and placed in it meat, vegetable and water. From a nearby fire, large stones heated very hot were successively taken, dipped and held in the water until the food was cooked. A variant of this method was known to the Arapaho and consisted in digging a hole, about the size of a cooking pot, carefully lining it with a piece of rawhide from the back of the animal and then proceeding as just explained. The Colorado Indians thus had a variety of ways of preparing their meals: broiling, baking and boiling.

In the old time they lighted grass, leaves, bark and wood by means of the fire-drill, one of the most primitive methods, soon replaced by flint and steel at the first contact with the whites.

Bowls were rare among the Western tribes. They were made of wood or of mountain-sheep horn. The best came from the Dakota, a Siouan tribe; the crudest were made by the Comanche and Ute of Colorado. Spoons were in general use, falling into two classes as to material and purpose. The buffalo horn spoons were employed like ours for eating purposes, while the mountain-sheep horn spoons were used more frequently in cooking. Knives for cutting flesh, skin and other things were made of flint flakes or of bone. But men and women were not slow in appreciating the superiority of the metal knives obtained from the traders. The same could be said for the bone bodkins. All this reminds us that our Colorado Indians, before they came in contact with the white men, either Spanish, French or American, were still in the Stone Age, all their implements being made of wood, stone, bone or horn, the use of metal being entirely unknown in the western plains. Pottery, so common in the Mississippi valley and so beautifully painted in the Southwest, was of a primitive type and somewhat rare in Colorado. The reason for this is clear. Pottery is bulky, heavy and breakable. All this makes it impractical for hunters always on the move over the plains and having no beast of burden nor carriage of any description. Even basketry did not answer well their needs.

The ideal and most natural solution for their wants in that line was found in the extensive and varied use of *skin*. The women knew well how to press pelts. By means of bone fleshers and scrapers they prepared the hides, treating them also with hot water and a mixture of brains, fat and liver, to obtain the soft tan finish given the buffalo and deer skins for making robes and certain bags. The first and simplest use of rawhide has already been alluded to, the hafting and binding of stone-headed clubs and mauls, to which must be added the Indian saddle made in imitation of the Mexican one with rawhide and sinew replacing nails and sewing material. The shrinkage of wet hide, on drying, holds firmly the pieces enclosed: stone, bone or wood.

The principal types of bags made of rawhide were first of all the parfleche. It is essentially a one-piece bag somewhat in the shape of an open envelope, then cleverly folded into a rectangular form fastened by means of small thongs. This convenient container, easily packed and carried, was primarily used in holding and carrying dried meat, fat, berries, etc., or even any utensil. A one-piece squarish bag, sewed on the side and closed by means of a triangular flap, was in common use among the women. In the small-sized ones they carried their sewing material, sinew, bodkins, etc., and in the larger ones their skin-dressing tools. A nearly cylindrical rawhide case, adorned with leather fringes, was employed by the men for carrying their feather headdress and other ceremonial objects. The rawhide bags were generally decorated with painted geometrical patterns.

A second and important class is that of the soft bags which are adorned with skilful designs obtained by combination of colored porcupine quills, later replaced by the glass beads of the white trader, preferred by the women on account of the variety of shades and ease of working. Cheyenne, Arapaho, Ute and Sioux made such bags, sometimes large and often in pairs. They were light, flexible and very convenient for carrying any kind of belongings. The pipe and tobacco bags were long, narrow and with generous fringes of leather at the bottom. The strike-a-light pouch was smaller and more fanciful in shape and decoration.

One might also mention the paint bags. Finally the modern use of horses led to the making of long, double saddle-bags. They are, like all the others, fringed, and also beaded all over.

Among important objects made of leather must not be forgotten the small round shield of tough buffalo hide, preferably from the neck of a bull. It was often adorned with feathers and painted on its outside face to represent a sacred symbol, some design of supernatural protective value, or a conventional sign recalling some exploit of the bearer.

The bison furnished, then, the Colorado Indians with material for making some of their tools, for sewing and hafting, and for the making of all sorts of most useful bags and shields. Yet that is far from being all. For the buffalo also presented the plains Indians with what they needed for *clothing*.

The men wore only a small apron of dressed skin, later replaced by the breech-cloth. But when appearing before strangers or at a meeting, they draped themselves in soft buffalo robes, worn horizontally, tail on the right side. The gaudily colored blankets of more recent years have displaced these beautiful tanned robes, formerly used by men and women alike. The typical footwear of the plains was the moccasin. It was made by the women from buffalo skin. In the North it was a one-piece, soft-soled moccasin; in the South the Arapaho, Comanche and Ute preferred a hard-soled moccasin and high leggings tied to the belt, while the women's leggings reached only to the knee and were held by garters. The shape of the toe and the heel fringes distinguished the tribes and allowed Indians to recognize friends and foes from traces left on dust and sand. The decoration of the moccasins also differed in designs, colors and meanings.

A one-piece dress, without sleeves, was commonly worn by the women among some of the Siouan tribes and among the Arapaho, Kiowa, Comanche, and Ute. The ordinary way of making a dress was by sewing together two deer skins, head down. The hind legs gracefully covered the arms like open sleeves, a place was reserved for the neck of the wearer, and a yoke was formed by the natural falling of the skin at front and back. Fringes were left all along the sides and bottom seams for decorative effect, and others were often added in rows in addition to other means of ornamentation. From tribe to tribe there were minor variations in the cut of the dress, but the general pattern remained the same, conditioned by the shape of the animal skin used. In a similar fashion men's shirts were made of deer skin.

There were also numerous customs in *hair* dressing and *head* ornaments. Men and women were bareheaded, the women parting their hair in the middle and braiding it in two long tresses. The men wore their hair in two braids also or loose on the back; and some, like the Kiowa, allowed a forelock to hang over their nose. But the hair of the face and other visible parts of the body was carefully removed with tweezers. All feathers placed on the head had some military significance and were not so profusely used as in recent times. The great war bonnet with long streamers worn on some occasions by high chiefs has been called one of the most beautiful headdresses invented by man. Like all primitive people, the Indians were fond of necklaces of beads, teeth, claws, and they liked also ear ornaments: bits of fur, metal rings, pins and chains. They painted their faces and portions of the body according to circumstances: war, various dances, etc.

The bison, already so amply used by the Indians, also furnished them with the essential material for their *dwellings*. Being of nomadic habits, hunters need a portable shelter, relatively light and easily folded, but strong enough to resist wind, rain or snow. It must, too, be readily put up and pulled down when the hunters are establishing camp or moving away. Nothing could answer better these many requirements than the *tipi* (or tepee) of the plains Indians. It is essentially a frame of long poles, covered with dressed buffalo skins. The fireplace occupies the center of the tent. The head of the family seats himself opposite the entrance, the others on the ground on both sides. Variations as to the size of the circular base of the tipi, or the number of poles of the frame first put up, or even the length of the poles showing above the tent proper, are found from one group of tribes to another. For instance, the Cheyenne gave their tents a wide base; the Arapaho made it narrow. Thus at a glance, an experienced warrior or hunter would recognize who were the occupants of a camp and would behave accordingly.

Strange to say, these roving Indians had very poor means of *transportation*. They were greatly handicapped by the fact that the fauna of the country did not present a single animal fit for carrying burdens or for pulling some sort of cart or wagon. And so the aborigines never invented the wheel or any carriage. All the belongings of the Indians of Colorado and of many other tribes were carried exclusively on human backs, mostly of the women, supplemented by dogs, the sole domesticated animal. The only means of transportation devised by the plains hunters was what is called the travois, essentially two tipi poles bound at one end, on which a pack was strapped. This primitive traveling apparatus was dragged by dogs. The northern tribes improved it somewhat. Later it was increased to fit the size of the horse, also used as pack animal and saddle mount. This allowed a much greater mobility for the Indians.

Thus we have seen that nothing from their environment could surpass the multiple usefulness of the bison for the Colorado Indians. From this king of the plains they obtained their principal food, for they ate his flesh, fat and marrow; with his bones they made tools; with his sinew they sewed and bound; with his skin they made all sorts of bags, shields, robes and moccasins and covered their abode. Chasing the buffalo controlled their principal activities; it made them nomadic and so shaped their very culture, both material and social.

Social Culture

Most of the plains Indians of Colorado lived in bands under a chief and sub-chiefs when the group was large. Such headmen had authority over a following of varied size on account of their recognized qualities as leaders, successful hunters and warriors. Within the groups of followers from one tribe the Indians, at least among Arapaho, Kiowa and Comanche, freely intermarried without those restrictions observed where the exogamic clan system was in force, as among some of the northern Siouan tribes. A man was allowed as many wives as he wished, but the average was generally three, more often sisters as conducive to harmony and cooperation. For, these Indians having neither slaves nor servants, the women had a heavy task to perform. Their work was endless and the burden increased with the size of the family and the possessions of the husband. To their lot fell the rearing of children, cooking, preparing skins, sewing and mending, making bags, robes, dresses, moccasins, quilling and beading, putting up the tipi, packing the dogs and carrying on the march a load on their own back besides the babies in their cradles. Assistant wives were thus welcomed to share in the incessant work; besides, they raised the social position of the first wife.

These bands, moving about at will, recognized their natural kinship with others of the same tribe, who spoke the same language, and had the same customs and costumes. But only on special occasions, such as a communal buffalo hunting or the organization of a large war party, did the bands gather and the *tribal government* function. This political organization was democratic, rather loose, and different with the various tribes. The Cheyenne, for instance, had four great chiefs, assisted by a council of forty members elected by the men of the bands of that tribe.

When the bands united in a tribal gathering, the leaders selected a suitable camp site. The groups distributed themselves around a circle, clockwise, starting with the first band near the entrance, which was reserved on the east side. The council tipi was erected in the middle of the central open space. The Cheyenne, the Arapaho and the Sioux had a special society, called upon only on such occasions, to serve as police in the camp and to transmit the orders of the chiefs or council. The plains Indians had also other men's societies, military or religious as to character and purpose, somewhat similar to our secret orders or fraternities. Beside these, the men were grouped in age-grades or classes forming closed societies with rituals, privileges and duties. These functioned in different ways, according to the tribes, but segregated naturally the Indians of about the same age. Finally, the Arapaho and Sioux had also some women's societies. These various organizations within the tribe, together with the camp circle, are two characteristic traits of the plains Indians and were found all over eastern Colorado.

Contrary to the customs of the Indians of the Northwest Coast, the amount of property did not necessarily determine *social ranking*. Personal deeds of valor, successful leadership in war, the killing of foes, the taking of scalps, the capture of horses and guns, and the like, constituted the basis for distinction. To keep the memory of such important and praiseworthy acts, the warriors used to "count" or tell their exploits at some meetings, or to depict them on buffalo robes or on the sides of their tipi. They acquired also the right to wear feathers of a certain kind and placed in a certain way on their heads, to paint in some recognized manner, and to adorn clothing and shield with standardized designs of one color or another. Thus, at a glance, one who knew how to interpret what he saw could tell the deeds of this or that brave. It developed both a type of picture writing and a system of military heraldry.

What about the *religion* of these Indians? It would be impossible to sketch satisfactorily in a few lines the religious concepts, at the same time vague and complex, of the Colorado Indians, or their mythology and folklore, of great interest from the viewpoints of psychology, literature and art. The animals most spoken of and represented in connection with mythological beliefs or magical practices are the buffalo, the thunder-bird or eagle, and a water monster in the form of a horned serpent.

The plains Indians had a strong mystical bent. They believed, for example, that each male member should enter into direct relationship with the divine power and have a personal religious experience. After being duly instructed by a priest or shaman, the youth would retire to an isolated spot and then fast, pray, meditate and expect a vision. From this resulted the obtaining of a supernatural helper or protective spirit, with the accompaniment of song or formula, taboo and finally a charm of some sort to be carried all the time. This practice was general among Cheyenne, Arapaho and Sioux, but not among Ute and Shoshoni. The Sioux often added to the other trials self-torture.

Among the most important *ceremonial objects* must be named the sacred bundles. They contained, carefully wrapped, the traditional paraphernalia of a tribe, a society or simply an individual. These religious objects, of various natures, represented great medicine; that is, they were endowed with supernatural or magic power in the eyes of the Indians and took their place in different rituals. The medicine arrows of the Cheyenne and the sacred pipe of the Arapaho were among the most famous treasures of the respective tribes.

The principal tribal ceremonies are known to us mostly

through the picturesque *dances* of the Indians of the plains. They are, properly speaking, acted communal prayers or ritualistic dramas, performed by the members of societies or groups entitled to do so by right of initiation or position. Hunting and war dances are possibly the more usual types. The so-called Sun Dance has been especially well studied for the Arapaho, but it was also practiced in various forms by many other tribes. A sun-pole was erected with a circular shelter, an altar was established, and the tribal sacred bundle was used on that occasion. Elaborate dancing took place, the performers wearing a variety of body-paintings. Torture, sometimes very cruel, was practiced according to the vow or purpose of each man. The Ghost Dance, based on a messianic belief, originated in the late eighties and rapidly spread from the plateau region over the plains, leading to troubles which came to a climax at the battle of Wounded Knee in 1890. It is said that the Cheyenne and the Arapaho still practice that modern dance in a modified form on their reservations.

A variety of more or less complex steps, the extensive use of body-painting and special costumes, the singing of inspired songs and sacred formulas, the accompaniment of rattles and drums, with the smoking of special pipes and sometimes the opening of medicine bundles constitute the characteristic elements of the Indian dances.

To this form of dynamic religious *art*, must be added another form, static and decorative, but also to a degree symbolical. By diverse means the Indians adorn their clothing, bags, shields, horse-trappings and tents. The women have a marked tendency to make use of geometric patterns. This may be due originally to the technique of their art, mostly depending on quills and beads as constitutive elements of their decoration of moccasins, dresses, bags and the like. But even the parfleche bags, where paint is used, are adorned with rectilinear designs. The simple elements entering into the composition of beaded surfaces often convey a meaning. But this symbolism changes with tribes and objects and even with individual interpretation. The men, on the contrary, are more inclined toward realism, being hunters and warriors. They use paints to draw freely on flat surfaces such as buffalo robes, tipis or shields. Moreover, they wish to depict their own exploits, war scenes and hunts. This led to a regular marshaling of the summary scenes represented, starting from the center of the robe and developing along a spiral line moving contrary clockwise. It led also to the simplification of the drawing, in some instances to the point of high conventionalism, equivalent to a pictorial writing. Some of the records thus represented have a real historic value as they refer to known encounters in which the American troops took part. The Sioux seem to excel in this art.

Relations with the Whites

The Indians of the western plains, as far as we know, had very little to do with the Spaniards or Mexicans who exercised a rather nominal jurisdiction over the territory now included in southern Colorado. The French, either Canadians or from the establishments in the Mississippi Valley, seem to have found the Indians in general friendly. These white men or half-breeds came individually or in small parties, mostly for trapping, trading, or buying furs and robes; they did not disturb the Indians in their peaceful enjoyment of the country. In fact they were welcomed as bringing to camps and trading posts metal knives, guns, powder, beads and the like, highly appreciated by the natives. But toward the middle of the nineteenth century and in the following period two facts radically changed the attitude of the aborigines in regard to the new comers, now mostly Americans.

First of all, the buffalo, which had fashioned, so to speak, the specialized culture of the plains Indians and represented their staple food and principal source of supply for tenting, clothing and other necessities, was rapidly diminishing, and the complete extermination of that noble animal was in sight. That fact was the deplorable outcome of the introduction of the horse, speeding up the chase; and more especially of the increasing number of guns, causing an excessive killing of the game; and finally of the demand of the white men for buffalo robes and furs, leading to the wanton destruction of animal life, and giving no peace to the herds vanishing from the prairies. For that capital reason our Indians extended their roving in quest of food, and came into conflict with neighboring tribes and incoming settlers. They were often hungry and like packs of famished wolves went on marauding expeditions, pillaging, killing, bringing upon themselves the bad will of the pioneers and the repression of the Army, as history can tell.

The second factor of importance is the following. While the Indians acknowledged the general right of each tribe to hunt over a certain territory and fought the bands encroaching upon their hunting grounds, they never believed that any man or group could actually pretend to the ownership of land or could prevent anybody from crossing it, chasing game over it, putting up his tipi or residing where he pleased. And then they saw the American settlers raising houses, fencing lots, establishing villages, building forts with stockades—trying to exclude them from such places, the first and rightful inhabitants of the region. They saw much game being killed by others while they, Arapaho, Sioux, Kiowa, had to go hungry, or beg and steal. Restricted in their primitive liberty, increasingly deprived of their hunting spaces, they naturally came to hate the new comers, who were treating them roughly, often beating them, and taking from them their heritage. The diseases brought by the whites, smallpox and measles for instance, decimated the natives. The bad whiskey sold them, rendering them as if crazy, and the advantage taken of them when under the influence of liquor, contributed also to ill feelings and quarrels often bloody. Everything in fact seemed against the Indians, who, seeing their country invaded, their rights ignored, their independence curtailed, their food vanishing, their very existence threatened, in desperation resorted to the most violent and treacherous warfare. It was a war of defense in their eyes and of revenge for all accumulated wrongs, a war without quarter asked or given, a war in which the Indians were bound finally to be defeated by their numerous, well-armed, and disciplined enemies, the proud savage falling bravely before the inexorable advance of a superior civilization.

Now all the Indians of the plains have left Colorado for their respective reservations in Wyoming and Oklahoma. Of the plateau Indians only the Southern Utes remain, on a reservation in the southwest corner of the State. What is left to recall the former inhabitants of Colorado? Of course these Indians occupy an important place in American history of the nineteenth century. They also, and especially those of the plains, have inspired many fine pages of literature, and beautiful drawings, paintings and statues, some of these adorning the public grounds of Denver and other places. Unhappily much of the folklore of the Colorado

Indians has been lost for lack of the systematic collecting done for other tribes. Again, too many pioneers have disappeared without leaving us sufficient accounts of the early days in this region, their struggle against the elements and their relations with the Indians. Thus another part of interesting and very human folklore is insufficiently recorded and will forever be incomplete.

The Indians had names for every important place and feature of the landscape. What is left of that? Naturally these strange and difficult designations were unknown to the whites or hard to pronounce, and the few which survive have often suffered in transcription. But many names of tribes, famous chiefs and the like have been given by the Americans to towns and counties, to mountains and rivers. A study of the origin or derivation of the geographical names of Colorado furnishes us with a few interesting facts on the subject. For instance, seven counties bear Indian appellations: Arapaho, Cheyenne and Kiowa, for the principal tribes; Ouray in honor of Ure, the most friendly chief of the Utes; Saguache or Sawatch, name of another Ute chief; Montezuma, a modern form of the name of an Aztec ruler at the time of the Spanish conquest, whose fame and legend reached as far north as Colorado; and Yuma, possibly after a small tribe of the Lower Colorado River. About fifty towns are called after Indian names, either of tribes or chiefs, or else by descriptive words more or less transposed in English spelling. Nine out of ninety-one rivers and six mountains or plateaus out of ninety-three are designated by Indian names. Finally, several towns and Denver in particular, call their streets after Indian tribal names. Thus the geography of the State of Colorado still bears witness of the Indian occupation and reminds the new comers of the former inhabitants.

SHORT BIBLIOGRAPHY

1. Bulletin 30, Bureau of American Ethnology
    HANDBOOK OF AMERICAN INDIANS NORTH OF MEXICO edited by Frederick Webb Hodge; two volumes; Government Printing Office, Washington: 1907.
2. INDIANS OF THE PLAINS by Clark Wissler.
    American Museum of National History, New York.
3. THE AMERICAN INDIAN by Clark Wissler.
    Douglas C. McMurtrie, New York: 1917.

4. THE INFLUENCE OF THE HORSE IN THE DEVELOPMENT OF PLAINS CULTURE by Clark Wissler.
    American Anthropologist, New Series, Vol. 16, pp. 1-25, Lancaster: 1925.
5. THE ARAPAHO by A. L. Kroeber.
    Bulletin, American Museum of Natural History, Vol. 18, Part I, New York: 1902.
6. SYMBOLISM OF THE ARAPAHO INDIANS.
    Bulletin, American Museum of Natural History, Vol. XIII, Article 7, New York: 1908.
7. THE CHEYENNE INDIAN by James Mooney.
    Memoirs, American Anthropological Association, Vol. I, Part 6, Lancaster: 1907.
8. THE FIGHTING CHEYENNES by George Bird Grinnell.
    Charles Scribner's Sons, New York: 1915.
9. THE CHEYENNE INDIANS, THEIR HISTORY AND WAYS OF LIFE by George Bird Grinnell.
    The Yale University Press, New Haven: 1923.
10. THE GHOST DANCE RELIGION IN THE SIOUX OUTBREAK OF 1890 by James Mooney.
    Fourteenth Annual Report, Bureau of American Ethnology, Part II.
    Washington: 1902.
11. THE SIOUAN INDIANS by W. J. McGee (Memoirs).
    Fifteenth Annual Report, Bureau of American Ethnology.
    Washington: 1909.
12. CALENDAR HISTORY OF THE KIOWA INDIANS by James Mooney.
    Seventeenth Annual Report, Bureau of American Ethnology.
    Washington: 1898.

CHAPTER 3

THE EXPLORATION AND SETTLEMENT OF COLORADO

COLIN B. GOODYKOONTZ

THE SPANISH ADVANCE

Although the northern boundary of Spain's possessions in America was indefinite, her authority certainly extended in more or less vague manner over the southern part of the present State of Colorado. Indeed, Spain claimed the whole of North America by virtue of the original discovery of Columbus and the Demarcation Line drawn by Pope Alexander VI in 1493. The other European powers naturally gave little heed to territorial pretensions so sweeping and uncertain. Much more substantial were Spain's claims based on the exploration of the interior, on the control of the Indians through conquest, missions and trade, and on the planting of colonies. From Mexico as a base Spanish explorers, missionaries and colonizers carried the authority of the Most Catholic Monarch far to the north in the sixteenth and seventeenth centuries.* The motives of the Spaniards were a medley of the practical and the fantastic, of the material and the spiritual. The same men who lusted for gold were thrilled with the prospect of finding strange places and weird people—the Seven Cities, Quivira, the Land of the Amazons, El Dorado. They conquered and exploited the natives—but who can separate exactly their greed and love of power from their missionary zeal?

The arrival in Mexico in 1536 of Alvar Nunez Cabeza de Vaca and four companions, including the blackamoor Estevanico, survivors of Narvaez's ill-fated expedition (1528), after their years of slavery and wanderings in Texas and Northern Mexico, stimulated interest in the northern regions. Cabeza de Vaca had seen nothing wonderful, but he had heard from the Indians about some large towns to the north of the land through which he had passed. In some manner the old legend of the Seven Cities** became at-

---

*Bolton and Marshall, *Colonization of North America*, gives a good brief account of Spanish exploration in the Southwest; Bolton, *The Spanish Borderlands*, is more readable. English translations of the original narratives of the more important Spanish expeditions into the Southwest in the sixteenth and seventeenth centuries may be found conveniently in Hodge and Lewis, *Spanish Explorers in the Southern United States, 1528-1543*, and in Bolton, *Spanish Exploration in the Southwest, 1542-1706*, both in *The Original Narratives of American History*, J. Franklin Jameson, editor.

**According to this legend, an archbishop and six bishops who fled from Spain in 714 after the defeat of King Roderick by the Moors, built seven cities on the mythical island of Antillia in the Atlantic Ocean.

tached to these northern towns, and thus the spirit of romance appeared to supplement cupidity as a motive for exploration. To test the stories of Cabeza de Vaca, Friar Marcos, Father Provincial of the Franciscan Order in New Spain, taking Estevanico as his guide, made a journey to the north in 1539. The Moor, who went ahead of the friar toward the close of the journey, reached Cíbola, one of the Zuñi pueblos in Northern Arizona. There he and some of the Indians who had joined the party en route were killed by the natives. The survivors of this massacre hurried back to Friar Marcos, who was a few days' journey behind. He pushed on until he came in sight of the pueblo where his guide had been killed. Its walls glistening in the sunlight told a story of gold and jewels to the credulous friar who, without further investigation, hastened back to Mexico with a tale sufficiently marvelous to raise excitement to fever heat. To Francisco Vasquez Coronado, governor of Nueva Galicia, was given the opportunity to become the Cortés of a new Mexico. At the head of a powerful expedition he set out from Compostela in 1540. Cíbola, which was reached without difficulty, turned out to be a squalid Indian village—and many were the curses hurled at Friar Marcos. Exploring parties were sent to the north, the west and the east. By the latter of these parties the villages of the Pueblo Indians in the upper Rio Grande Valley were discovered, and thither went Coronado and his army to spend the winter as the unwelcome guests of the natives. Among the Pueblo Indians the Spaniards found a captive slave taken from one of the tribes of the Great Plains who told them some wonderful stories of a country lying far to the east called Quivira. According to this cheerful liar, whom the Spaniards called the Turk, there was in that country a river "which was two leagues wide, in which there were fishes as big as horses, and large numbers of very big canoes, with more than twenty rowers on a side". Even more marvelous was the statement that "the lord of that country took his afternoon nap under a great tree on which were hung a great number of little gold bells, which put him to sleep as they swung in the air". Taking the Turk as guide, Coronado set out to find "Gran Quivira" in the spring of 1541. His route was southeast into central Texas, and then north into Kansas. Despite the fact that Quivira proved to be nothing more than an insignificant village of the Wichita

Indians, the myth hung on and the name long remained on maps of North America. Coronado returned directly to the Pueblo villages, and so probably passed to the east and south of the limits of Colorado. In the following year he went back to Mexico with his army; the results of the expedition were so disappointing that for forty years the Indians in the upper Rio Grande Valley were not again molested by the whites.

Meanwhile a less rapid but more effective advance was being made up the great central plateau of Mexico by miners, ranchers and missionaries. By 1580 mines and missions were to be found as far north as Santa Barbara in the southern part of the present State of Chihuahua. As the northern frontier of New Spain approached the Pueblo region, interest in it was revived. The missionaries were concerned about the souls of the hundreds of Indians there assembled; soldiers and colonists still cherished hopes of finding gold and silver in the northern mountains; the officials of both Old and New Spain were now attaching more importance than formerly to the northern frontier because of their fear that some English "Sea-Dog" like Sir Francis Drake, who had recently invaded the Pacific, might find the Strait of Anian— an imaginary passageway connecting the Atlantic and the Pacific —and thus endanger Spain's power in North America. Following the preliminary expeditions of Rodriguez (1581) and Espejo (1582-1583), elaborate preparations were made for the permanent occupation of the Pueblo country. The official expedition departed from Nueva Vizcaya in 1598 under the command of Juan de Onate; the natives were soon subdued, and the colony of New Mexico planted. In their hopes of finding great stores of precious metals, the Spaniards were again disappointed; the province did, however, become a flourishing missionary center.

How far north the limits of New Mexico extended, no one knew. Although no settlements were planted within the limits of Colorado during the seventeenth and eighteenth centuries, it was nevertheless within the sphere of Spanish influence, and into it on various occasions expeditions were sent for exploratory or punitive purposes. The first of these expeditions, so far as is now known, was made about the middle of the seventeenth century when one Juan de Archuleta was sent from Santa Fé with a few soldiers to bring back some Taos Indians who had fled to a place known to the Spaniards as El Quartelejo, sixty or seventy miles east of the site of Pueblo.* Apart from the fact that the foot of European now perhaps for the first time trod the soil of our State, the expedition had no particular significance. Half a century later the records disclose a similar *entrada*: in 1706 Juan de Uribarri was sent out to bring back some Indians who had likewise run away to El Quartelejo. With this party was Juan de L'Archevêque, one of La Salle's assassins, who was at this time a trader in Santa Fé. This expedition was significant chiefly because the friendly Apaches, through whose territory the party passed, reported that white men in the East were supplying their enemies, the Pawnees, with fire arms. In support of this assertion they produced a gun which L'Archevêque identified as a French weapon. Naturally the Spaniards were interested and eager to find out more about the activities of their Gallic rivals. In 1719 Governor Valverde, who led an expedition to the north of the Arkansas River in Colorado for the purpose of punishing some Utes and Comanches who had been disturbing the frontiers of his province, returned with rumors of French activities west of the Mississippi. Fortunately for the peace of mind of the officials of New Spain his report, which indicated that wherever the French were they were not in the immediate vicinity of New Mexico, arrived in time to show how groundless were the fears of the governor of Parral, who had just sent word that he understood that a force of six thousand Frenchmen was encamped only seventy leagues from Santa Fé.**

The French danger, although grossly exaggerated, was not imaginary. La Salle, it is true, failed in his attempt to plant a colony in Texas (1684), but his compatriots established themselves in the Illinois country and at Biloxi, near the mouth of the Mississippi River, in the closing years of the seventeenth century. The French soon began to trade with the Indians living on the western tributaries of the Father of Waters. Their motives were economic and political, the acquisition of furs and territory; in both they threatened Spanish suppremacy in the West.

To resist French encroachments on the northeastern flank of

---
*There is an accurate and concise summary of Spanish expeditions into Colorado in Thomas, "Spanish Expeditions into Colorado", in *Colorado Magazine*, I, 289-300.
**Dunn, "Spanish Reaction Against the French Advance Toward New Mexico", in *Mississippi Valley Historical Review*, II, 348-362.

New Spain, missions and presidios that had been abandoned in Texas at the close of the seventeenth century were reoccupied; to cope with the French on the northern frontier, plans were considered for the establishment of a new colony with mission and presidio at El Quartelejo, near the Arkansas River in Colorado. Orders were also issued that a reconnaisance expedition be dispatched from Santa Fé to find out just what the French were doing among the tribes that roamed the Great Plains to the northeast of New Mexico. This expedition, which set out in June, 1720, was commanded by Don Pedro de Villasur. The route followed was probably the one usually taken by the Spaniards in their journeys to the Arkansas country; to Taos, then over the Sangre de Cristo Mountains, to the Las Animas (Purgatoire), down it to the Rio Napeste (Arkansas), and on to El Quartelejo, which was near at hand. From the place last named they went in a northerly direction to the North Platte in western Nebraska where they were ambushed by a band of Pawnee Indians. Only about twelve of the party of more than one hundred escaped to tell their alarming story in Santa Fé, where it was believed at first that the French were responsible for the massacre. Of this there is no proof, although it is possible that some French traders were with the Pawnee when the attack was made.

So great was the alarm in New Mexico that some timorous souls talked of abandoning the province; others more resolute considered the establishment of a buffer settlement to the north and east of Santa Fé. Neither was done. In America, as in Europe, a long period of rivalry between France and Spain was coming to a close. A Bourbon now sat on the throne of Spain. The two powers, united in the Family Compact, met defeat together in the Seven Years' War (1756-1763). At the close of the war France ceded Louisiana west of the Mississippi to Spain to recompense her ally for the loss of Florida, and to prevent it from falling into the possession of her victorious rival, England. The Mississippi River thus became the boundary between Spanish and English possessions in North America. With the removal of the French from the Mississippi Valley there disappeared one powerful stimulus that for a time had kept the Spaniards keenly interested in the land to the north and east of New Mexico; the Anglo-Americans, who were just beginning to cross the Alleghanies, were hardly near enough to provide an equal incentive for watchfulness and activity. In the northwest, however, a new interest was being aroused: the Russian menace was looming up in the northern Pacific, and entirely too many English ships were finding their way into those waters. In order to check foreign encroachments on the northwest coast, old plans for the establishment of a colony in Upper California were recalled, and the foundations for a new frontier province were laid with the sending out of the Gálvez-Portolá expedition in 1769.

In the case of the officials and inhabitants of New Mexico there were more immediate motives for sending expeditions to the north and west, such as the desire to find mines and to control the Indians. In 1765 Juan Maria de Rivera, bent on investigating reports of mines in the La Plata (Silver) Mountains, led an expedition northwest from Santa Fé to the San Juan River, and continued in a northerly direction to the stream known to us as the Gunnison. Never before, so far as we know, had a white man advanced that far on our Western Slope. There are reasons for believing that in the decade following the return of the Rivera party several private trading or prospecting companies visited this part of Colorado; at any rate, at the time of the Domínguez-Escalante expedition in 1776 the more important physical features of the country through which the friars passed in southwestern Colorado were referred to by names still in use.*

The Domínguez-Escalante expedition was indirectly a result of the settlement of Upper California. By 1776 the Spanish missions in that province stretched as far to the north as San Francisco. But so far removed from the other northern provinces of New Spain were the California missions and presidios, that it seemed imperative that communication be opened by land with Pimería Alta (Arizona) and New Mexico. From Pimería Alta the attempt was made in 1774 by Juan Bautista de Anza and Father Garcés to find a road to California, but without conspicuous success. It was then suggested that an attempt be made to find a trail between Santa Fé and Monterey. For this purpose, and also to establish friendly relations with the Indians along the way, two Franciscan friars, Francisco Athanasio Domínguez and Silvestre Velez de Escalante, with twelve companions, set

*Hill, "The Old Spanish Trail", in *Hispanic American Historical Review*, IV, 444-473.

out from Santa Fé in July, 1776. The route they followed to the La Plata Mountains, and on by way of the Dolores, the San Miguel, and the Uncompahgre to the San Xavier (Gunnison), was much the same as that taken by Rivera ten years earlier. From the Gunnison they continued in a northerly direction across the rivers known to us as the Grand and the White to the Green River in the northeastern part of the present State of Utah. On account of the lateness of the season they abandoned their attempt to reach California, and returned to Santa Fé in January, 1777. The Domínguez-Escalante expedition, although it failed to accomplish its primary purpose, is generally regarded as the most important journey of exploration made by the Spanish in Colorado.

For some reason, perhaps because of the rough character of the land where the Rio Grande enters New Mexico, the Spaniards were slow in following that stream up into the San Luis Valley. Not until 1779 do we find a record of such an expedition; in that year Juan Bautista de Anza, then governor of New Mexico, led a military force into the San Luis Valley and across the mountains to the waters of the Arkansas near the site of Salida, for the purpose of punishing some Comanches who, under their leader Cuerno Verde (Green Horn), had been murdering Spanish settlers. In the closing years of the eighteenth century there were perhaps other official expeditions from New Mexico into the present state of Colorado, and doubtless several private trading ventures. Certain it is that in the opening years of the nineteenth century the New Mexicans appeared to be familiar with the San Luis Valley, the passes over the Sangre de Cristo Range, and the southern tributaries of the Arkansas.

The American Approach: Pike

The days when Spain's power in New Mexico stood secure in its isolation were passing. Now come the Americans—at first, only as a cloud as small as a man's hand in the eastern sky.

From the Peace of Paris (1763) to the close of the American War for Independence (1783) Spain and England shared most of North America with the Mississippi River as the dividing line. In 1783 the United States took the place of England on the eastern side of the river; in 1800 Napoleon compelled Spain to retrocede

Louisiana to France, and then, in 1803, in spite of pledges to the contrary, sold that vast territory to the United States. The boundaries of Louisiana had never been determined. But of one thing the Spanish could be sure: the aggressive, young nation on the Atlantic seaboard had thrown its frontier too close to their northern provinces for comfort. Nor were indications of the approach of the Americans long lacking: in March, 1807, Spanish soldiers escorted into Santa Fé Lieutenant Zebulon Montgomery Pike and his ragged men who had recently been found on the Conejos River, a tributary of the Rio Grande.

Lieutenant Pike was one of several men who had been sent to explore the Louisiana Purchase. Lewis and Clark went up the Missouri and down the Columbia to the Pacific; William Dunbar and George Hunter explored the Washita River; Thomas Freeman ascended the Red River for about six hundred miles; Pike was sent first to find the source of the Mississippi and then to explore the country around the headwaters of the Arkansas and Red rivers. General Wilkinson, Pike's superior officer, in his letter of instructions, said:

> As your Interview with the Commanches will probably lead you to the Head Branches of the Arkansaw and Red Rivers you may find yourself approximated to the settlements of New Mexico, and therefore it will be necessary you should move with great circumspection, to keep clear of any Hunting or reconnoitring Parties from that Province, and to prevent alarm or offence, because the affairs of Spain and the United States appear to be on the point of amicable adjustment, and moreover it is the desire of the President, to cultivate the Friendship and Harmonious Intercourse of all Nations of the Earth, and particularly our near Neighbors the Spaniards.*

The motives of General Wilkinson in sending Pike into the Southwest are still obscure. Wilkinson, an intriguer, was involved in the Burr Conspiracy; he may have sent Pike off toward the frontiers of New Mexico in order that the latter might be arrested by the Spaniards, taken to Mexico, and thus put in position to gain information that would be of use in case a filibustering expedition were launched against New Spain. This information, of course, would be just as useful if the United States should go to war with Spain; and war was imminent because of the dispute over the boundaries of Louisiana.

The Spaniards were naturally concerned about the activities

---
*Bolton, "Papers of Zebulon M. Pike", in *American Historical Review*, XIII, 813.

of the Americans in the Southwest, especially since both laid claim to Texas. News of the proposed Pike expedition having reached Santa Fé, Lieutenant Malgares was sent out in the summer of 1806 to explore the disputed regions, to establish friendly relations with the Indians, and, if possible, to intercept and turn back the American party. The Malgares expedition was much more pretentious than that commanded by Pike; there were one hundred dragoons of the regular army and five hundred mounted militia, with two extra horses and a mule to each man, and ammunition for six months. The two expeditions did not meet; when Pike reached the country of the Pawnee Indians he learned that Malgares had already been there and had returned to Santa Fé. The contrast between the two expeditions is brought out clearly by Captain Chittenden:

> There is a profound significance in the almost simultaneous presence of these two expeditions upon the boundless prairies that separated the frontier settlements of their respective countries. One was looking into the future and paving a way for the irresistible expansion of his people. The other was clinging to the past and watching with distrustful eye the too rapid progress of a rival power. Both were visiting the wild inhabitants of the plains and seeking with presents and speeches and grandiloquent pictures of the greatness of their respective nations, to secure their attachment. In this preliminary skirmish between the two powers, which were even then, did they but know it, preparing the way for inevitable conflict, the advantage was on the side of the Spaniard. Between the powerful and well-appointed expedition of Malgares and the small and poorly-equipped handful of men with Pike the contrast was great, and to the untutored mind of the prairie inhabitant there could be no doubt of the outcome of a trial of strength between their governments. He could not see the forces behind these outward manifestations—the expanding vigor of a young nation and the decadent energies of the old; but in due time he came to know.[*]

Pike left St. Louis in July, 1806. His immediate objects were to escort a band of Osage Indians to their home on the Osage River, to attempt to arrange a permanent peace between the Osage and Kansas nations, and to establish friendly relations with the Comanches. After having performed his missions among the Indians, Pike with fifteen men went up the Arkansas River, entering the limits of the state of Colorado on November 11, 1806. Pike was the first official American explorer, but not the first citizen of the United States, to enter Colorado. On November 23 the site of Pueblo was reached, and there a rude breastwork

---
[*]Chittenden, *American Fur Trade of the Far West*, II, 495.

of logs was built to serve as a defence for the party while Pike with three companions went up the Fountain River to explore the country around the high peak which now bears his name. Their attempt to climb to the top of the peak was a failure, as is revealed in an interesting manner in Pike's narrative:

> *Thursday, 27th November.*—Arose hungry, thirsty, and extremely sore, from the unevenness of the rocks on which we had lain all night; but very amply compensated for our toil by the sublimity of the prospects below. The unbounded prairie was overhung with clouds, which appeared like the ocean in a storm, wave piled on wave, and foaming, whilst the sky over our heads was perfectly clear. Commenced our march up the mountain [Cheyenne], and in about one hour arrived at the summit of this chain; here we found the snow middle deep, and discovered no sign of beast or bird inhabiting this region. The thermometer which stood at 9° above 0 at the foot of the mountain, here fell to 4° below. The summit of the Grand Peak, which was entirely bare of vegetation, and covered with snow, now appeared at the distance of fifteen or sixteen miles from us, and as high again as that we had ascended; it would take a whole day's march to have arrived at its base, when I believe no human being could have ascended to its summit. This with the condition of my soldiers, who had only light overalls on, and no stockings, and were every way ill provided to endure the inclemency of this region, the bad prospect of killing anything to subsist on, with the further detention of two or three days which it must occasion, determined us to return*.

The reunited party continued up the Arkansas as far as the Royal Gorge, and then crossed over into South Park, probably by way of Oil Creek.** They ascended the South Platte, which Pike thought might be the Yellowstone, and then crossed the mountains to a stream supposed by Pike to be the Red, but which really was the Arkansas a few miles below the site of Buena Vista. The leader with two companions went up stream about twenty-five miles; then, as the whole party followed the river in its downward course, they returned to their old camp near the Royal Gorge—and discovered that they had gone in a circle. On the site of Cañon City a small blockhouse was built. Here Pike left two men with the horses and a part of the baggage. With the others he set out to cross the Sangre de Cristo Range in the dead of winter in search of the Red River. His route was up Grape Creek into Wet Mountain Valley and across the range by

---
*Pike, *Exploratory Travels Through the Western Territories of North America* (reprint, Denver, 1889), 207.
**Coues, *The Expeditions of Zebulon Montgomery Pike*, II, 464.

Sand Creek Pass. The men suffered intensely from the cold and lack of food; at one point two of the party were left behind temporarily because they could no longer walk on their frozen feet. On January 30, 1807, Pike reached the Rio Grande, which he professed to believe was the Red River, near the site of Alamosa. He went down the river to the Conejos, then up the latter about five miles, and made camp on its northern bank. There Pike built a fort which was far more pretentious than those temporary structures he had hastily erected on the sites of Pueblo and Cañon City. The stockade was built twelve feet high and thirty-six feet square of heavy cottonwood logs; an abatis of small pointed stakes was set up, a moat four feet wide was dug and filled with water, and a rampart of earth was thrown up. Why such elaborate preparations for defence? For protection against the Spaniards, of course. But how were the Spaniards to be informed that Americans had come into their territory? By sending a member of the party, Dr. Robinson, into Santa Fé. Upon what pretext? To collect a debt for William Morrison, a merchant of Kaskaskia, from one Baptiste LaLande, who had failed to render an account. If Pike thought he was on the Red River and not on the Rio Grande, as he said, the question naturally arises how he thought Dr. Robinson would ever get to Santa Fé by going down the river. The arrival of Dr. Robinson in the settlements of New Mexico produced the result Pike had expected: a military force was sent out to find the American intruders. The Spanish officer was very polite; Pike was very much surprised when informed that he was on the Rio Grande, and much chagrined to think that he had erected a blockhouse and flown the American flag on territory incontestably Spanish!

From Santa Fé, Pike and his men, the whole party again united, were taken to Chihuahua and finally allowed to return to the United States by way of Texas. By the time of Pike's return the Burr Conspiracy, whatever it was, had collapsed; the country contained no more vociferous patriot that General Wilkinson; the threatened war with Spain had been averted. There was no immediate military use for Pike's information about the Southwest. As a contribution to geographical knowledge, however, the expedition was very important, and as a forerunner of the American advance it was of tremendous significance.

MEXICAN LAND GRANTS AND SETTLEMENTS

After a decade of revolutionary disturbances Mexico achieved independence in 1821. From the outset of her national existence her title to two-thirds of Colorado was clear, because only two years earlier Spain and the United States had come to an agreement about the western boundary of Louisiana. By this treaty (1819) the United States gave up its claim to Texas and accepted the Arkansas River as a boundary line west of the one hundredth meridian; from the source of the Arkansas a line was to be drawn north to the forty-second parallel. Thus Mexican authority, in succession to that of Spain, was undisputed in the southern quarter and western half of Colorado.

The new Republic fell heir to a vast but sparsely settled territory. In order to encourage settlement, laws were passed in 1824 and 1828 under which large grants of land might be made to *empresarios*, or to reward men for their services to the state. There was an abundance of land, and so the grants were large; the land had little value, and so frequently no attempt was made to determine accurately the limits of a grant. This loose system of disposing of the public domain was of interest to the United States because by the Treaty of Guadaloupe Hidalgo (1848), which ended the Mexican War, our government pledged itself to respect valid titles to land in the ceded territory; American land officers and judges were called on to untangle the snarl of Mexican land grants in New Mexico and California. Some notion of the causes and nature of the disputes which arose may be obtained from Mr. Justice Miller's remarks about the difficulty of adjusting claims based on the California grants; they apply with equal force to those of New Mexico:

> Some idea of the difficulties which surround these cases may be obtained by recurring to the loose and indefinite manner in which the Mexican government made the grants which we are now required judicially to locate. The government attached no value to the land and granted it in what to us appear magnificent quantities. Leagues instead of acres were their units of measurement, and when an application was made to the government for a grant, which was always a gratuity, the only question was whether the locality asked for was vacant and was public property. When the grant was made no surveyor sighted a compass or stretched a chain. Indeed, these instruments were probably not to be had in that region. A sketch, called a diseño, which was rather a map than a plat of the land, was prepared by the applicant. It gave, in a rude and imperfect manner, the shape and general out-

line of the land desired, with some of the more prominent natural objects noted on it, and a reference to the adjoining tracts owned by individuals if there were any, or to such other objects as were supposed to constitute the boundaries*.

Of the Mexican land grants affecting Colorado the first in general interest is probably the Maxwell Grant. On January 8, 1841, Carlos Beaubien and Guadalupe Miranda petitioned Governor Armijo of New Mexico for a grant of land to the east of Taos. In their petition they pointed out that of all the provinces in the Republic of Mexico, New Mexico was one of the most backward "in intelligence, industry [and] manufactories"; they lamented the idleness, vice and crime of the day, and hinted that conditions might be improved by the establishment of colonies. They asked for a tract of land on which to raise sugar beets and stock, and to establish manufactories of cotton and wool. Then followed just such a description of the land desired as Mr. Justice Miller depicted above. It embraced, roughly, a large part of present Colfax County, New Mexico, and an irregular tract in the southwestern corner of Las Animas County, Colorado. Possession of this vast tract of over a million and a half acres was given in the customary manner: mounds were erected to indicate the limits of the grant; a magistrate took the grantees by the hand, "walked with them, caused them to throw earth, pull up weeds, and show other evidences of possession". After the United States acquired New Mexico in 1848, a surveyor general was appointed to investigate claims to land based on the Mexican grants. He approved the grant to Beaubien and Miranda, and on June 21, 1860, Congress confirmed their title to some 1,700,000 acres of land. Soon thereafter title passed to Beaubien's son-in-law, Lucien B. Maxwell, famous western trader and scout. The subsequent history of the grant,—its transfer to the Maxwell Land Grant Company, an English syndicate, the fights between the company and the squatters on the land, the various lawsuits that arose,—is an interesting story that cannot be told here. The patent as finally issued by the United States Government in 1879 carried the northern line of the grant almost to the city of Trinidad.**

---
*Rodriguez v. United States, 1 Wall., 587.
**House Report 457, 35 Cong., 1 Sess., 245 House Report 321, 36 Cong., 1 Sess., 247; on the Maxwell Land Grant I have found helpful an unpublished thesis prepared by Miss Bess McKennan of Trinidad.

THE EXPLORATION AND SETTLEMENT OF COLORADO 55

Equally provocative of strife was the Las Animas Grant made in 1843 to Cornelio Vigil and Ceran St. Vrain. Their claim was bounded, roughly, by the Maxwell Grant on the south, the Arkansas River on the north, the Las Animas (Purgatoire) on the east, and the Huerfano on the west. Although the surveyor general recommended in 1857 that this entire tract of about four million acres be confirmed to Vigil and St. Vrain, Congress was not as generous as in the case of the Maxwell Grant. Falling back on the letter of the Mexican colonization law, which had limited the amount of land that could be granted to one individual to eleven square leagues (nearly 49,000 acres), Congress voted to grant twenty-two square leagues to the two claimants. From this amount was to be substracted the lands of those who held title to a part of the original estate under grants or promises made by Vigil or St. Vrain; so generous had they been in their sub-grants that practically nothing was left to be divided among their heirs. Some men, especially those financially interested in the Las Animas Grant, contended that the refusal of the United States to confirm the grant with the boundaries fixed in 1843 was an act of bad faith; in behalf of the Government, on the other hand, it was pointed out that grants in excess of eleven square leagues to one person were illegal under Mexican law, and that it was not in keeping with American policy to grant such large sections of the public domain to a few individuals.*

Large grants of land were made also in the San Luis Valley. In October, 1842, a considerable part of our Conejos County was granted to José Maria Martinez, Antonio Martinez, Julian Gallegos and Seledon Valdez. It was not until 1854 that a permanent settlement was made on this grant. In August of that year José Maria Jaquez selected a site for a colony at Guadalupe on the Conejos River. While final preparations were being made to move to the new location, the colonists were joined by Lafayette Head of Servilleta.** Head was a Missourian who had gone to Santa Fé as a private in the Mexican War. At the expiration of his term of service he took up his abode in New Mexico, where he quickly rose to a position of prominence. He was the out-

*House Report 457, 35 Cong., 1 Sess.; Senate Report 228, 36 Cong., IV; House Report 1253, 52 Cong., 1 Sess.; Las Animas Land Grant Company v. United States, 179 U. S. 201; Decisions of Department of Interior Relating to Public Lands, I, 266.
**Meliton Velasquez, in Alamosa Journal, Oct. 22, 1925; for this reference I am indebted to Dr. Leroy Hafen of the State Historical Society, Denver.

standing figure in the Conejos colony, and later held posts of honor and trust under the governments of both New Mexico and Colorado. In spite of the fact that actual settlements were made on the Conejos Grant, claims to land under it were not confirmed by the United States Government, partly because of technical defects, partly because much of the land had been taken up under the Federal land laws.*

The Conejos Grant was on the west side of the Rio Grande. On the east side of that river, in present Costilla County, a large tract of land was given in 1843 to Luis Lee and Narciso Beaubien, both of Taos. Up to the time the two beneficiaries were killed in the Taos massacre of 1847, no attempt had been made to plant a colony on this land. In 1849 Carlos Beaubien, father and heir of Narciso, having purchased the interest of the heirs of Luis Lee, established a settlement on the Costilla River about one mile south of the Colorado-New Mexico boundary line. Within the next five years several other settlements were made on the grant within the limits of Colorado; among them were San Luis (1851), San Pedro (1852) and San Acacio (1853). This vast estate, which was generally known as the Sangre de Cristo Grant, having successfully stood the test of investigation by the officials of the United States, passed into the hands of William Gilpin, ex-governor of Colorado, in 1864. By him it was sold to an English company which in turn sold the southern portion of the grant to a Dutch syndicate, thus producing the division of the tract into the Trinchera Estate in the north and the Costilla Estate in the south.**

To the north of the Sangre de Cristo Grant, in present Saguache County, lay "Baca Grant No. 4", which was confirmed to the heirs of Luis Maria Baca by Congress in 1860. This tract of nearly one hundred thousand acres was transferred first to William Gilpin, and then to an English company. It later was called the Crestone Estate. Another of the minor estates was the Nolan Grant, which lay to the south of the Arkansas River and west of the Las Animas Grant; title to it finally passed to one of the subsidiary companies of the Denver and Rio Grande Railroad, and on a part of it South Pueblo was laid out in 1872.

*Report of Secretary of Interior, 1904, 100; Hafen, "Mexican Land Grants in Colorado", in Colorado Magazine, IV, 92.
**Blackmore, Colorado, Its Resources, Parks and Prospects, 168; House Report, 457, 35 Cong., 1 Sess.; Decisions of Department of Interior Relating to Public Lands, XI, 203; Tameling v. United States Freehold and Emigration Company, 93 U. S., 644.

THE EXPLORATION AND SETTLEMENT OF COLORADO 57

Buried in old newspapers and dusty records is a romantic story of the struggle for the control of the Mexican land grants. In general, the heirs and descendants of the men who received these vast estates realized little from them. The outstanding exception was Lucien B. Maxwell, who lived in a sort of barbaric splendor in his home on the Cimarron, and who is said to have received more than a million dollars for the Maxwell Grant. The speculator who by fair means or foul obtained a claim to the whole or even a part of one of these estates looked forward to the time when its mineral and agricultural resources would make him richer than Croesus. And then there were the squatters, the pioneer farmers or ranchers, who settled on the grants either ignorantly or wilfully; they sometimes resisted even to the point of bloodshed the attempts of the agents of the great land companies to expel them, as in the Stonewall Valley on the Maxwell Grant, near Trinidad, in the summer of 1888.*

In the settlement of Colorado the Mexican land grants had a two-fold significance. The uncertainty and confusion in land titles that long prevailed in the southern part of the State retarded its settlement by the Anglo-Americans.** On the other hand, there was no cause to worry over such matters when the grants were made; it was on them that the first settlements by white men, other than traders and trappers, were made in Colorado. On the Las Animas Grant a few scattered settlements were made in the Mexican period; as early as 1847 John Hatcher, an employee of Vigil and St. Vrain, tried to raise crops on the Purgatoire a few miles east of the site of Trinidad. The settlements on the Maxwell Grant, prior to 1859, were south of the Colorado line. In the San Luis Valley there were at least several hundred people of Mexican or Spanish descent when the gold seekers came; their descendants are still to be found in certain parts of the Valley, thus reminding us of our connection with the old Spanish Empire.

One of the most pleasing manifestations of Spanish influence in Southern Colorado is in its nomenclature. For the melodious and euphonious names of so many of our mountains, rivers, and towns we must give thanks to Spanish and Mexican explorers, traders and settlers. Some of the names, such as Sangre de

---
*Denver Republican, Sept. 1, 1888.
**Denver Tribune, July 14, 1871.

Cristo (Blood of Christ), Trinidad (Trinity), Las Animas (the Souls), San Juan (Saint John), and Dolores (Sorrow), remind us of the religious faith of the Spaniards; others are descriptive, such as Mesa Verde (Green Table-land), Huerfano (Orphan), Rio Blanco (White River), La Junta (the Junction), La Plata (the Silver), Costilla (Rib), and Colorado (reddish brown).

TRAPPERS AND TRADERS

Even before Mexico gained independence (1821) enterprising traders and trappers from the United States appeared on its northern frontier. The first of these to enter Colorado, so far as we now know, was James Pursley or Purcell. His story is recorded briefly by Pike, who met him in New Mexico in 1807; as early as 1805 he had traded with the Indians on the South Platte, had gone with them into South Park, and had, as he told Pike, found in Colorado flakes of gold which he carried in his shot pouch for months. Pike's description of New Mexico and its people doubtless called attention to the possibility of developing an overland trade between that remote province and the American communities on the Missouri River. News of the Hidalgo revolution and the expectation that a more liberal commercial regime would be inaugurated in Mexico, led to the McKnight trading expedition to Santa Fé in 1812. Unfortunately for these pioneers of the Santa Fé trade, the Hidalgo revolution failed; they were thrown in prison by the Spanish authorities and kept there nine years, or until the success of the revolutionary movement under Iturbide. Distressing but not so tragic was the experience of the Chouteau-De Munn party; after three years of arduous toil trapping on the Platte and Arkansas rivers (1815-1817), they were visited by a Spanish force and ordered into Santa Fé where all their furs were confiscated.*

The agreement on a boundary line between American and Spanish territories in the Southwest in 1819, and the success of the Mexican Revolution in 1821, removed some of the difficulties that had beset American trappers and traders who had ventured out to the borders of New Mexico. Beginning with William

---
*The standard account of the fur trade of the West during this period in Chittenden, *American Fur Trade of the Far West*; there is an excellent account of the early fur trade and exploration of Colorado by Hafen in State Historical and Natural History Society, *History of Colorado* (Baker and Hafen, editors), I, chap. VI.

Becknell's trading expedition in 1821, caravans regularly crossed the plains to Santa Fé until the railroad made this mode of conveyance obsolete. The "desert route" of the Santa Fé Trail cut the corner of Baca County, Colorado; the longer route followed the Arkansas to Bent's Fort, and then turned off up the Timpas toward the site of Trinidad and Raton Pass.*

At the same time the Santa Fé trade was developing it was becoming safer for American trappers to approach the frontiers of New Mexico. Certainly the Glenn-Fowler party in 1821-1822 met with a much more cordial reception in Santa Fé than did the McKnight party a decade earlier. The Glenn-Fowler party is worthy of remembrance in Colorado history because camp was made on the site of Pueblo and there was built the first habitable and inhabited dwelling constructed by private citizens within the limits of the State. This "fort" was built for protection against the Indians while Colonel Glenn went to Santa Fé; Fowler, who was left in charge of the party on the Arkansas River, describes the situation as follows:

> We are now In the Hart of the Inden Cuntry and Emedetly on the great Ware Road—not only of one nation against the others—in the Road to all the Spanish Settlements With Which the Indeans on this Side of the mountains are at War—So that our Setuation is not the most Plesent kind—We have no meet In Camp—and Con Clude to Send two Hunters out With Horses in the morning to kill Some meat Intending to Set the ballence of the Hands at work to build a Hous and a Strong Peen for the Horses at night**

On the receipt of news that Colonel Glenn had met with a friendly reception in Santa Fé, the whole party went to New Mexico; before their return to the States in the spring of 1822 some time was spent in trapping on the Rio Grande as far up as Wagon Wheel Gap.

In the late twenties and the thirties the most important group of trappers operating in Colorado was the one associated with the Rocky Mountain Fur Company. In 1822 William H. Ashley and Andrew Henry of St. Louis formed a partnership for the purpose of engaging in the fur trade on the upper Missouri River. By 1825, as a result of competition with the Missouri Fur Company, and the discovery of virgin field in the Great Basin and on the western slopes of the Rockies, they began to

---
*Hulbert, *The American Transcontinental Trails*, V. (Santa Fe Trail).
**Coues, *The Journal of Jacob Fowler*, 75.

concentrate their energies in the region now covered, roughly, by the states of Wyoming, Idaho, Utah and Colorado. They introduced a new method of conducting the business: instead of building forts or trading houses, they relied on an annual rendezvous at some suitable place in the mountains. A sheltered valley, centrally located, well-watered and well-supplied with grass would be selected. To it at a specified time in the summer would come men from St. Louis with supplies to exchange for furs, the trappers who had spent the preceding months in their solitary employment, and frequently friendly Indians. After a week or two of revelry and bartering, the men scattered; the trappers went back into the wilderness, while the furs were taken to St. Louis. Among the better known of these meeting places were Pierre's Hole in eastern Idaho, Jackson's Hole in western Wyoming, Cache Valley on Bear River north of the Great Salt Lake, and Brown's Hole in northwestern Colorado. In 1826 the business was transferred to Jedediah Smith, David E. Jackson and William Sublette, the ablest and most experienced of Ashley's lieutenants; they in turn sold out in 1830 to Thomas Fitzpatrick, Milton G. Sublette, Henry Fraeb, Jean Baptiste Gervais, and James Bridger. Smith and Bridger and Sublette are names to conjure with in the exploration of the Far West, but to tell in detail the story of their wanderings even within the limits of Colorado is impossible in this brief sketch. Suffice it to say that they followed the rivers to their sources and explored the mountain parks; they, more than any other group of men, were the real pathfinders of the West.

Colorado was also visited in this period by many "free" or independent trappers who sometimes erected rude forts for protection against the weather or the Indians. Of these early trading posts, as distinguished from the more temporary structures of Pike and the Glenn-Fowler party, the first to be erected in Colorado seems to have been the one built by the Bent brothers and Ceran St. Vrain about 1826 on the Arkansas River fifteen or twenty miles above the site of Pueblo. Of St. Vrain mention has already been made in connection with the Las Animas Land Grant; the Bent brothers, William, George, Robert, and Charles, belonged to a prominent family of St. Louis. For thirty years their name was almost synonymous with the fur trade of Colorado. The post built by the Bent & St. Vrain Company in 1826 is of little consequence; in 1828 they began to erect a larger fort farther down the Arkansas River. Bent's Fort, or Fort William as it was sometimes called, was finished in 1832. It stood on the north bank of the river ten or twelve miles above the mouth of the Purgatoire. It was the most important trading post in Colorado and one of the most famous in the West. Ruxton, an early traveler in the Far West, has left a vivid description of this fort and some of its early denizens:

> Bent's Fort is situated on the left or northern bank of the river Arkansas, about one hundred miles from the foot of the Rocky Mountains—on a low and level bluff of the prairie which here slopes gradually to the water's-edge. The walls are built entirely of adobes—or sun-burned bricks—in the form of a hollow square, at two corners of which are circular flanking towers of the same material. The entrance is by a large gateway into the square, round which are the rooms occupied by the traders and employes of the host. These are small in size, with walls colored by a whitewash made of clay found in the prairies. Their flat roofs are defended along the exterior by parapets of adobe, to serve as a cover to marksmen firing from the top; and along the coping grow plants of cactus of all the varieties common in the plains. In the center of the square is the press for packing the furs; and there are three large rooms, one used as a store and magazine, another as a council-room, where the Indians assemble for their "talks", while the third is the common dining-hall where the traders, trappers, and hunters, and all employes, feast upon the best povender the game-covered country affords. Over the culinary department presided of late years a fair lady of color, Charlotte by name, who was, as she loved to say, "de onlee lady in de dam Injun country", and who moreover was celebrated from Long's Peak to the Cumbres Espanolas for slap-jacks and pumpkin pies.
> Here congregate at certain seasons the merchants of the plains and mountains, with their stocks of peltry. Chiefs of the Shian, the Kioway, and Arapaho, sit in solemn conclave with the head traders, and smoke the "calumet" over their real or imaginary grievances . . . .
> In the corral, groups of leather-clad mountaineers, with "decks" of "euker", and "seven up", gamble away their hard-earned peltries. The employes—mostly St. Louis Frenchmen and Canadian voyageurs—are pressing packs of buffalo skins, beating robes, or engaged in other duties of a trading fort . . . .
> The appearance of the fort is very striking, standing as it does hundreds of miles from any settlement, on a vast and life-less prairie, surrounded by hordes of hostile Indians, and far out of the reach of intercourse with civilized man; its mud-built walls inclosing a little garrison of a dozen hardy men, sufficient to hold in check the numerous tribes of savages ever thirsting for their blood. Yet the solitary stranger passing this lone fort, feels proudly secure when he comes within sight of the "stars and stripes" which float above the walls.*

---

*Ruxton, *Life in the Far West*, 189-191.

The site of the fort had been selected with reference to trade with Santa Fé on the one hand and with the Indians on the other. It was in the buffalo country, a region frequented by the Utes, Arapahoes, Cheyennes, Comanches and Pawnees. According to Thomas J. Farnham, who visited the fort in 1839, from "fifteen to twenty thousand savages ready and panting for plunder and blood" sometimes gathered around this outpost of civilization*. The Bents were skilful in their dealings with the Indians, and so this lonely fort stood until it was destroyed by its own master in 1852. In a fit of anger that grew out of delays in his negotiations for the sale of the fort to the United States Government, William Bent wrecked it, and then built "Bent's New Fort" farther down the Arkansas Valley, near the present line between Bent and Prowers counties.

There were other more ephemeral trading posts in the Arkansas Valley: both Farnham** and Dr. Wislizenus*** in 1839 refer to El Puebla, a small trading post four or five miles west of Fort Bent; in 1842 a group of independent trappers built "the Pueblo" on the site of the present city of that name. The latter post remained the abode of a small group of Mexican and half-breed traders and trappers until 1854 when all but one of its seventeen inhabitants were killed by a band of Ute Indians;**** from then until the time of the gold rush no one appears to have lived at the junction of the Fountain and the Arkansas.

In the thirties and forties an important group of trading posts was to be found on the South Platte below the site of Denver. Fort Lupton was built in 1836 or 1837 by Lieutenant Lancaster P. Lupton, who had accompanied Colonel Henry Dodge and the First Dragoons to the Rocky Mountains in 1835. Realizing the possibilities of the fur trade, Lupton resigned his commission in the United States Army and built a trading post on the South Platte about a mile north of the present town of Fort Lupton. About 1837 Louis Vasquez, a well-known early trader, built a post, the ruins of which may still be seen on the Fort Vasquez Ranch about a mile and a half south of the town of Platteville.

---
*Farnham, *Travels in the Great Western Prairies*, in Thwaites, *Early Western Travels*, XXVIII, 164.
**Farnham, *op. cit.*, 173.
***Wislizenus, *A Journey to the Rocky Mountains in the Year 1839*, (Missouri Historical Society, 1912), 141; Wislizenus calls it "Peebles' Fort".
****Hafen, "The Fort Pueblo Massacre and the Punitive Expedition Against the Utes", in *Colorado Magazine*, IV, 49-58.

THE EXPLORATION AND SETTLEMENT OF COLORADO 63

To compete with Lupton and Vasquez, the Bent brothers and St. Vrain built a post on the South Platte in 1837 or 1838 about a mile and a half south of the mouth of St. Vrain Creek. It was called Fort St. Vrain, or sometimes Fort George, in honor of George Bent. No one of the South Platte trading posts ever rivaled Fort Bent in importance. Although a well-defined trail was marked out by the Mexican traders who visited these northern posts, they were not as easily reached as Fort Bent; nor were they as well located with reference to the Indian trade. Fort Vasquez was abandoned about 1842; Fort St. Vrain was "fast falling into ruin" when Francis Parkman passed in 1846; Fort Lupton, although not in use as a trading post, was still in a fair state of preservation during the early settlement period, and was sometimes used as a place of refuge during the Indian wars of the sixties.*

There were at least two trading posts on the Western Slope. Robideaux's fort on the Gunnison River was built in the late thirties by Antoine Robideaux, a French trader from St. Louis. In Brown's Hole on the Green River in northwestern Colorado there was Fort Crockett. Dr. Wislizenus, who visited it in 1839, described it as "the worst thing of the kind" he had seen on his journey; so poverty stricken was this establishment, the property of three American traders, Thompson, Gray and Sinclair, that it was known to the trappers as Fort Misery.

EXPLORERS AND TRAVELERS

The fur traders ordinarily left no record of their wanderings; travelers with literary tastes and official explorers did, for which we are thankful, although the result has been to give us a distorted notion of the importance of some of these men as "pathfinders". Some of the later official expeditions did not get far off the beaten path; those that did frequently had to depend on the guidance of some scout or trapper.

After Pike's expedition to Colorado the next official exploring party to enter the limits of the State was the one commanded by Major Stephen H. Long. This expedition was the outgrowth of attempts made at the close of the War of 1812 to check British

---
*Hafen, "Early Fur Trade Posts on the South Platte", in *Mississippi Valley Historical Review*, XII, 334-341.

influence among and to strengthen American control over the Indians of the Northwest.* New forts were built; a new method of regulating the fur trade was introduced; a great expedition was prepared for the purpose of impressing the natives with the power of the Great Father at Washington. Unfortunately, the plans for this elaborate expedition up the Missouri River were blocked in Congress in the winter of 1819-1820; then as a "half-hearted apology to the public for its failure, a small side-show was organized for the season of 1820 in the form of an expedition to the Rocky Mountains". Major Long and his command went up the South Platte past the site of Denver to the entrance to South Park, where a futile attempt was made to enter the mountains. The outstanding achievement of the expedition was the ascent of Pike's Peak, for the first time by white men, by Dr. Edwin James, chronicler of the party, and a few companions; for several years thereafter this landmark was frequently called James Peak. On the return trip to the States the party divided, some going down the Arkansas, the others crossing over to the Red River. Historically the Long expedition was significant chiefly on account of the unflattering description published regarding the land lying to the east of the Rockies; Long, more than any other man, was responsible for the idea of the "Great American Desert". He wrote:

> In regard to this extensive section of country, I do not hesitate in giving the opinion, that it is almost wholly unfit for cultivation, and of course uninhabitable by a people depending upon agriculture for their subsistence . . . Agreeably to the best intelligence that can be had, concerning the country both northward and southward of this section [in the vicinity of the Canadian], and especially to the inferences deducible from the account given by Lewis and Clark, of the country situated between the Missouri and the Rocky Mountains above the river Platte, the vast region commencing near the sources of the Sabine, Trinity, Brases, and Colorado, and extending northwardly to the forty-ninth degree of north latitude, by which the United States' territory is limited in that direction, is throughout of a similar character. The whole of this region seems peculiarly adapted as a range for buffaloes, wild goats, and other wild game; incalculable multitudes of which find ample pasturage and subsistence upon it. This region, however, viewed as a frontier, may prove of infinite importance to the United States, inasmuch as it is calculated to serve as a barrier to prevent too great an extension of our population westward and secure it against the machinations or incursions

---

*Goodwin, "A Larger View of the Yellowstone Expedition, 1819-1820", in *Mississippi Valley Historical Review*, IV, 299-313.

THE EXPLORATION AND SETTLEMENT OF COLORADO 65

of an enemy that might otherwise be disposed to annoy us in that part of our frontier.*

The subsequent official exploration of Colorado can be dismissed quickly. Neither the expedition under Colonel Henry Dodge in 1835 nor the one under Colonel Stephen Kearny in 1845 traversed new or unknown territory; both were significant chiefly in connection with our relations with the Indians living on the Great Plains. The most famous of the later official explorers of Colorado was the romantic Captain John C. Frémont. Five times between 1842 and 1848 this "Pathfinder of the West" appeared in Colorado. In 1842 and again in 1843 he visited a region east of the mountains that had been many times explored. In 1844, on his return from his first journey to Oregon and California, Frémont entered Colorado at Brown's Hole on the Green River and crossed the limits of the State from west to east passing successively through North, Middle, and South Parks; he left by way of the Arkansas River. His third western journey, the one of 1845, brought him into Colorado for the fourth time; his route was up the Arkansas to its source, across Tennessee Pass, and down the White River to the Green. This expedition is historically significant because it put Frémont in California in time to share in the American conquest of that province. The acquisition of territory on the Pacific coast stimulated interest in the building of a transcontinental railway; in 1848, Frémont, now a private citizen, appeared in the rôle of railway engineer. With the financial assistance of St. Louis capitalists, Frémont set out in that year to find a feasible line for a railroad through the mountains of Colorado; in order that he might examine the proposed route under the most unfavorable conditions, he tried to cross in winter. Despite warnings from trappers and mountaineers he set out from Fort Bent in November, 1848. The Sangre de Cristo Range was crossed with little difficulty, but the foolhardy attempt to cross the mountains at the head of the Rio Grande in the midwinter had disastrous results. One-third of the men and all of the animals were lost. The survivors made their way back down the valley of the Rio Grande to New Mexico, where a new party was recruited; Frémont continued his journey to California by a more southern and less lofty route.**

*Thwaites, *Early Western Travels*, XVII, 147.
**Bigelow, *Memoir of the Life and Public Services of John Charles Fremont*.

In 1853 Captain Gunnison of the United States Army made a more successful attempt to find a route for a transcontinental railroad in the region where Frémont had failed. Congress in the spring of that year had authorized several surveys of possible Pacific railway lines. To Captain Gunnison was assigned, roughly speaking, the line of the thirty-ninth parallel; his route was over the Sangre de Cristo Range, across Cochetopa Pass, and down the Gunnison and the Uncompahgre into Utah, where he and seven other members of the party were killed by Indians near Sevier Lake. Lieutenant Beckwith, who succeeded to the command, led the survivors to Salt Lake; there the surveys along the forty-second and thirty-ninth parallels merged. Tracks of the Denver and Rio Grande Railway, although not those of the main line across the mountains, follow closely Captain Gunnison's route. His fellow engineers, who about the same time explored routes that correspond roughly to the present lines of the Northern Pacific, the Union Pacific, the Santa Fé, and the Southern Pacific, reported individually that roads could be built through the parts of the mountains they had traversed. It was thus apparent that physical obstacles were not insurmountable. Actual construction, however, was impossible at the time without Federal aid, and sectional rivalry made it impossible for Congress to agree on a route; a land grant for the first Pacific railway was not voted until after the Southern delegation had withdrawn from Congress following the outbreak of the Civil War.

Brief mention should also be made of the journeys in Colorado in the thirties and forties of the private individuals who are remembered in this connection because of the books they wrote. Thomas Farnham's *Travels in the Great Western Prairies* gives an account of a journey made to the Columbia River in 1839 by a small band of Oregon emigrants. Instead of following the ordinary Oregon Trail, they tried a much more difficult route which took them up the Arkansas to its source and down the Blue and the Yampa to Brown's Hole on the Green. Before Farnham left Brown's Hole en route for Oregon, Dr. F. A. Wislizenus, an Illinois physician, who had been as far west as Fort Hall, arrived on his homeward journey. The latter's route through Colorado took him to the headwaters of the North Platte and across the mountains to the South Platte near the trading posts of Lupton, Vasquez and St. Vrain. From the South Platte he crossed the Divide to the Arkansas, down which he returned to the States.*

Between 1841 and 1843 many parts of Colorado were visited by Rufus Sage, a trapper and trader, whose *Rocky Mountain Life* is full of interesting descriptions and some strange fancies, as, for instance, his notion that the frequent storms of rain, hail, snow and wind in the Pike's Peak country had some connection "with the vast quantities of minerals lying embeded in its hills and valleys". Much less extensive were the travels of Francis Parkman, who in 1846 passed along the eastern base of the mountains from Fort Laramie to the Arkansas; the charm of his *Oregon Trail* is not lessened by the fact that it is the narrative of a journey through a region that was already well explored. Frederick Ruxton's *Wild Life in the Rocky Mountains* is an account of the experiences of an English traveler who entered Colorado by way of the San Luis Valley in 1847; after crossing in mid-winter to the tributaries of the Arkansas, he hunted in South Park and along the eastern base of the mountains for several months. For definite information about the fur trade and trading posts, the location and habits of the Indians, and Mexican interests in Colorado in the thirty years preceding the coming of the gold seekers, we are dependent to a large extent on the writings of these travelers and explorers.

It is obvious from what has been written above that Colorado was not *terra incognita* in 1858 and 1859. There were then several small Mexican communities in the San Luis Valley, and there had been ephemeral settlements of Mexicans and half-breeds on the Arkansas and its southern tributaries. Traders from Santa Fé and Taos were well acquainted with the passes across the mountains in the southern part of the State; from New Mexico clearly defined trails reached out to the South Platte and the Arkansas rivers. Through southwestern Colorado there was the Old Spanish Trail stretching out toward Utah. Traders, trappers and explorers, both official and unofficial, had visited North, Middle, and South Parks, the headwaters of the North and South Plattes, the Arkansas, the Rio Grande, and had been on all the

---
*Wislizenus, *A Journey to the Rocky Mountains in the Year 1839* (Missouri Historical Society, 1912).

other principal streams of Colorado. Again and again the South Platte and the Arkansas had guided parties of men into the limits of Colorado or had pointed the way back to the States.

With the decline of the fur trade in the forties and fifties passed the great days of the trading posts; in their stead came the Government forts. The first in Colorado was Fort Massachusetts, which was built in the San Luis Valley in 1852 as a means of protection for the white settlers against the Ute Indians; in 1858 Fort Garland, six miles distant, took its place. The second of the official forts was established in 1859 when "Bent's New Fort" on the Arkansas River was taken over by the Federal Government, and renamed Fort Wise in honor of Governor Henry Wise of Virginia; in 1861, after the secession of Virginia, the name was changed to Fort Lyon in commemoration of the valiant services of General Nathaniel Lyon, who was killed in the battle of Wilson's Creek, Missouri, in August of that year.

THE GOLD RUSH

In the early fifties there was less interest in that part of the Rocky Mountains enclosed within the limits of Colorado than there had been in the two preceding decades. The fur trade had declined in importance, but nothing had appeared to take its place. The chief overland trails passed either to the north or to the south of the lofty mountains in which the South Platte and the Arkansas take their rise. The transcontinental railroad was still a dream. The agricultural frontier was no farther west than central Iowa and eastern Kansas. On the prairies there was room for indefinite expansion, and on beyond lay the "Great American Desert". So far as any one could foretell the Utes would not soon be disturbed in their mountain hunting grounds, and the Arapahoes and Cheyennes would be allowed to enjoy without molestation from the whites the land along the eastern base of the mountains between the Oregon and Santa Fé trails which had been granted to them by a treaty made in 1851. Colorado was remote, not easily accessible, and uninviting. All this was changed suddenly and violently by the discovery of gold on the South Platte and its tributaries in the summer of 1858.*

---

*For the gold rush see chapter by Willard in this volume.

The Exploration and Settlement of Colorado

In times of prosperity the cry of "Gold!" is enough to set thousands of eager men on the run; in a period of depression, such as that following the Panic of 1857, economic unrest and unemployment push from behind those for whom the lure of gold alone is not a sufficient inducement. Owing to the fact that it was late in the summer when the rumors of the discoveries of gold made by the Russell party reached the Missouri Valley towns, only a few hundred men ventured out to the "diggings" that autumn. The first gold seekers came mainly from the middle western and southern states. They were imbued with the speculative spirit of the frontier and were interested in the establishment of towns as well as in the digging of gold. They could do both, and, indeed, some of them undoubtedly realized that gold could be obtained more quickly and easily by the sale of town lots than by back-breaking exertions with pan and shovel. Slight discoveries of the yellow metal near the mouth of Cherry Creek were probably responsible for the selection of that spot as a place of abode for the men who chose to spend the winter of 1858-1859 in the Pike's Peak country. As early as September 7, 1858, Montana City was laid out by members of the Lawrence party on the east bank of the South Platte about four and a half miles south of the site of the State Capitol.* Within two weeks some members of this group became dissatisfied with the site selected; they believed that a better location for a town was to be found just east of the mouth of Cherry Creek, and there on September 24, they laid out St. Charles City. Late in October Auraria was founded on the opposite bank of the creek. In November the site of St. Charles was "jumped" by the Lecompton-Leavenworth party in order that their town of Denver might be established thereon. Montana City soon disappeared leaving Denver City and Auraria to contend for supremacy in the Cherry Creek district.

It was not alone at the mouth of Cherry Creek that new "cities" were projected by idle and ambitious men during the autumn and winter of 1858. A group of squatters on the east bank of the Fountain River called their hamlet Fountain City; it disappeared when the town of Pueblo was laid out in the vicinity

---
*There is a detailed account of the orgin of Denver in Smiley, *History of Colorado*, I, 223ff.

in 1860. At El Paso City, so named on account of its nearness to Ute Pass, a few cabins were built in the spring of 1859; it was superseded in the following summer by Colorado City. In February, 1859, Boulder City was laid out on a generous scale by a group of promoters who expected that the town that commanded the approach to Boulder Cañon would be the metropolis of the mountains. During this winter the town of Colona was started on the Cache la Poudre by men who had visions of its future greatness; it died after the town of Laporte was started nearby in 1862. In December, 1858, Arapahoe City was laid out on Clear Creek about two miles east of the site of Golden; it did not advance beyond the paper stage until the great rush of the following year. When the spring of 1859 opened there were no fewer than seven insignificant "cities" planted at the base of the mountains between the Arkansas on the south and the Cache la Poudre on the north. As yet there had been no discoveries of gold of sufficient magnitude to warrant the optimism of their founders. But the laying out of towns by squatters on the public domain did not take much time or money—and if the mountains should prove to be rich in gold, some of the new towns were bound to grow by reason of their locations on the streams and at the passes into the hills.

And the gold was there! The discoveries of George Jackson and John Gregory in the spring of 1859 insured the immediate future of Colorado. At the Jackson diggings the town of Idaho Springs grew up; in and around the more famous Gregory diggings Blackhawk, Nevada City, and Mountain City, which was later absorbed by Central City, were started. Early in the spring of 1859 a rush toward Pike's Peak was started by the men who had been waiting impatiently for winter to break in order that they might be among the first to reach the distant land of gold. This early rush spent its force quickly because the word had already gone out, as a result of the meager discoveries of the preceding autumn, that the whole thing was a humbug. Then came news of the strikes made by Jackson and Gregory; the result was a stampede across the plains in which perhaps one hundred thousand men took part. After June most of the "Fifty-niners" headed for either the Gregory or the Jackson diggings. By the first of June, according to Hollister,

Gregory Gulch, from North Clear Creek to the confluence of Eureka, Nevada, and Spring Gulches, was crowded with canvas tents, log shanties, and bough houses, as thick as they could stand, . . . It was estimated that there were five thousand people in the gulch.*

The first mining camps were soon overcrowded, and as the latecomers arrived and found no favorable openings they scattered by the thousands to prospect the hills in all directions. Most of those who came to Colorado in 1859 had had no previous experience in digging gold; until they picked up enough information to make their searching worth while, they were doomed to rush from the scene of one strike to that of another. Some of them made the circuit of the camps and then went home rich only in their experiences. Apart from the discoveries of Gregory and Jackson on the North and South Forks of Clear Creek (how soon its waters were muddied!), the other principal strikes of the year 1859 were on Boulder Creek and its tributaries, in South Park, and on the Blue River on the Western Slope. The finding of a profitable placer about twelve miles northwest of Boulder early in 1859 was followed in April by the discovery of an outcropping of gold on the side of an adjacent mountain to which was given the name of Gold Hill. In South Park camps at Tarryall, Fairplay, and Jefferson City appeared in the summer and autumn of this year. Prospectors crossed over to the headwaters of the Blue River on the western side of the Continental Divide, and developed a mining district in which the town of Breckinridge was established the following year (1860).

Meanwhile the "cities" which had been established at the edge of the foothills had had varied experiences. Denver and Auraria flourished in 1859 because through their streets passed most of the men bound for the mines, and to them came the returning miners to spend their gold dust—if they had any. At Colona and El Paso City the first effect of the appearance of the mining camps on Clear Creek was to drain off practically the entire population. The abandonment of the site of El Paso City opened the way for another group of speculators to lay out Colorado City in the late summer of 1859. And what a crop of new "cities" sprang up! Golden, at the entrance to Clear Creek Cañon, was founded in June; by the close of the year it had a

*Holister, *The Mines of Colorado*, 76.

population of seven hundred and was ready to challenge the supremacy of Denver-Auraria in the Pike's Peak country. Two miles to the north of Golden the town of Golden Gate was laid out; five miles to the south Mount Vernon appeared in the autumn; two miles to the east Arapahoe City, which had been projected in the preceding December, now acquired some inhabitants. Cañon City was laid out in 1859, but until the spring of 1860 its site was graced by a single cabin; its founders hoped that it would stand in the same relation to the camps in South Park that Denver, Auraria and Golden did to those on Clear Creek.

Tens of thousands had come to Colorado in 1859; thousands had gone home by the end of the season; but several thousand were left to spend the winter in the new towns. In January, 1860, the legislature of the self-created Territory of Jefferson sent a memorial to Congress and the President in which the population of the Pike's Peak country was estimated at eight thousand, distributed as follows:

> The population of Denver is about 1,100; of Auraria, 1,000; Golden City, 900; Arrappahoe, 400; Colorado, 300; and Mountain City, 800; while in the other portions of the Territory there is population enough to swell the sum to about 8,000; nearly all of which are male adults so that were the usual number or proportion of females and children added, the total population would be about 40,000.*

In the spring of 1860 the plains were again alive with men bound for Colorado; for about two months in the late spring and early summer the arrivals were estimated at about five thousand a week. Among the new mining camps opened during this year were Buckskin Joe, Hamilton and Georgetown. The outstanding development, however, was the discovery of Colorado's richest placer mines in California Gulch near the site of Leadville. At the height of the excitement fully five thousand people were gathered in and around the principal camp, Oro City. Not all of these, of course, were engaged in mining; many there were who sought the precious metal in less laborious and less honorable ways than by arduous toil with pick and shovel, pan and rocker; many were "floaters", swept in the rushing tide of humanity from one new camp to another, always hopeful of better luck in the untried

*House Mis. Doc., 36 Cong., 1 Sess., No. 10.

El Dorado. The mercurial temperament of the miners and the ephemeral character of some of the camps of the period is well illustrated by the experience of Mr. Irving Stanton. Some of the members of his company reported a rich strike at the head of Beaver Creek, east of Fairplay. When the other members of the company arrived they found a large number of men already there. Then, as Mr. Stanton tells the story,

> A miner's meeting was held and a new district organized under the name of Australia Gulch. A code of laws was adopted, officers—president and a recorder—were elected. These offices with all the honors and emoluments, were conceded to the discoverers. The simple machinery of a mining district was put in operation for business. No work worthy of note had been done by our party. Their find was only a good color in the grass roots, and some of the old prospectors, a little cautious of new discoveries, commenced to prospect the gulch for themselves. The result was that in a few days we were left, Robinson Crusoe-like, monarchs of all we surveyed, sole claimants, in undisputed possession of all the hidden treasure of Australia Gulch, and it still remains hidden to this day, for we could not find it and no one since has tried.*

By 1861 the excitement in the Pike's Peak country had largely subsided. The guns at Fort Sumter announced the arrival of stirring days in the East and the South. New El Dorados appeared in Montana and elsewhere in the West to attract the restless miners. Many of those who had joined in the gold rush had gone back to the States convinced that gold digging did not pay; it has been estimated that gold to the value of about ten million dollars was found in Colorado in 1859 and 1860—only one hundred dollars for each of the "Fifty-niners"! But the placer mining of the early days was easy and remunerative compared with the quartz mining of the middle sixties. After the placers had been worked, the miners naturally turned toward the veins and lodes from which the dust and nuggets had come. The disintegrated quartz near the surface of the ground yielded its golden treasure with little difficulty; but as the veins were followed into the interior the returns became less adequate. The miners knew that there was gold in the rocks, but their metallurgical processes failed to save enough of it to make mining pay. Some mines and mills were closed; in others fantastic machines and weird processes were tried only to add to the confusion of a

---

*Stanton, "Early Days in Colorado", in *The Trail*, II, 8-9.

depressing period. In 1866 a traveler through Colorado described conditions at Central City as follows:

> Over the hills as far as eye can reach, and up and down the valleys, stand the lonely stamp mills, with their high iron chimneys, . . . from only a few of which could smoke be seen to issue. Now and then from one here and another there came a dull heavy sound, like the falling of a hugh weight on some solid body, showing that some of the stamps were in motion, though most of them were silent as the tomb; no smoke, no sound, and no living thing seen about the innumerable tenements.*

The depression in mining was aggravated by the high freight rates charged for the transportation of food, supplies, and machinery to Colorado; and the high rates were explained, in part, by the Indian wars during and immediately following the Civil War. Under such conditions it is not surprising that the Territorial Census for 1866 showed a total population of only twenty-eight thousand.

Colonies and Town Companies

By the end of the sixties Colorado was well on the way to recovery. The mining industry had been put on a more substantial basis by the introduction of better metallurgical processes; the Civil War was over and more men were turning their eyes toward the agricultural frontier; the Indians were no longer a serious menace along the main roads to Colorado; the agricultural possibilities of the Territory had been discovered. Indeed, the market value of the grains, hay and vegetables produced in Colorado in 1869 was estimated at three and a half million dollars—almost as much as the output of the mines for that year. Especially important was the approach of the transcontinental railroad. The completion of the Union Pacific Railway in 1869 was followed quickly by the building of two roads into Colorado. In June, 1870, the Denver Pacific joined Denver to the main line of the Union Pacific at Cheyenne; in August of that year the Kansas Pacific reached Denver, thus giving direct communication with St. Louis.

Both the Denver Pacific and the Kansas Pacific were land grant railroads. They were anxious to sell their land, not only to raise money to pay the costs of construction, but also to create a constituency along their tracks. Unfortunately for them a

---
*Hoyt, "Over the Plains to Colorado", *Harper's*, June, 1867, 8-9.

large part of their land lay in a region known, even as late as the close of the Civil War, as the "Great American Desert". In 1867 General John Pope, who was in command of the Department of Missouri, which included Colorado, wrote in one of his reports that there was a belt of land never less than five hundred miles wide stretching from Canada to Mexico along the base of the mountains, which was "beyond the reach of agriculture and must always remain a great uninhabited desert"*. Despite the fact that men had already demonstrated the practicability of farming in Colorado, the old notion died slowly. Before Easterners could be induced to buy railroad land or to take up Government land along the roads, it was necessary to educate them in regard to the nature of the country and to point out the opportunities that awaited farmers in the semi-arid regions of the West. The principal land selling agency for the Denver Pacific and the Kansas Pacific railroads was the National Land Company. It and other organizations interested in securing agricultural settlers for Colorado emphasized the prodigious crops which bore witness to the fertility of the soil; the superiority of irrigation over reliance on Providence for rain; and the steady markets in the mining camps and towns for what was raised on the farms.

At a time when such inducements were held out to prospective settlers in Colorado, would-be pioneers throughout the East, the South and the Middle West were looking toward the frontier. The Civil War had retarded but not stopped the Westward Movement. At the close of the War the movement was accelerated: the process of economic readjustment in the North, the disorganized state of society in the South, the more liberal land policy of the Federal Government as shown in the passage of the Homestead Law, either tended to drive or lure people out to the farm lands of the West.

The agricultural colony was the distinctive mode of settlement in Colorado in the early part of the seventies. The colony plan of settlement was not new, but it had not been generally used on earlier frontiers, except in colonial New England, because the pioneers were too individualistic and the distance traveled by the ordinary frontiersman in going to a new home was usually not great enough to warrant such an organization. At the close

---
*House Ex. Doc., 39 Cong., 1 Sess., No. 76, 2.

of the War many settlements were planned for Nebraska, Kansas and Colorado on the basis of community migration. The increase in distance between the old home and the new may have had something to do with the change in method. The success achieved by the Mormons in Utah through coöperation probably called attention to the value of this method of settlement in the semi-arid West; only through community action, ordinarily, could an irrigation system be installed. It was pointed out, also, that the colony would furnish community life with schools and churches from the outset, thus mitigating the loneliness of frontier life.

The first of the agricultural colonies to settle in Colorado was the German Colonization Company which was started in Chicago in the summer of 1869 by Carl Wulsten. His purpose was to reduce the cost of migration to the West through the economies of coöperative endeavor, thus enabling poor German workingmen of that city to take advantage of the Homestead Law. The members of the colony bound themselves to work together for five years; a site was selected in the Wet Mountain Valley; the prospective colony town was named Colfax after the man then Vice-President of the United States; a petition was sent to Congress asking for a grant of forty thousand acres of land. Although the grant was not made, Wulsten and his followers, about two hundred and fifty in number, left Chicago in February, 1870. Their attempt to establish a cooperative colony was a failure. The leader was arbitrary and impractical; there was dissension in the ranks; their first attempt to raise a crop at an elevation of eight thousand feet or over met with little success. In the late summer and autumn of 1870 the colony began to break up. Some of the members left for Denver, Pueblo or Cañon City; others stayed in the Valley, made an informal division of the property, secured land from the Federal Government, and became prosperous settlers.[*]

The most famous of the Colorado colonies, and the model after which at least two others were patterned, was the Union Colony at Greeley. It had its inception in a visit made to Colorado in the autumn of 1869 by Nathan C. Meeker, agricultural editor of the *New York Tribune*. On his return to New York

---

[*]Willard and Goodykoontz, *Experiments in Colorado Colonization, 1869-1872* (*University of Colorado Historical Collections*,¡III), 29-133.

Meeker issued through the *Tribune* a call for a meeting of all persons interested in the establishment of an agricultural colony in Colorado. Horace Greeley, editor of the *Tribune*, had long been interested in humanitarian projects, and naturally gave his support to this enterprise which combined social relief and economic gain. His name was given to the colony town which was founded in the spring of 1870. A splendid site was chosen in the valley of the Cache la Poudre, near the Platte; land was obtained from the Denver Pacific Railway Company and from the Federal Government. By October, 1870, there were about eight hundred colonists in Greeley; they were thrifty, industrious and temperate people who had come mainly from the New England and North Central states. In contrast to the coöperative German company, the Union Colony was semi-coöperative; the colony secured land, laid out the town, divided the town lots and land among the members, and constructed the necessary irrigating ditches, in return for the membership and initiation fee of one hundred fifty-five dollars. Otherwise the members owned property, traded and carried on other business on a purely individualistic basis.*

The rapidity with which raw land had been turned into the abode of several hundred people in the summer of 1870 under the Union Colony plan, and the evident success of the experiment, led in the following year to the establishment of two similar colonies in northern Colorado. The St. Louis-Western Colony, which had been launched at Ayres Point, Illinois, in the autumn of 1870 by the Reverend Andrew C. Todd, pastor of a Reformed Presbyterian Church, was planted at Evans. The town of Evans had been laid out in the autumn of 1869 when the Denver Pacific Railroad was being built; for a few months, while it was the temporary terminus of the railroad, it flourished, then languished after the line was completed to Denver in the following year. From this unhappy state it was rescued temporarily when it was chosen as the site for the St. Louis-Western Colony in 1871. The other colony to be founded that year on the Greeley plan was the Chicago-Colorado Colony at Longmont. Agents of the National Land Company had much to do with its organization; they made plans for the meeting in Chicago in November, 1870, at which the

---
*Willard, *The Union Colony* (*University of Colorado Historical Collections*, I); Boyd, *A History: Greeley and the Union Colony of Colorado*.

colony was launched, and they helped secure members. A tract of land was selected in the northeastern corner of Boulder County near the hamlet of Burlington, many of whose inhabitants joined the colony and helped found the town of Longmont nearby.*

The colony idea having met with popular favor, promoters and speculators took over the name, but discarded such features of a real colony as did not suit their purposes. In the Union Colony, for example, an organization of prospective settlers was formed outside Colorado, a committee was sent to select a site for the colony town, the officers of the colony secured land and distributed it among the members and made arrangements for the construction of irrigating ditches; there was a semblance of mass movement of the colonists to the new home. In the pseudo-colonies a group of promoters secured control of a tract of land, divided it into farms or town lots and sold to any buyer who appeared. The most interesting of the speculative enterprises that masqueraded as a colony was the "Southwestern Colony", membership in which was secured by the purchase of lots in the "colony town" of Green City. The promoter, David S. Green, took up two sections of Government land on the South Platte about twenty-seven miles below Greeley. The land having been laid out into more than five thousand town lots, the promoter and his associates carried on an active selling campaign, especially in the southern and border states. Some bona fide settlers bought lots and went to the new town to live; a few skilled artisans were induced to go there by false promises of employment; many bought lots in the expectation that a thriving city would spring up—perhaps a river port, if we are to give credence to a strongly established tradition that advertising circulars were distributed by the promoters showing a steamboat tied to a wharf in Green City. After a few years of precarious existence both colony and city became a memory.

Not all town development companies used methods as questionable as those employed by the promoters of Green City; when honestly managed the business of taking up a tract of land, platting it as a town, and selling the lots was perfectly legitimate. Sometimes the venture was a failure, as at Platteville, Monument and New Memphis; sometimes it was a partial success as at Fort

---
*Willard and Goodykoontz, *op; cit.*, 137-330.

Collins, where a company was formed in 1872 for the purpose of building a town on an abandoned military reservation on the Cache la Poudre River. Certain of the so-called colonies of this period were formed by companies affiliated with the Denver and Rio Grande Railway Company. This railroad, unlike the Union Pacific and the Kansas Pacific, did not receive a grant of twenty sections of land for each mile of track; it was built mainly by private capital. As an inducement to invest money in the railroad the shareholders were given the opportunity to take stock in subsidiary companies formed for the purpose of laying out and developing new towns along the road. It was thus that Colorado Springs was started in 1871 by the Fountain Colony, and South Pueblo in 1872 by the Central Colorado Improvement Association. In order that the new towns in which the company was especially interested might flourish, other towns along or near the track sometimes received shabby treatment. Castle Rock, the county seat of Douglas County, was not made a station stop when the stations were established because that would interfere with the neighboring town of Douglas which the company was sponsoring*. Residents of Colorado City complained because their town, once the Territorial capital, was passed to one side, and overshadowed by the new town of Colorado Springs, a child of the railroad. The people of Pueblo had a grievance because, in violation of a pledge given when bonds were issued to aid in the construction of the Denver and Rio Grande Railway, the company moved its station from the north side of the river, where the city was located, to the opposite bank where its own town of South Pueblo was being developed.

Directly and indirectly the colony and town development companies were responsible for bringing thousands of settlers to Colorado; by them the Territory had been well advertised in the Middle West, in the East and in the South, and even in England. At a time when the future of Colorado was still uncertain, the colonies served a useful function by drawing attention to the opportunities that there awaited the homeseeker.

At the same time the agricultural colonies were being founded along the eastern base of the mountains, there was a revival of interest in mining as a result of the rich discoveries made in the

---
*Weekly Rocky Mountain News, July 15, 1874.

San Juan country in the southwestern corner of the Territory. Out of the rush into this remote region grew such towns as Lake City and Silverton in 1874 and Ouray in 1875. The ores were found on land that had been reserved for the Ute Indians by an agreement made in 1868. As usual the miners paid no attention to an Indian treaty, and, as usual, the natives were forced to accept a new agreement (Brunot Treaty, 1873) in which they ceded the mineral lands desired by the dominant race. The San Juan mines were remote and difficult of access. Until they were reached by branch lines of the Denver and Rio Grande Railway in the eighties, one of the principal routes to them lay through the San Luis Valley. Towns grew up along the way as outfitting points and way stations; one of the most important of these was Del Norte which was established on the Rio Grande in 1872.

Statehood

Colorado's struggle for statehood ended in 1876. Between 1870 and 1876 the population of the Territory had grown from forty thousand to about one hundred thousand. Mining, especially in Gilpin and Clear Creek Counties and in the San Juan country, was on a paying basis. Prosperous farming communities had been established on the irrigable lands east of the foothills. The farms did not, however, extend far down the Platte or the Arkansas; the whole eastern part of the new State was still a buffalo range or grazing country. Practically the whole of the Western Slope, save for the San Juan mining camps, was unsettled, and much of it was legally within the Ute Reserve. South of Pueblo, the chief town on the eastern side of the mountains was Trinidad, which was even then hardly more than a Mexican village. In the San Luis Valley there were a few thousand Mexican farmers and ranchers, but already Anglo-American settlers were coming in to found towns and to engage in farming. In addition to the Denver Pacific, the Kansas Pacific and the Denver and Rio Grande railways, Colorado was served by the Santa Fé, which had advanced up the Arkansas Valley as far as Pueblo, and by the Colorado Central, which had built a line from Denver to Blackhawk on the North Fork of Clear Creek. Altogether the new State could boast about eight hundred miles of railway lines. But rapid as had been the growth in population in the early seventies, the Centennial State was still sparsely settled in 1876; for each of its one hundred thousand inhabitants there was a square mile of land.

In the latter part of the seventies the outstanding feature in the development of Colorado was the finding of rich silver ores at Leadville. Ever since 1860 there had been some placer mining in California Gulch, but it had been conducted on a small scale after the excitement of the early sixties had died down. About 1877 it was discovered that the heavy black rocks and sand that had caused the placer miners so much annoyance all the while were full of lead and silver. Hitherto Colorado had been the land of Gold; now it became the Silver State. Days of great excitement followed the disclosure of the richness of the carbonate of lead ores at the new Leadville camp. Helen Hunt wrote of it in 1878, while it was still in its picturesque state,

> In six months a tract of dense, spruce forest had been converted into a bustling village. To be sure, the upturned roots and the freshly hacked stumps of many of the spruce trees are still in the streets . . . the houses are all log cabins, or else plain unpainted board shanties. Some of the cabins seem to burrow in the ground; others are set up on posts, like roofed bedsteads. Tents; wigwams of boughs; wigwams of bare poles, with a blackened spot in front, where somebody slept last night, but will never sleep again; cabins wedged in between stumps; cabins built on stumps; cabins with chimneys made of flower-pots or bits of stove pipe,—I am not sure but out of old hats; cabins half roofed; cabins with sail cloth roofs; cabins with no roofs at all,—this represents the architecture of the Leadville homes. The Leadville places of business are another thing; there is one compact, straight street, running east and west, in the center of this medley of sage brush, spruce stumps, cabins and shanties . . . The middle of the street was always filled with groups of men talking. Wagons were driven up and down as fast as if the street were clear. It looked all the time as if there had been a fire, and the people were just about dispersing, or as if town meeting were just over. Everybody was talking, nearly everybody jesticulating. All faces looked restless, eager, fierce. It was a Monaco gambling room emptied into a Colorado spruce clearing.*

As a result of the fabulous discoveries at the "Camp of the Carbonates", Leadville was reported as the second largest city in the State in 1880 with a population of about fifteen thousand. There was a revival of interest in mining all through the mountains; wherever the ore resembled the Leadville product there was excitement. The discovery of such ores in the Wet Mountain Valley in 1878 led to a rush to the vicinity of the Rosita gold

*H. H., "To Leadville", in *Atlantic*, May, 1879, 574-575.

mines, and the establishment of Silver Cliff, which for a time ranked next to Denver and Leadville in population. Rich deposits of carbonate of lead were found also near the head of the Roaring Fork of the Grand River, and there in 1880 the town of Aspen was started.

Gunnison was another town that shared in the prosperity of the period. Its founder was Sylvester Richardson, who had been geologist and physician with the Parsons prospecting expedition of 1873. He had realized something of the mineral and agricultural possibilities of the Gunnison Valley and in 1874 had organized in Denver a stock company for the purpose of establishing a town therein. About twenty-five cabins were built the first season. Gunnison was isolated and only a few miles east of the Ute Reservation; until the late seventies it remained an unimportant, straggling, frontier village. Then came the excitement at Leadville, and Gunnison shared in the boom because carbonates were found in the vicinity. History students at Western State College have written regarding this period in the history of Gunnison:

> In the spring of 1879 the rush began. Prospecting was conducted on a tremendous scale. An entire new town organization was effected . . . Thousands came weekly. A correspondent writing to the Pueblo *Chieftain* from Parlin's ranch, on May 17, 1880, says that on the day previous he counted two hundred fifty teams bound for Gunnison, Ruby, Gothic. "One would think", he says, "that there must be an end of this procession, but the end is not yet, for far away on the Saguache road, there is a long line of white wagon covers".*

The creation of new mining camps in the mountains attracted the railways. The traffic of Leadville was a prize for which both the Denver and Rio Grande and the Santa Fé companies strove vigorously. The key to Leadville is the Royal Gorge; after struggles, both physical and legal, the victory was finally won by the Denver and Rio Grande, which reached its goal in Leadville in 1880. Meanwhile the Colorado Central Railway Company was building a line from Golden to Cheyenne. The completion of this road in 1877 was followed shortly by the founding of the town of Loveland at the crossing of the Big Thompson, and of Berthoud on the Little Thompson.

Except for the first gold rushes, Colorado's period of most

Historical Sketches of Early Gunnison, 19.

rapid growth was in the decade ending in 1880. In 1870 the Territory had a population of about forty thousand; in 1880, the State, then four years old, had nearly two hundred thousand inhabitants. Nearly all parts of the State had shared in the increase. Lake County, on account of Leadville, had shown the greatest growth; its population had increased from five hundred to nearly twenty-four thousand. Clear Creek, another mining county, had grown from fifteen hundred to nearly eight thousand; Arapahoe County, which then included Denver, from less than seven thousand to more than thirty-eight thousand; El Paso, with Colorado Springs as its chief town, from one thousand to nearly eight thousand; Boulder County, partly on the plains and partly in the mountains, from two to ten thousand. In the Arkansas Valley, Las Animas and Rocky Ford, both more or less the result of railway construction, were among the new towns that appeared on the map in this decade. The valley of the South Platte east of Evans, on the other hand, was not yet the pathway of a railroad. That lack, together with the fact that the State, which held considerable land there, was not yet trying to dispose of its property, may explain the delay in settling the lower Platte Valley. It was still largely a cattle range, although since the early seventies there had been a few farmers around Sterling.

The future of Colorado looked bright in 1880· the silver mines were pouring out their flood of precious metal; real estate values were rising; on the Eastern Slope there was a narrow belt of irrigated land near the mountains, while cattle numbered by the tens of thousands fattened on the grasses of the plains; on the Western Slope the pioneers were impatiently waiting for the opening to settlement of the old Ute Reservation.

As one of the results of the White River Ute massacre in 1879, in which Nathan C. Meeker, founder of Greeley and Indian agent lost his life, the cry was raised "The Utes must go"*. By an agreement made in 1880 the Utes abandoned, save for a fifteen-mile strip in the extreme southwestern corner of the State, the reservation secured to them by the treaties of 1868 and 1873. The new treaty cleared the way for the settlement of the valleys

---
*On this point I have been helped by an unpublished thesis on the Ute Uprising of 1879 written by Miss Olive Carr of Brighton.

of the Gunnison, the Grand, and the White rivers. Throughout the State there was rejoicing. The Ouray *Times* said:

> Sunday morning the Utes bid adieu to their old hunting grounds and folded their tents, rounded up their dogs, sheep, goats, ponies and traps, and took up the line of march for their new reservation, followed by General McKenzie and his troops. This is an event that has been long and devoutly prayed for by our people. How joyful it sounds, and with what satisfaction one can say, "The Utes have gone". The great menace to the advancement and development of this grand southwestern country is no more. Eastern people can now come to this section in the most perfect security. Besides it throws open to the dominion of white men one of the most fertile and beautiful valleys in all of Colorado; a valley that will be to those who are so fortunate as to become owners of its broad acres, a happy land of Canaan.*

Already farmers and promoters were at hand waiting for the opportunity to pick out the best lands and most likely town sites. In the autumn of 1881 Grand Junction was founded at the confluence of the Grand and Gunnison rivers; in December Delta was platted at the junction of the Gunnison and the Uncompahgre. In January, 1882, the Montrose townsite was located, while Glenwood Springs was founded in August of that year by the Defiance Land and Town Company. The town of Meeker grew up near a military post which was maintained on the White River for a few years following the Ute uprising of 1879. The valleys of the Gunnison, Grand, and Uncompahgre rivers were quickly settled by farmers who soon discovered that certain parts of this region are by climate and soil peculiarly adapted to the growing of fruit; farther north, the valleys of the White and the Yampa and their tributaries, furnished grazing for large herds of cattle and flocks of sheep.

In the late eighties the outstanding development in the settlement of Colorado was the movement of farmers into the semi-arid, non-irrigable region in the eastern part of the State. Hitherto much of the land in this section had been thought worthless except as a cattle range. By the eighties the day of the cattle man was passing; the day of the "nester" was coming. As the frontier was pushed farther and farther westward, and as the available land suitable for agriculture was taken up, land-hungry farmers ventured out on the less desirable lands of western Kansas and Nebraska. By 1886 the overflow from these states

---
Denver Daily Times, Sept. 12, 1881; this reference was brought to my attention by Miss Grace Burnham of Boulder.

was making its influence felt in eastern Colorado. A few years of unusually heavy rainfall in this region seemed to prove the soundness of the theory generally held that as land was brought under cultivation, rainfall increased. The railroads whose lines ran through this sparsely settled country were quick to spread the good news. The Burlington Road, which had reached Denver in 1882, issued a pamphlet in 1887 in which the following statement and explanation of the remarkable change in the climate of eastern Colorado was made:

> The rain belt has moved westward to within less than eighty miles of Denver . . . In fact an entirely new "rain belt" has been created within the past five years. For sixteen years—from 1870 to 1886—men entered this arid zone, built houses, plowed the sod, sowed grain, and attempted to farm. They lost their money, their time, and in many cases their courage. Many of them returned east to live off their wives' relatives. Other men took the abandoned houses and farms, and in time these became bankrupt too. All men of intelligence *knew* that the "arid zone" was unfit for agricultural purposes. They *knew* the physical configuration of the land lying west of the arid belt, and which controls the climate, could not be changed. The settlers, eager for land and homes, continued to pour into the dry region. At last they have been rewarded. They have secured from two to four consecutive crops of grain. So much rain now falls in the eastern portion of the arid lands of Colorado that it is no longer fit for a winter range for cattle. If sufficient rain falls to destroy the nutriment in the grass during the winter, then there is sufficient rainfall to grow wheat to perfect maturity. What has brought about this great change cannot be accurately determined; . . . The winds blow from the same directions they did, but they are not sirocco-like. The rain storms come from the west generally, and in the past the west wind was a dry wind. In our opinion, the change is due to the extensive irrigation of land lying along the eastern base of the Rocky Mountains. Great rivers, which head in perpetual snow banks, have been turned into irrigation ditches, and the water which formerly ran wastefully into the Gulf of Mexico has been turned on to the arid plains. There it soaks into the soil. The wind sweeping over the land sucks up a large portion of it. There is then moisture in the air and it is precipitated on the high lands of eastern Colorado and the adjoining country.*

For a year or two the movement of farmers into eastern Colorado attracted little attention in the State, except to call forth occasionally a prediction of failure from those unconvinced about the feasibility of farming without irrigation. To the surprise of those who had predicted failure, the experiment was apparently a success. Late in 1887 a representative of the Denver

---

*Burlington Route, *Eastern Colorado* (Lincoln, Neb., 1887), 4-5.

Republican visited the "rain-belt" and reported that the people were prosperous and that the country was filling up rapidly. He wrote:

> The condition of the people in these new sections is gratifying in the extreme. They have raised sufficient to feed them through the winter and have some to sell. The corn and all else was grown upon the sod but with results that far exceeded the most sanguine anticipations of the veterans who have seen the development of Kansas and Nebraska. To these the "rain-belt" section of Colorado is now what those states were six years ago. These men form a large percentage of the new settlements, and their influence amongst the influx of population in Colorado from other States has the effect of calming the doubts of those less experienced in the development of the newer states . . .
> The entire country along the Burlington Railroad in Colorado east of Denver is pretty generally settled. The most of the residents having gone in during the past summer, their farms as yet have not assumed much beauty as regards outward appearances, nor has much been done toward building fences and pretentious structures; but the lands for from one to ten miles on each side of the road are dotted here and there with newly-erected cottages.*

Bright prospects in the "rain-belt" in the late eighties were followed by drought and depression in the early nineties. There had been no permanent change in climatic conditions; the rainfall became normal again, or perhaps abnormally slight, and the crops dried up. Farms were abandoned; whole counties were almost depopulated. Many towns, such as Akron, Burlington, Holyoke, Haxtun and Wray, had been started during the boom period; now they dwindled in size. The unfortunate people who had made this ill-advised experiment in agriculture had had a bitter experience, but some good came out of it, however, because both the Federal Government and the States of the semi-arid West began systematic investigation to determine what crops are best adapted to dry lands and what methods of cultivation are best to use. Drought-resistant crops, special tools and peculiar methods of cultivation were introduced. Dry farming was thus put on a scientific basis, and in the early part of the twentieth century a new wave of settlement swept over the plains of eastern Colorado. Abandoned farms were re-occupied; dead towns were brought to life; new towns were founded.

While the crops of eastern Colorado were being burned up by the drought of the early nineties, there were scenes both cheering and disheartening for the people of the mountain districts.

**Denver Republican*, Jan. 1, 1888.

Silver mining received an artificial and temporary impetus by the passage of the Sherman Silver Purchase Law of 1890, but the price of the white metal continued to drop. The finding of rich ores by N. C. Creede in 1890 in a section of the San Juan country called at first "King Solomon's Mines", led to a stampede to that district and the founding of the town of Creede. From 1891 to 1893 it was at the height of its glory, and, in the words of the Creede *Chronicle,*

> It was day all day in the daytime,
> And there was no night in Creede.

Here were found all the romance, all the excitement, all the tawdriness of the typical mining camp. Cy Warman said:

> Life in Creed was of necessity rapid. The doings of a day comprised a cycle of time. Locations were made in the morning, sold at noon, and jumped at night. The arrival of a freight train with the rising sun, indicated a new place of business at sunset.*

Richard Harding Davis described Creede in 1892 as a village of fresh pine:

> There is not a brick, a painted front nor an awning in the whole town. It is like a city of fresh card-board, and the pine shanties seem to trust for support to the rocky sides of the gulch in which they have squeezed themselves. In the street are ox-teams, mules, men, and donkeys loaded with ore, crowding each other familiarly, and sinking knee deep in the mud. Furniture and kegs of beer, bedding and canned provisions, clothing and half-open packing cases, and piles of raw lumber heaped up in front of the new stores —or those still to be built—stores of canvas only, stores with canvas tops and foundations of logs, and houses with the Leadville front, where the upper boards have been left square instead of following the sloping angle of the roof.
> It is more like a circus tent which has sprung up over night and which may be removed on the morrow, than a town, and you cannot help but feel that the people about you are a part of the show.**

The show ended suddenly in 1893 when Congress, at the insistence of President Cleveland, repealed the Sherman Silver Act under which the Federal Government had been buying practically the entire output of the silver mines of the United States. The loss of this artificial market, together with the closing of the mints of India to the coinage of silver, dealt a blow to the mining industry from which it has never fully recovered. Fortunately, however, it was just at this time that Cripple Creek

*Warman, "Creede", in *Colorado Magazine,* I (May, 1893), 169.
**Davis, *The West From a Car Window,* 59-60.

began to disgorge its flood of gold, and many of the men thrown out of work by the closing of the silver mines found employment there. In January 1891, the site of Cripple Creek was a cattle ranch. Several months followed Bob Womack's noisy and drunken announcement of his discovery of gold before much interest was manifested in a region which had been prospected so many times before, and which had not yet rid itself of the stigma of the Mt. Pisgah hoax, in connection with which one "Chicken Bill" had "salted" a mine. The rush to Cripple Creek did not set in until the autumn of 1891. By the spring of 1892 men began to realize and exaggerate the wealth of a wonderfully rich mining district. According to the Colorado Springs *Evening Telegraph* in February, 1892,

> The mineral belt grows larger every day and the deeper the holes go down, more and stronger indications make their appearance to convince the experienced that the camp is a world-beater and here to stay. Even if the bottom should drop out of every hole there would be enough free milling ore on the surface to keep thousands of men busy for years to come.*

As in every other mining camp in Colorado, the glory of Cripple Creek has faded. Not that mining has been abandoned there or in scores of other mountain towns; thousands of men still make a living wage in the industry and occasionally a rich pocket of ore is struck from which the returns are ample. But in general the cost of production is so great that mining does not pay well. The result has been a sharp decline in the population of the mountain counties. Camps once famous are all but deserted. Central City, with 552 inhabitants according to the Census of 1920, lives in the greatness of its past; in the whole of Mineral County, which includes Creede, there were 779 people at the last report; Tarryall had 107; Fairplay, 222; Gold Hill, 51; Cripple Creek, 2,325; Leadville, 4,959; Aspen, 1,265; Silver Cliff, 241; Ward, 74.

The losses in the mining camps have been more than made up in the mountain parks where agriculture and cattle raising can be carried on, and on the farms and in the industrial centers on the plains. Denver and Pueblo have grown into important industrial cities, and together they contain almost one-third of the total population of the State. The building of the Moffat

---
*Colorado Springs Evening Telegraph, Feb. 4, 1892; for this reference I am indebted to Mr. Robert Newman of Colorado Springs.

Road has opened to exploitation the natural resources of a region larger than the State of Connecticut. During the last quarter of a century the agricultural development of the San Luis Valley has attracted attention both within and without the State. Between 1900 and 1920 the population of Alamosa, in the San Luis Valley, grew from 1,000 to 3,000; Brighton from 366 to 2,715; Brush from 381 to 2,103; Fort Lupton from 214 to a thousand; Lamar from 987 to 2,512; Fruita from 126 to 1,193. Verily, agriculture, a stone rejected by the first builders of Colorado, has become the chief cornerstone.

The decline of mining has had the effect also of decreasing the number of foreign born white inhabitants of the State. Mining camps were noted for the heterogeneity of their population. According to the Census of 1870 there were 6,599 foreign born in Colorado out of a total population of 39,864, or 16.5 per cent. In 1880, when mining was at its height, the foreign born numbered 39,790 out of a total of 191,126, or 20 per cent. In 1900 they comprised 16.8 per cent of the population; in 1910, 15.9 per cent; in 1920, 12.4 per cent. In 1910 only three counties, Baca, Conejos, and Costilla, had less than five per cent of foreign born whites in their total population. Of course, it must be remembered that in both Costilla and Conejos counties there are many Spanish speaking people who are native born American citizens. In 1920, in addition to the three just named, ten others, Moffat, Rio Blanco, Montezuma, Saguache, Rio Grande, Alamosa, Archuleta, Yuma, Kit Carson, and Kiowa, had less than five per cent of their inhabitants in the class of foreign born. In 1910 between twenty-five and fifty per cent of the inhabitants of Gilpin, Clear Creek, Lake, Pitkin, Gunnison, Ouray, San Juan, San Miguel, and Dolores, all mining or mountain counties, were foreign born; in 1910 only San Juan and Lake remained in this group.*

In general Colorado has passed beyond the frontier stage, and yet in many parts of the State frontier conditions may still be found. With a total population of 939,629 in 1920, and a land area of 103,658 square miles there were on the average only 9.1 persons per square mile in Colorado. Ten counties, Moffat, Rio Blanco, Dolores, Jackson, Grand, Gunnison, Saguache, Hinsdale, Mineral, and Park, had fewer than two inhabitants per square

*Statistical Atlas of the United States, 1924, 195

mile; it will be observed that these are all mountain or western counties. Twenty-two counties had between two and six inhabitants per square mile. Exclusive of the City and County of Denver, only four counties, Boulder, El Paso, Pueblo, and Otero, had in 1920 as many as eighteen to forty-five residents per square mile.

Superficially the settlement of Colorado has been accomplished—and within the span of one human life. There are men and women still living in this Semi-centennial year of the University of Colorado who remember the gold rush, who recall with horror the Indian wars of the sixties, who heard the whistle of the first locomotive in the Territory, who watched the buffalo give way to cattle on the eastern plains of the State and they in turn to the farmer. Aeroplanes and motor-cars, radios and "movies", are all about us—but the frontier is just behind.

Chapter 4
EARLY RANGE DAYS
Joe Mills

From the dawn of history the trend of civilization has been westward. In ancient times ambitious rulers sought to conquer western peoples; in medieval days, bold navigators ever strove to venture further out upon western seas. Progress has ever harkened to the voice of the Occident.

Lewis and Clark, returning from their epoch-making explorations of the northwest with reports of endless plains and virgin forests, of fertile valleys and mighty mountain ranges, first fired the imaginations of the eastern settlers and set the more adventurous to dreaming of taking the trail they had lately blazed into the unknown. The discovery of gold in California in 1848 and in Colorado in 1859, fanned these smouldering desires into flame, and thousands of daring men and women, from every station in life—for no calling had a corner on courage—severed secure family ties and left the sure comforts of home for the glamorous perils of the unknown West. The lure of the wilderness called them, that storied land of far horizons, of rolling prairies and trackless deserts and unexplored mountain mazes, offered too great a challenge for their bold spirits to ignore. They longed to conquer that untamed empire, they wanted a share in the winning of the West. On horseback, in spring wagons drawn by horses, in covered wagons hauled by oxen, with all their movable worldly possessions, in single small groups and in great organized armies, they trekked westward.

Buffalo trails were worn into wagon roads, which came to be called the Union Pacific and the Santa Fe trails, according to their respective destinations. At the foot of the Rockies the emigrants turned north or south, depending upon their predetermined objective. Some of the more venturesome left the bison-cut paths and penetrated the mountain barriers, returning laden with furs. Trappers followed the cañons that lead into the jumble of lofty ranges and harvested the crop of pelts, which they found prime and to be had for the taking. Gold-seekers rushed feverishly on, each striving to be first at the scene of rumoured fabulous strikes and chafing under the unavoidably slow progress and exasperating delays. Many of the train, compelled by illness or misfortune, or impelled by agrarian inclination and the promise of the fertile untilled land, dropped out before they reached the intended end of their journey and settled down to furrow and cultivate the unturned prairie sod.

These pioneers were far from cities and the sources of supply. Adopting the habits and customs of the Indian, they reverted to the primitive. They fished and hunted and trapped for a livelihood, they used the skins of animals for clothing, they camped or tented and cooked in the open. Campfires burned all along the trails where scouts in picturesque fringed buckskin dress and long, Samsonian locks, guided the still-advancing wagon trains through that strange land of hostile savages. Thus did Kit Carson and Jim Bridger and other knight-errants spend their chivalrous lives.

During this period thundering herds of buffalo migrated north and south with the seasons. Their hides brought a dollar each on the market. Hide-hunting became a business. Hunters waited at water-holes along the streams. They slaughtered the animals by the thousands, skinned them, and left their carcasses to rot. The plains were turned into foul shambles over which buzzards wheeled and coyotes yammered and grey wolves howled and fought.

Even those huge herds could not long survive such senseless, uncontrolled slaughter. After a few short, flourishing years the hide-hunting industry began to languish. The aborigines considerately invented the legend of the "Lost Herd" to excuse the white man's lust to kill. A subtle change crept over the vast land. Thin steel threads were stretching out across the plains up to the mountain passes. The beaver and other fur-bearers were going the way of the buffalo.

But the pioneers, resourceful by nature as well as by necessity, quickly adapted themselves to the changing conditions. The limitless prairies, overgrown with high grass, offered excellent, and seemingly inexhaustible, pasturage for livestock. They brought in rangey, long-horn cattle from the Texas plains, descendants of old breeds introduced by the Spaniards. Toll was taken of the wild horse bands, and imported domestic horses usurped their pastures. Both cattle and horses were turned loose to graze; there were no fences, the range was free. Each owner marked his stock for the purpose of identification. Thus "brands" came into common use. Distant neighbors turned stray stock back toward its home range.

With these pioneers widely scattered over the sparsely populated land and with their straggling herds began the cattle industry of the West. Compared to the highly specialized systems of today their management was crude and unscientific. However they solved many problems by which their successors profited, as, for instance, whether cattle could graze through the northern winters and, if so, whether such herds could compete with those hordes streaming up the Chisholm trail. To them too must go the glory of wresting the land from the Indian and making it safe for occupation, the glory of reclaiming the desert and developing the wilderness.

In 1848 the American farmer had scarcely come as far west as the Mississippi. By 1860 there were ranches scattered along the Overland Trail in Nebraska for a hundred and fifty miles west of the Missouri. The northern ranchers pushed westward very slowly because they had to drive the Indians before them and because as they progressed they left their base of supplies farther and farther behind. In 1867 the railroad reached Wyoming, and the cattleman at last had profitable connection with a consuming market for his wares.

In Colorado, the cattle industry first started along the Arkansas river, in the southeastern part of the state. The driving of cattle northward in great numbers began in 1866. Immense herds, and their attendant herders on horseback, called cowboys, followed the route known first as the Chisholm trail, later, variously as the Fort Griffin, the Dodge City, the Northern, the Northwest, and the Texas. From 1866 to 1885 the cattle driven northward into Kansas, Nebraska and Colorado numbered three to five hundred thousand a year. Herds numbering from a few hundred to many thousand grazed their way northward along worn trails, all the way from the middle and southern plains of Texas. They sold from ten dollars a head for the scrubs and "she stuff" to "twenty straight on the prairie" for the four-year old steers.

As the industry grew there came into existence the rancher

or cattleman, and the cowboy. These latter were not only sons of the pioneers, but disappointed gold-seekers, and adventurers from all parts of the United States, though mostly from Texas, and even from England. Strange intermingling of classes took place upon the cattle ranches: English noblemen rode the range as common cow hands and married rancher's daughters; business and professional men from the stern New England shores and the Old Dominion rode herd. Fathers in the effete east sent their wayward sons west, hoping the virile life there might reform them. All this amalgamation made for democracy. Social barriers were broken down. The high-born aristocrat of Europe and the settler's son shared the perils, the joys and the adventures of ranch life in common. Soon a distinctive, democratic spirit, free from class prejudice, manifested itself. Men were judged by their personal achievements and deserts, not by their backgrounds nor wealth. They were accepted for themselves, no questions asked, until they showed themselves unworthy of friendship. Men lived primitively, lived and loved and fought greatly, sometimes even with wild abandon. They were fearless, loyal to their friends, faithful to their families, liberal-minded, great-hearted, magnificent. This cordial, generous, free from pettiness, spirit still characterizes the West.

To the women of those days should go more praise than to the men. Their unfaltering devotion and patient heroism saved many a ranch from failure. They had to endure the monotony as well as the hardships of the life. They were practically marooned in isolated shacks, oftentime without the gentler companionship of their sex. They performed a continuous round of daily drudgery, far from enlivening scenes. The plight of the pioneer woman has never been adequately chronicled by the historian. Besides the dullness and drudgery, they suffered the constant dread of marauding Indians. The red men valued white squaws highly and abducted them at every opportunity. As their captives they knew lives of revolting misery.

Schools were unknown in the "cow country" and overworked mothers tutored their children as best they could. They taught them the three R's and trusted to life to complete their education. The children were born to the saddle and imbibed a knowledge of cattle and horses and range lore with their milk. What they lacked in higher education they made up in aptitude and resourcefulness. True, the cultured adventurers from Europe and the east contributed to their learning and were as entertaining as the troubadours of old.

Despite the strenuousness of their work and the dangers it entailed, the cowboys were a care-free lot. The frontier towns that sprang up along the Chisholm trail catered to their pleasure and preyed upon their weaknesses. Gambling, gun-fighting and wild carousals filled their leisure hours. They ate coarse food, slept on the ground, and met with fortitude whatever misfortunes befell them. They rode for weeks at a time, combing the range for stray stock. During feuds over water rights or ranch boundaries they fought loyally for their employers and continually risked their lives in defense of their interests. All this for the paltry wage of a dollar a day, or less.

Riders, or cowboys, were necessary because it was impossible to fence such unbounded areas as most of the ranches comprised. Each ranch had its own mark or brand and this design burned or branded upon its stock identified them. The old stock, all so marked, was turned upon the open range, and twice each year there were "round-ups". Hundreds of cowboys scattered far and wide and drifted the cattle toward a central point. Here the new calves were branded and the herds separated so that each owner might claim his own.

Naturally so many cattle roaming over such a wide territory, far from the protection of the home ranch, excited the cupidity of dishonest men. Organized gangs of "rustlers", or thieves, cultivated a nice cunning in brand tampering, and stole thousands of head of cattle, changed their brands, and boldly sold them in the market places.

There was no legal machinery in those remote regions, no courts of justice. It was the custom of the range to give every man a fair show, to decide all questions upon their merits, without fear or favor, or consideration of personal feelings or social connections. The cattlemen organized vigilance committees to detect and prosecute these thieves who were threatening the cattle business. The vigilantes meted out prompt, awe-inspiring, crime-deterring justice. They were judge, jury, and executioner.

Through his heroic fights against the rustlers the Southern

and Western cowboy achieved immortal fame. He had no idea he was heroic, it was all in the day's work. Yet many a one actually died with his boots on in defense of his employer.

Hangings were frequent in the days of the rustlers and each section had its official (?) hanging tree, on which thieves were strung up and left swinging, a gruesome warning to others. I once examined such a tree growing on the banks of the Cache la Poudre river. It was a cottonwood, standing apart from its neighbors, as though shunned by them because of its monstrous fruit. Its joints were gnarled and swollen, its limbs distorted and broken. Nearly all bore evidence of once having been accomplices of the hangman and seemed to writhe at the haunting memory. The whole tree had the air of extreme weariness, of premature old age; its foliage drooped as though about to shrivel and drop off; yet it did not die for nearly twenty years after I saw it.

When, some four centuries ago, Cortez set out on his two years' exploration and conquest of Mexico, he brought with him the first horses to tread American soil, great chargers, bred from Arabian sires. As the expedition forced its way into the hostile land many of these animals went lame or in some such way became unfit for service and were abandoned. These noble nomads turned feral and were the progenitors of the wild horses that later swarmed over the plains and valleys of Southwestern America. Inbreeding dwarfed the stock, but the struggle to survive in the strange, peril-fraught environment developed their speed and endurance. They became wiry and wary, tough and sinewy, with an unconquerable love of freedom, and an uncanny instinct for avoiding capture. Many are the round-up tales of super-stallions that have out-run and out-witted their human pursuers.

Different sections applied different terms to these wild strains. However, all use the appellation first given them by the Spaniards, "broncho", meaning rude or rough. In time the various names used to describe wild horses were applied to domesticated ones as well, and broncho, contracted to "bronc", mustang and cayuse (kiuse) are now used interchangeably.

The hunting and capturing of wild horses by roping or trapping became a sideline of the cattle business. Here were thrills that more than compensated for the monotony of riding herd. The captured bronchos were useless until "broken" although the breaking of a horse commonly added but ten dollars to its value. Cowmen had a saying expressive of this valuation. Seeing a rider with a handsome saddle on a broken wild horse, they would remark, "There goes a hundred dollar saddle on a ten dollar cayuse."

The breaking of wild or half-wild horses became a profession in the West. Riders of rare skill were discovered, and in rare instances developed, though for the most part the top-notchers in the riding game, as in other fields of excellence, are born, not made.

Out of the necessity of wild-horse taming grew that most spectacular exhibition of cowboy skill, the rodeo, almost the only surviving phase of the epic West available to the tenderfoot, or to the westerner, for that matter. Here are reproduced the activities of the cowboy, his life on the open range, the calf-roping and branding, the bull-dogging, the steer-riding, the broncho-busting of the cow country. To these are added a sort of vaudeville, trick riding, and fancy stunts with the lasso. Real, not synthetic, cowboys, crowned with the typical "four-gallon" Stetsons and shod with the pointed-toed, high-heeled boots of the range, stake their reputations and hazard their lives attempting to ride unbroken horses, both bronchos and thoroughbreds. From that tense moment when they climb aboard their blind-folded mounts and are shot out of the chutes they make a gallant picture, as, waving their hats and slapping their bucking steeds with them, spurring and shouting, they dash across the arena, preserving throughout the whole performance the debonair grace of a circus rider. Most of them stick on the required thirty seconds but some have to be rescued or "picked up" before the time limit is up for there are occasional "outlaws" that refuse to submit to gentling. These are valued highly for rodeo performances. The West has known many "bad actors" among the captured wild horses, of which Old Steamboat was one of the worst, or rather best, according to the rodeo promoter's point of view.

The West is everlastingly indebted to the horse. Without his mount the cowboy would have been helpless, and the cattle business could never have been developed. The cowman has always recognized this, and even the crudest of them treated their horses well. The gentler side of the cowboy was revealed in his association with his "little cayuse"; he always looked to the comfort of his mount before he did to his own. No matter how late he made camp nor after how long a ride, he first ministered to his four-footed comrade. Nor would he tolerate another man's abusing his own horse. He looked on at men abusing each other to the limit of endurance, shooting and fighting to the death, and never presumed upon their privilege nor sought to interfere, but let one of them abuse his horse—! Such a fellow he regarded with the same consideration he gave a rattlesnake!

Each stage of development of the cattle industry had its peculiar problems. In early years, when settlers were few, it was the Indians, who trailed the prairies in bands large enough to attack the widely-separated ranches. Then, the rustler took toll of the livestock. Later, when the region became more thickly settled, there were feuds over claim boundaries, where once grazing land had seemed so illimitible. Then, too, sprang up trouble over water rights. Besides these there were natural enemies, flood and drought and fire, plague of grasshoppers and ticks and tick fever.

Through it all the cattlemen never thought of quitting. It was their custom to help each other in times of distress, and the greater the emergency the more they sacrificed to meet it. They gave ungrudgingly of both property and service. If rustlers raided one, his neighbors rode with him to avenge the raid, and risked their lives in his defense. The history of the West is emblazoned with the heroic deeds of simple men who laid down their lives for their friends.

Far out on the plains a cowboy took up a homestead, married a neighboring rancher's daughter, and started in the cattle business with twenty head of stock. Slowly, as the years passed, more and more cattle bearing his brand, the J. C., appeared upon the range. For twenty years he and his wife toiled and prospered. Then trouble overtook them. Rustlers drove off most of their herd, Indians stole their saddle stock, and set fire to the ranch buildings. Then a prairie fire swept over the region, destroying their remaining cattle and literally obliterating the ranch. The rancher and his wife found themselves advanced in years, without a roof over their heads, or a single steer, or money to procure either. Their plight was hopeless. Yet they were dauntless. The same fire that had swept away their earnings had also ruined a neighbor. Twenty miles away a rancher and his wife had perished in the fire, and had left five small children parentless. The owners of the J. C. borrowed a wagon, drove over to the orphans, adopted them, and began life all over with the added responsibilities of an adopted family. Such an occurrence was not out of the ordinary in cattle land.

As time passed the primitive ranch methods were improved. The gaunt, long-horned Texas steers were supplanted by Herefords and other breeds that were more profitable. Horses were bred up. Graded highways were built to replace the old crooked roads. Railroads reached further and further into the range country. In the middle eighties the stockmen were at the height of their prosperity. Then came the collapse of the horse market, owing to the rapid substitution of electricity for horse power.

The free range of the West is gone; the land is fenced. The squatters who followed the cattleman homesteaded all of it, and spoiled that which was privately owned by cultivating the land adjacent to it and making it too valuable for cattle ranging. Big corporations squeezed out many of the homesteaders by securing control of the water rights. The homesteaders resented this injustice and fought back with true western spirit. Be it to their everlasting credit that though not always infallible in their judgment, they never lacked the courage to fight for their convictions.

The early range days have left an indelible impress upon the West. The gold rushes of the late forties and fifties lured thousands of emigrants beyond the Mississippi, but it was the cattle industry that made it possible for them to settle permanently. The cattle industry made possible the development of the West. It inspired the building of railroads. It saved the day for Colorado when other industries failed.

Gone are those wild, free days. But the brave spirit of those gritty pioneers will live forever. Their dauntless courage in the face of tremendous odds, their superb surmounting of every difficulty, their generosity, and even greater than these, their simple-hearted democracy, have made the West a land of wholesome, valley-deep, mountain-high, traditions. The splendour of their lives casts a glamourous glow over our less colorful, less heroic ones.

Colorado is still the old West, bluff and hearty, unsophisticated, fair-minded, rich in her heritage from those epoch-making days. The covered wagon, the buffalo and the free range are gone, but campfires still burn along cow trails and picturesque cowboys still enjoy the wide, open spaces. So long as cattle dot the plains, range days will exist. The traditions of those pioneer cattlemen are as deeply inscribed upon the hearts of their descendants as the trails they blazed were cut upon their beloved land!

Chapter 5
THE GOLD RUSH AND AFTER
James F. Willard

Small quantities of placer gold had been found from time to time in what is now the State of Colorado before the discoveries that led to the gold rush of 1858-1859. William Gilpin, who had visited the mountains with Frémont and who later became Territorial Governor of Colorado, had told stories of gold in the Rockies to an unmoved world; others had found gold, though little of it, and then, in 1858, wise after the event, told of their discoveries. Some men doubtless invented their tales in order to share in the publicity given to the early Peakers. As none of these finds of gold led to active exploitation of the streams and mountains they may be left without further mention in this brief sketch.

The movement toward the Rocky Mountains in search of gold owed its origin to the reputed great success of a company that reached the district surrounding the present site of Denver in June, 1858. This company, composed of Georgians, Missourians, Kansans and Cherokee Indians, is known in Colorado history as the Russell Company. Shortly after this company reached the mountains another, of independent origin, known as the Lawrence Company, reached the vicinity of Pike's Peak in search of gold. The movement that followed was stimulated by hard times in the Mississippi Valley, the result of the panic of 1857.

It is necessary to keep in mind when reading of the movements of the early gold hunters that they did not enter into an entirely unknown land. Nor did they venture into an uninhabited wilderness. There were a number of trappers and traders in the Rocky Mountains and along their eastern slope. There was one trading post, Bent's Fort, near Pike's Peak. By Fort Laramie, which lay to the north of the gold region, went the wagons of emigrants bound for Utah or the Northwest and the fort with traders, trappers, and visiting Indians formed a centre of gossip for the mountain district. Along the Arkansas by Bent's Fort went a part of the Santa Fé trade. What is more there was cross traffic between the northern and southern routes along the base of the mountains. When the early companies reached the foothills of the Rockies they met mountain men from whom they learned the names of the streams and of the peaks. After they had discovered gold these same mountain men and other wayfarers carried the news to Fort Laramie from whence it sped down river to the towns of the Missouri Valley and westward to Utah. Others carried the news to Taos and the New Mexican country. To one who reads of the rapidity with which the news spread it seems as though within the snowy range of the mountains there was a powerful station broadcasting in every direction hundreds of miles across the hills and mountain valleys.

The Russell Company journeyed toward the mountains to investigate a report of gold found at Ralston Creek. The reason why that particular stream formed their goal is not easy to discover. Rumors of gold in the Rockies were afloat in the Missouri Valley in 1857, but they were far from definite. The Lawrence Company which was influenced by these rumors went to Pike's Peak to find gold. It may be that the Russell Company owed its more definite information to John Beck, a Cherokee Indian and a returned Californian who had been to the base of the mountains and found gold there. Whatever the reason William Green Russell and his brothers decided in 1857 to organize a company to prospect for gold during the following summer. The Russells got together a party in Georgia, Beck organized a group of Cherokees and a few white men in the Indian Territory, and a small party was formed in Missouri of men from Ray and Bates counties and a scattering few from elsewhere. These parties came together in May and June, 1858, on the southern route to the mountains. Luke Tierney, one of the members of the company gives the total number of gold seekers as one hundred and four and divides them as follows: Georgia, 19; Missouri, 27; Cherokee Nation, 58*.

On the twenty-fourth in the evening, or the twenty-fifth of June, the former is Tierney's statement, the company reached its destination, Ralston Creek, near the present site of Denver. "Here," writes Tierney, "according to the statements of the returned Californians, we were in the immediate vicinity of the

---

*Luke Tierney, *History of the Gold Discoveries on the South Platte River*, p. 10. Tierney includes the few Kansans among the twenty-seven from Missouri.

gold mines". The members of the company prospected the region and were promptly disillusioned, for they found only a few particles of gold. Several days of anxious search brought no better results and the majority of the men were so discouraged by the fourth of July that they determined to return home. They went, leaving about thirty to continue the search. This number was soon reduced to thirteen and this small group, known as the Georgia Company, made the first discoveries of gold in reasonably paying quantity. Gold was found in several places but the name of Cherry Creek was prominent in the stories carried to the outside world despite the fact that it yielded little placer gold. It was the news of these discoveries in July that spread through the mountains and the Missouri Valley and caused the excitement of the autumn months. Curiously enough Oliver P. Goodwin is reported in the *Weekly Kansas Herald* of the twenty-fourth of July as having arrived on the preceding Wednesday, from Fort Bridger with the following news: "On the head waters of the South Fork of Platte, near Long's Peak, gold mines have been discovered and 500 persons are now working there." The distorted news of the earliest meagre finds of the Russell Company had found a credulous host.

The Lawrence Company was organized in April, 1858, and left the city on the 24th and 25th of May for Pike's Peak. Following the southern route it arrived at Bent's Fort on the 28th of June. On the fifth of July the company met two wagons of the Russell Company deserters and learned from them the discouraging results of the first expedition. During the months of July and August they prospected in the southern part of the reputed gold region. Hearing of the discoveries on the South Platte they moved northward and arrived at the new diggings on the second of September. William B. Parsons, one of the company, tells the story: "There we found five or six men engaged in mining, and, although they had very inferior tools, they were making respectable wages. We immediately went to work, and found that although things had been considerably exaggerated, we could do well, and had a good prospect for the future."[*]

Gold had been found in the streams near the present site of Denver in July and the following weeks and it did not take long

---
[*]*Lawrence Republican*, October 28, 1859.

for the news to reach the Missouri Valley. The exaggerated account from the *Weekly Kansas Herald,* quoted above, seems to have received no attention in the papers. Then in August came more definite news. The *Missouri Republican,* of St. Louis, published an item from the *St. Joseph Gazette* on the twenty-fifth of August on discoveries near Fort Laramie, and doubted the story. Four days later the same paper published a despatch from Kansas City dated August 26 chronicling the arrival of Monsieur Bordeau and party from Pike's Peak. They came for outfits to work in the mines on Cherry Creek. A few days more and most of the doubters were silenced, for a letter came down from a man who had visited the mines, a specimen of gold was brought into Rulo, Nebraska, and Mr. John Cantrell arrived in person with three ounces "which he dug with a hatchet in Cherry Creek and washed out with a frying pan."*

There was immediate and unreasoning excitement in the river towns for times were still hard in the valley and the New Eldorado promised relief from all financial worries. Some of the earlier reports promised great riches. On the thirty-first of August the *St. Louis Republican* sent forth to the world the story, emanating from Leavenworth, that two men had "washed out $600 in one week". Much less modest sums were soon to figure in the newspapers.

As the news spread men from the relatively near-by points of Fort Laramie and the towns in New Mexico and Utah hastened to the mines. Then the more distant towns of the Missouri Valley fell into line. Mr. Buttan, a member of the Lawrence party, left the mines on the twentieth of September and reported that there were already about one hundred men there and more arriving daily. He stated that on his way down he met from seven hundred to one thousand emigrants. This statement is found in the *Lawrence Republican* of the 28th of October. There are notices of parties forming and departing from various places in Kansas, Nebraska, Missouri, Iowa, Ohio, and even far away Michigan. In several instances a member of the company agreed to write to the home paper about the adventures of the group. William O'Donnall wrote of the activities of a second Lawrence Company, General William Larimer about the

**Lawrence Republican,* September 2, 1858.

Leavenworth men, and A. A. Brookfield and others about the Nebraska City boys. Some of these men continued to write during the winter and ensuing spring. There were many volunteer correspondents. Thus the western country was kept well informed of the progress of the first migration.

With the advance of cold weather there was a cessation in the movement westward, and the same weather conditions caused a number of the gold seekers to leave the mines. They came down to the Missouri Valley towns to purchase supplies for the next season or because they had had enough of placer mining and all its ways. The optimists were in the majority and some of them told great tales. Mr. Cantrell said that he could make $17 to $20 a day with pick and pan; others reported $10 to $30 a day as the results of their mining; but the usual estimates of returns ran from $3 or $5 to $10 or $12 a day, with emphasis upon the larger sums. The largest sum reported as having been taken by an individual in the mines was $6,000, and $3,000 and $2,000 were also mentioned. It is is perhaps unnecessary to add that these large sums were purely apocryphal and that the large sum noted would probably cover all the gold washed out by all the miners during the autumn and early winter months. However, gold was brought down from the mines, flake gold as it was called, shown to everyone on the way, and later exhibited in drug stores, newspaper offices and saloons. Who could doubt the stories when they had actually seen and handled the gold dust? The newspapers spread the glad tidings and everywhere in the West and Middle West men began to prepare for the spring migration to Cherry Creek. Some of the discontented who had been to the mines and had found the situation there far from roseate, called the whole affair a humbug, even a damned humbug. They were answered with vigor by the optimists; the newspaper editors of the river towns were glad to support the cause of the latter, for a great migration meant prosperity to the merchants in the struggling settlements on the Missouri.

The late winter months were spent in preparation for the spring rush to the mining district. Companies were organized not only in the Missouri Valley but also throughout the region east of the Mississippi. The newspapers were full of sage advice concerning the proper outfits for the prospective miners. Guides and maps of the routes were published. Of the guides, that issued by William B. Parsons in Lawrence during the month of December seems to have been the earliest.* Others followed. The maps were more or less accurate according to the knowledge or bias of their makers. As many of the maps were local products, issued in order to attract attention to one town and one route, they were at times very indefinite in their designation of other towns and routes. A map drawn up by E. L. Berthoud in Leavenworth shows the various routes, but of the rival towns notes only Lawrence. The *Lawrence Republican* of the third of March, 1859, grew indignant over the entire omission of Lawrence from Pearman's map of the gold regions. Each of the river towns put forward a claim during the winter and spring to be the best outfitting point for the prospective miners. Even St. Louis, far down the river, modestly claimed that its goods were the cheapest and that the up-river merchants charged exorbitant prices for everything they had to sell.

The battle of the routes, which was directly connected with outfitting, was one of the most interesting events of the period preceding and following the opening of the spring migration. Though bloodless it was of vital interest to all concerned. The various towns lying on the Missouri as it turns to the north could be reached by steamboat or railroad, and then arose the problem of the selection of the route westward. From the southern part of the bend of the river there led the Southern Route by the Santa Fé road, and also by way of the Kansas and Smoky Hill Fork, the Smoky Hill route. From points farther north there lay the route by the Republican Fork and the Northern or Platte Route. Each town claimed the best or shortest road to Fort Riley or Fort Kearney, which were the assembling points on these routes, and then expatiated on the advantages of the roads to the mines. Nebraska City made much of its Great Central Route to Fort Kearney and unquestionably it stood at one end of the shortest route from the Missouri to the fort. Most of the towns laid emphasis upon the cheapness of their supplies and the advantages of their western route. Atchison and St. Joseph favored the Northern Route; Lawrence the Smoky Hill Route and Kansas City the Southern Route. The battle went on merrily during

---

*The Gold Mines of Western Kansas. Published for the author and sold at twenty-five cents a copy.

the winter and spring over the distance to the mines, the condition of the roads, the best supplies of wood, water, and grass. Then the Peakers came and decided the matter for themselves. Leavenworth, from which men could take with comfort any but the Northern route, and they could even go by that highway, had, if not the best arguments, at least the greatest success in the warfare. Soon its position as an outfitting and starting point was made doubly secure by its selection as the eastern end of the route followed by the Leavenworth and Pike's Peak Express. This stage line chose a route almost midway between the Republican and Smoky Hill routes, avoiding so it was thought the disadvantages of each.

While the merchants laid in stores, the wheelwrights built wagons and the newspapers wrangled over the merits of their respective routes. At the same time companies were organizing in the East preparatory to the spring migration as soon as the roads opened and the steamers could bring them to their starting points. While all this excitement prevailed in the "States" the miners in the West settled down for the winter.

A considerable number of the men who had reached the mines in the late summer or autumn returned to the valley as winter approached, but many remained to mine a little, to form towns and build houses, to take up farms, and to discuss mining and politics when they could not work. It is clear that mining languished during the winter, but that house and town building flourished. Scores and even hundreds of log cabins were built in the new towns, not only for the accommodation of the builders, but also to sell or rent to the men who were sure to come in the spring. Of the towns the earliest was Montana, the work of the Lawrence men. It was started early in September, 1858, on the Platte to the north of the Denver of today. During the following months Auraria, St. Charles and Denver City were all founded on the present site of Denver. Arapahoe City was laid out near the site of the present Golden and El Paso to the south where Colorado City now stands. El Dorado City and Fountain City both in the southern district were begun and to the north in February Boulder City started on its career. In connection with the latter event A. A. Brookfield, one of the founders wrote in March, 1859, "I did not come out here for town speculation but after we made what are considered by far the best discoveries of the 'precious metal' we thought as the weather would not permit us to mine, we would lay out and commence building what may be an important town, *provided* the mines prove of the richness we expect." Though some of the miners had left for home, while others had gone to Laramie, or to the building of the old St. Vrain's Fort, even to New Mexico, there remained in the mining district during the winter about five hundred of the more optimistic or the more far-sighted. Mining might not pay well, but house building had a potential value and selling shares in the town companies was attractive and might prove remunerative.

The first groups of the gold hunters of the spring migration were those formed in the Missouri Valley towns. As early as February, 1859, a small company called a "packing company", using Indian ponies instead of wagons for the transportation of their goods, left Lawrence for Cherry Creek. In March the rush began, despite the warning of old timers, and increased in volume during the months of April and May. What a rush it was! Every boat that came up the river to the starting points was filled with Peakers. As they landed they were greeted by the merchants, or runners for the merchants, who wished to sell them rifles, provisions, mining utensils, tents, oxen, the inevitable whiskey, and all other things needed on the plains and in the mines. The pages of the newspapers bore startling or attractive Pike's Peak advertisements of all sorts and, so it is said, in Leavenworth and elsewhere, hotels, saloons, and other establishments, by their signs and placards, tried to draw to themselves the attention of the gold seekers. Many of the latter placed the slogan Pike's Peak on the sides of their wagons and so carried the tale across the plains.

By the several routes a motley lot of men and conveyances started toward the mines in the spring of 1859. The earlier gold seekers had been organized into companies and had set forth in the dignified large wagon, with its white top, drawn by oxen or mules. The men who went out in the rush of the following spring were in a hurry; they went in companies or small groups and many were without the money with which to purchase an expensive outfit. So there were all kinds of means of conveyance from the prairie schooner to the pack on the back of a pedestrian. There are many references to the heavy and slow wagon. Along side of these went light wagons of various sorts drawn by horses or mules. Some men rode on horseback across the plains. There were many hand carts, large and small, drawn by the Peakers themselves. Most of these seem to have had crews of eight men, serving two at a time. A hand cart is thus described in April: "The cart is constructed pretty much after the fashion of a 'go-cart', only being minus the legs or supports in front to keep it level while standing. A cross-piece is attached to the ends of the shafts, while the space between is occupied by the locomotive powers, who push against the cross-rod." In most cases, however, the hand carts are said to have been pulled or drawn. A few men pushed wheelbarrows with all their worldly goods loaded on them. There are at least two references to light wagons drawn by dogs toward the mines. Decidedly the most curious conveyance invented was the Westport Wind Wagon. With wheels some twenty feet in diameter, and large sails, its omnibus body was to accommodate over twenty people. It is perhaps needless to say that it was a failure. The number of men who started for the mines with handbags, black carpetbags, or packs on their backs was large, how large it is impossible to state. One contemporary observer writes: "Those who observed the character of this emigration this spring, must have noticed the vast number who were totally unprepared for an expedition of this kind. A black carpetbag, an extra pair of boots, and a substantial suit of clothes, with, in every case almost, a rifle and gun, and perhaps six-shooter, generally constituted their outfit for a trip of one thousand miles. Of mining implements, or anything to aid in separating the particles of gold from the earth, the exhibition was a scanty one."[*] Through the accounts of and by the Peakers there runs a thread of exaggeration and burlesque, yet even sober observers were wont to lay stress upon the bizarre equipment of many of the emigrants and upon the medley of means of transportation. Many observers record that, by the month of May, an emigrant train was but rarely out of sight of others either to the east or the west.

The goal of most of the emigrants was the Cherry Creek district, though some were attracted by the mines to the north and south. When they reached Denver City or Auraria in April and May they found towns with many log houses, a number of

---

[*]*Missouri Republican*, April 21, 1859.

saloons and stores. These, like the other towns of the mining district were decidedly frontier towns with the roughness and enthusiasm of their kind. The residents of the embryonic cities were glad to greet the newcomers and to sell them town lots and whatever they might need. Some of the Peakers were convinced that the majority of the inhabitants of Denver and Auraria were speculators in town lots. One who returned home in May is reported to have stated that, "As soon as he and his party arrived at Denver City they were surrounded by town speculators, all eager to make them rich by selling them lots at low figures. This seems to be the whole and sole business of the inhabitants of Denver City and Auraria".* Allowing for the exaggeration of a disappointed gold hunter, the rivalry between the Denver City and Auraria lot-holders seems to have been intense. In the month of May, when the hopes of many of the men who were seeking gold had been dashed to the ground, there was much disorder in the frontier towns. Prices were high, provisions scarce and hard times the order of the day. The disillusioned, who had expected to reap a rich harvest with little effort, were discontented and ripe for disorder.

From the towns the gold seekers went to the mines in the vicinity. The methods of placer mining used by those who had reached the mines during the autumn and early winter were crude and unsatisfactory. What is more most of the men were inexperienced. The usual plan of operations was that of pick, shovel, and pan, and the pans were those used in cooking. From the start the yield of gold was estimated by the pan. In October, 1858, it is reported that James Rooker had made a rough rocker out of a split hollow log and that he was doing well. In November the Russell Company is said to have been using quicksilver. More rough log rockers are mentioned before the winter set in. During the winter many long sluices and the shorter Long Tom, which was a sluice box, were made in the mining district. The spring migration brought many men unprepared for mining despite the efforts of the stores in the border towns to sell them a complete equipment including Long Toms, rockers, and gold pans. But by that time a large number were using better implements, even hydraulic pumps and pipe lines, and quicksilver.

---
* *Missouri Republican*, June 1, 1859, quoting from the *St. Joseph West* of May 30.

The Gold Rush and After

The gold that was found was placer gold, called scale, float or drift gold. It was very fine and was found in the creek beds and in the South Platte bottom. The broad and sandy beds of the rivers and streams flowing out of the mountains offered a wide field of operations. In these beds the miners dug trenches or holes seeking for the bed rock above which the gold was found. The estimates of the depth at which the gold bearing sand or "dirt" was found vary from two to fifteen feet. As the streams were small in the spring the miners had often to carry their pans of "dirt" many yards before they reached the water needed for washing it. By the winter at least claims were staked out, the usual size, so it is stated, being fifty by one hundred feet.

Mining was hard work, much harder work than that to which many of the emigrants were accustomed, and it was soon found that it did not pay. After a day's labor in April and May a miner might have but a few cents to show for all his pains. When the first day's yield was matched by that of several more the men became discouraged. Mr. Barney, who arrived in May, describes his own experience with his usual inimitable humor: "I have had three day's experience in gold digging. The first didn't reach the auriferous color, though I washed about a thousand panfuls. The second day about the same number with a shade of yellow dirt, which inspired courage. Third day, near as I can judge, having no means of measuring or weighing, I secured about the sixteenth part of a new cent's worth of the genuine article".* To most, not gifted with Barney's sense of humor, such a result was a tragedy. With little or no money, their hopes blasted, the disappointed men turned back toward home. To the Missouri Valley came the news that the Pike's Peak gold region was a humbug and this news was reinforced late in April and in May by the appearance in person of those who had failed to make their fortunes.

The return of the miners, which began in April, 1859, was a stampede in May. Down the routes went disappointed and angry men who spread the bad news as they traveled. A few went down the Platte in small flat-bottomed boats. To the men on their way to the mines the news they received from the returning miners spelled disaster and many gave up long before they came in sight of the mountains. Those who went on had hardships

---
* Libeus Barney, *Early Day Letters from Auraria.*

to face, for a large number were unprepared for a long journey. Along the Smoky Hill Route especially there was suffering and even starvation. The month of May seemed, therefore, to mark the beginning of the end of the gold excitement. Even the optimistic editors of the papers in the river towns began to doubt the richness of the mines and some were convinced that the Pike's Peak bubble had "busted".

At the time when the discouragement of the gold seekers was approaching its nadir there came the news of discoveries of exceeding richness in the mountains. Many of the early miners had noticed, as they worked up the streams toward the foothills, that there was or seemed to be more gold dust. They had, therefore, predicted that with the coming of spring the rich deposits would be found in the Rockies. A few had ventured into the mountains in the autumn and winter in an attempt to verify these predictions only to be deterred by the snow and ice. It remained for George A. Jackson and John H. Gregory to realize the hopes of the miners.

During the first week of May there came to the towns in the mining district first rumors and then direct evidence of the discoveries of Jackson and Gregory. Jackson's Diggings were what were called bar diggings, true placer mines, and were located on Chicago Creek as it empties into Clear Creek at Idaho Springs. Gregory's discovery was made on the hillside of a small ravine between the present Black Hawk and Central City in the valley of the North Fork of Clear Creek. The mines there were called quartz mines. The miners found at first rotten or disintegrated quartz on the sides of the hills and worked downwards along the lodes until they reached the hard rock. Then their troubles began. Up to that time they broke up the loose quartz, carried the ore in sacks or otherwise down to the streams, washed it in sluices and collected the gold with the aid of quicksilver. Of the two districts Gregory's became immediately the more renowned and was the goal of the majority of the gold hunters.

The news of the new discoveries caused the desertion of the little towns along the mountains by their inhabitants. Then, rather slowly at first, the glad tidings were carried down the routes. On the tenth of June the Pike's Peak Express coach reached Leavenworth. On that day the *Leavenworth Times* issued an extra. In it under the heading IMMENSE GOLD

DISCOVERIES! PIKE'S PEAK A GLORIOUS REALITY! was printed a long letter from Henry Villard telling of the discoveries, of the rush to the Gregory district, and of the marvelous yields of the quartz leads. Gregory himself is said to have taken out $1,100 in five days. From Leavenworth the news was sent by telegraph to St. Louis and from there to the East. Though some editors were sceptical because of what had happened before, the arrival of gold dust in fairly large quantities soon dispelled their doubts. The march of the Peakers to the Rockies was resumed.

The population of the mountain mining region grew by leaps and bounds. When William N. Byers, editor of the *Rocky Mountain News*, reached the Gregory Diggings on the twentieth of May, he found about twenty men there and only two quartz leads had been opened. About two weeks later he estimated that there were about three thousand men in the mines, about thirty leads satisfactorily prospected, and several hundred claims being worked. Henry Villard, writing on the eleventh of June, states that there were about six thousand men in the mountains. During the following weeks the estimates run as high as ten thousand men and in July one observer notes that there were about fifteen thousand in the mountain districts. The hillsides were in the first weeks dotted with the tents or rude shacks of the miners, but cabins quickly appeared. Horace Greeley visited the Gregory Diggings in early June and notes in his *Overland Journey* that about one hundred cabins were being built and "three or four hundred in immediate contemplation". "As yet", he adds, "the entire population of the valley sleep in tents, or under booths of pine boughs, cooking and eating in the open air. I doubt that there is as yet a table or chair in these diggings, eating being done around a cloth spread on the ground, while each one sits or reclines on mother earth". Sluices lined the creeks, to which the busy miners carried their loads of "dirt". In the midst of the Gregory Diggings, Mountain City was founded late in May. It is described early in June as containing over two hundred dwellings. "The pine trees are being levelled to the ground, streets opened, and the axe and hammer sounding in every direction . . .". Stores appeared, saloons and gambling houses, hotels, express offices and a printing office. Lawyers' and physicians' signs were hung up. Town life had invaded the mining district. Within a short time Central City, the successor of Mountain City, was an established town with substantial buildings and a prosperous air. The foundations of several considerable fortunes were laid in the district about it.

While many succeeded in the mines, and while there are verified stories of rich yields, there were numerous cases of failure. James Robinson and five other men reached the mines late in May. In Jackson's Diggings they worked for six days and made just six cents. In the Gregory Diggings they averaged twenty-five cents a day. Others had similar tales to tell. One man reported that the "mines will not pay as well as staying at home with one's wife". The work of mining was hard work, the leads though numerous, were not sufficient to provide everyone in the crowded district with a paying claim, and many miners did not know how to get out the gold. Byers writing from Omaha on the tenth of July, advised no one to think of going to the mines without serious consideration. But many lazy, ignorant or thoughtless persons went, failed and returned to their homes in the autumn of the year 1859, went to work for other men, or went off to other diggings.

Within a very short time after the opening of the mining districts in the mountains it was found that some sort of organization must be adopted if confusion in the matter of claims was to be avoided. On the ninth of May a miners' meeting was called in the Jackson Diggings. The assembled miners drew up a set of by-laws regulating the size of claims, and the method of marking them. Officers were chosen. On the eighth of June the miners in the Gregory Diggings met, defined the boundaries of their district, and passed a series of resolutions relating to claims, water rights and the settlement of disputes. On the sixteenth a more formal set of laws was adopted. During the winter months a miners' court was created. Other mining districts were quickly formed with codes of laws, elected officers and courts. The names of most of the districts were undistinguished. Some were named after the original discoverers, Jackson, Gregory, and Russell, others were given place names, Pleasant Valley and Spring Gulch, while still others were named Wisconsin, Bay State, Eureka, Independent. The Shirt Tail District, in Clear Creek County, bears a name that carries with it the flavor of pioneer days. As the months passed the codes of law became more comprehensive. At times considerable attention was devoted to criminal matters. It is interesting to note that some districts excluded lawyers from practicing in the courts, and that some forbade saloons or gambling halls within their limits. There was a strain of puritanism in the mining camps at first along side of the independence and wild ways that charm present day writers of western tales.

Though the interest of the miners during the year 1859 was first centered about Cherry Creek and later in the districts just noted, there was a considerable broadening of the field of mining operations as the year passed. Both the early and late discoveries already described soon failed to satisfy the desires of the multitude. What is more the original districts were soon overcrowded. There was, therefore, a considerable number of unemployed or adventurous spirits, men ready to move anywhere in response to the news of rich finds and almost as ready to give up quickly if their hopes of quick returns were not realized. There were several minor stampedes during the year in consequence of the presence of these men in the camps.

Early in the year "shot" gold, which was coarser than "flake" or "float" gold, was found in Boulder Creek. So a number of miners went there. A. A. Brookfield wrote from Boulder City on March sixth "Our mines are all the talk of Auraria and Denver". The Boulder placer mines like many others soon disappointed the miners. As the spring advanced the miners continued to move into the mountains and in June quartz gold was discovered in Gold Gill. The Horsfal lode proved to be rich and the district prospered.

During the spring months some men crossed the Continental Divide into South Park and as early as May there were stories of shot gold there, but also of frozen ground and cold weather. Gold was soon found across the range in paying quantities on the South Fork of the South Platte, near where Como stands, near at hand at Fairplay, on the Blue River near the present Breckenridge, and on the Swan River. These were all placer mines and some of them proved to be rich. The news of the discoveries in South Park, on the headwaters of the Platte, came to Denver and the mining camps late in July and there was great excitement. More reports arrived and one writer reports that on his arrival in Denver

City on the sixteenth of August "The whole community was in a perfect stir in regard to the new discoveries on the head of the South Platte and Colorado". The emigration across the Divide was estimated by the same writer to number about five thousand men, of which number all but about five hundred returned. As it was with this migration so it was with most of the others. When rumors of returns as large as one hundred to one thousand dollars a day in other places were in the air the adventurers could not rest contented with the small individual earnings they were able to make where they were.

The story of gold and silver mining in Colorado since 1860 is one that may not be told in any detail in this place. All that will be attempted is a brief sketch of the development of the mining industry with special emphasis upon certain outstanding events.

The period from 1860 to 1868 was notable in at least two respects. It was then that eastern capitalists ventured for the first time to invest largely and with what proved to be mistaken zeal in Colorado mines. It was also an era of enthusiastic but poorly conceived "processes" in the treatment of ores, culminating in the sounder methods of Professor N. C. Hill.

In 1863 gold advanced rapidly in price because of the war needs of the government and the use of paper money. This drew the attention of financiers in the East to the possibilities of gaining riches by investment in the mines of Colorado. In 1863 and early in 1864 there were therefore formed a large number of companies for the exploitation of these mines and there was also a lively stock boom in the eastern financial centers. Large amounts of machinery of a very modern and often useless type were freighted to the Territory, many mills were erected, high salaried officials were placed in charge of operations and the companies hoped for quick and large returns. Many a miner in Colorado won a competence by selling claims or day dreams, for it was far more profitable to sell than to work underground. The boom, however, soon collapsed and left the mining industry with a bad name.

Once the era of excited speculation was over the mining camps settled down again to steady work in the mines. The period was, however, one of much discouragement, for the placer mines and surface workings on the sides of the mountains were being exhausted and the miners had reached either the solid rock with free gold or had opened veins of refractory ores. There was ample gold ore but the stamp mills saved only a little over half of the metal even when the rock contained free gold. The numerous "processes" of the time proved to be inadequate for the handling of the refractory ores. The method devised by Professor Hill and utilized under his direction by the Boston and Colorado Smelting Company at Black Hawk saved the day. The smelter of this company was opened for business in January, 1868. Its product was a copper matte and this was sent to Swansea in Wales for final reduction. In the seventies the company took up the production of gold and silver bullion and moved its plant to Argo, close to Denver.

During the late sixties and the first half of the next decade new fields and new mines were opened in various parts of the Territory. These served to keep up the production of the precious metals despite the decline of some of the early districts. Georgetown, in Clear Creek County, became a silver camp; rich silver mines were found at Caribou; the gold and silver mines in the San Juan country were opened, and such mines as the Smuggler, near Telluride, and the Mary Murphy in Chaffee County, bore witness to the possibilities of any mountain district. The increased production of silver in the early seventies shows a division of interest among the miners. During the ensuing years, after the discoveries at Leadville and Aspen, Colorado became a silver State and the output of the less precious metal became far greater in value as well as in volume, than that of its rival, gold.

The men who had worked the placer gold mines in California Gulch in the early sixties had passed over and about the site of the later town of Leadville without discovering the rich deposits of silver that were hidden there. They were not hunting for silver and, what is more, the silver was not free but found in a carbonate of lead. In 1874 W. H. Stevens, while engaged in placer mining, discovered the ore and staked out his first claim. In 1877 the rush to the new mining district began and continued in 1878 and 1879 with ever increasing volume. Leadville was decidedly a new and glorious El Dorado.

As there was no railroad into the district in Lake County until 1880 the migration was over the poorly made highways. Some of the immigrants came by the quickly formed stage lines, others in freight wagons, many in light wagons, others on horseback and a large number on foot with or without a pack mule. The town of Leadville was organized early in 1878, but those who reached it then found its dwellings to be largely tents and rude shacks with a few substantial log cabins. By the sides of its streets, and at times in the streets themselves, were still the stumps of the trees that had been cut down a few weeks or months before. By the end of 1879, however, Leadville had taken on a metropolitan air. Saw-mills had worked and were working night and day pouring out lumber for the homes of the citizens and for the business houses. Comfortable dwellings had appeared and with them hotels, banks and business blocks, saloons and dance halls, gambling houses and houses of ill fame, theatres and other places of amusement. Along side of these the citizens had brought into being a water system, a fire department, a system of lighting the streets and homes with gas, and last, but not least, a more or less efficient system of police. Before the end of the year 1879 three newspapers brought the news of the outside world to the citizens.

The Leadville of 1878 and 1879 was, like most mining camps in the early days, the scene of much excitement and a great deal of disorder. All kinds and conditions of men came to the city, but through all of them ran the desire to gain wealth with the least possible delay. The miner and the banker, the card sharp and speculator, the theatre manager and the owner of a saloon, had at least that much in common. With riches all about them, with new strikes every week, and with mining claims as well as real estate increasing in value by leaps and bounds, all but a few men lost their heads and shared in the general excitement. Chestnut Street and later Harrison Avenue were filled with men during the day, all talking eagerly. Some were selling town lots, others mining claims, but all were excited. At night bedlam broke loose and the crowds and the noise continued until daybreak. Many of the saloons, gambling houses and other resorts remained open all night and bands played to entice the miners to them. It is reported that one theatre opened at about midnight in 1879 and closed at four in the morning.

But the lurid side of the life of Leadville is only a part of the story. Out of its mines poured millions of dollars' worth of silver. That the mines had in these early days to be guarded by heavily armed men to protect the owners from claim-jumpers and more simple-minded thieves is true, but that does not affect the story of riches. From the Camp Bird mine, from the mines on Fryer Hill, and from dozens of others, thousands of tons of rich ore were taken to the smelters about the city. Fortunes were quickly made and often quickly lost, but the wealth of Colorado was materially increased by the output of these mines.

One effect of the discovery of the silver mines at Leadville was to stimulate prospecting elsewhere. Prospectors from Leadville made the discoveries that laid the foundation of Aspen and that caused the rush to that place in 1879. Mines were opened in Silver Cliff in 1879 and in other places and the San Juan Country became more prosperous. To each of the new districts there was the usual rush of disappointed miners from other camps, in each towns quickly arose, and in these towns the tumultuous life of Leadville was reproduced on a smaller scale. Then came a slow or rapid decline both in the excitement of the inhabitants and in the mineral production of the district.

The eighties witnessed the reign of silver in Colorado, but no startling discoveries of the character of those made at Leadville. Then in 1891 and 1893 two districts were opened, one of which nearly rivalled, while the other surpassed the richest of earlier days. The first was the district centering at Creede, and second that about Cripple Creek. Once again and for the last time on a large scale were reproduced the scenes of the Gold Rush.

Thousands of adventurers hastened to the mines discovered by N. C. Creede in the spring of 1891 near the town that bears his name. Before the railroad built by David H. Moffat reached the town late in that year the stampede was of the older type. The old wild ways reappeared in the town with the saloon, dance halls and gambling houses. The excitement in the streets, approaching a riot, was reenacted. Bad men were there and as a contemporary observer stated, "many who were reckless". But Creede and all the silver camps were soon to meet a serious check upon their development. In 1893 the Sherman Silver Purchase Act was repealed and none but the mines with rich ores could be operated at a profit. There was a sharp decline in the total value of the silver ore produced in 1894 and since then, though much silver is mined, there has been a rather steady decline in the volume and value of the mineral mined in Colorado. Colorado struggled to remain a great silver State to no avail.

With the opening of the mines at Cripple Creek in 1891 and 1892 we come to the last of the great mining camps in Colorado thus far discovered. To those who have lived in the state for many years, however, there is always hope, for what has happened in the past may happen again.

In the year 1891 Bob Womack, a rancher, found rich gold ore near the small stream called Cripple Creek and laid out his claim. In that year other claims were staked out and the news began to spread. But Creede was attracting much attention and the Mount Pisgah hoax of a few years before in the region of Pike's Peak was still remembered and consequently few men took the news seriously. The town of Cripple Creek was started, however, and the following year the movement into the district began in earnest. It reached great heights in 1893. There was the usual mixture of sober business houses and more or less questionable places of amusement in the town. One improvement was made, for electricity lighted the streets and the homes. Cripple Creek mining stocks sold freely in the eastern States and the buying and selling of claims in the district was brisk. From the Portland, Independence, Golden Cycle, Mary McKinney, and other mines came marvellous yields of gold. Unlike those in many another mining district, a number of these mines are still producive.

Cripple Creek more than other metal mining camps has been burdened with labor troubles. The strike of the miners in 1894 had to do largely with the matter of hours of labor. It was finally settled, after a large amount of disorder, by the grant of an eight-hour day. In 1903-1904 there was a more serious strike, lasting for about a year and a half. There was serious disorder, the State militia was called out for a long period, and everyone concerned, including the State government, lost enormous sums of money. The strike was largely sympathetic in character, the miners of Cripple Creek being called out by the Western Federation of Miners in order to force their rules upon the Colorado Reduction and Refining Company at Colorado City. With the assistance of the military forces of the State the Mine Owners' Association and the Citizens Alliance suppressed disorder, crushed the unions and wrecked the influence of the Western Federation in the camp.

Since the days of the rush to Cripple Creek there have been no like movements in Colorado save, on a much smaller scale, that to the Boulder District during the tungsten boom of the years of the World War. The rise in the cost of labor and of mining materials after 1918 has caused a slow but steady decline in the value of the precious materials produced in the State.

Most of the mining towns of early days are now mere shadows of their former selves. A number have been completely deserted, others still hold on to a semblance of life despite boarded up houses, and deserted stores; only a few are active and reasonably prosperous. Yet in the lobbies of the hotels of the moribund towns and in other gathering places a visitor may still hear of new discoveries by hopeful miners, of the Mother Lode that is just about to be found, and of the return of prosperity to the camp "next year". Prospectors are still grub-staked to search for gold and silver and wander through the mountains seeking for lost mines and the end of the rainbow. Some day they may find what they seek.

Chapter 6

EDUCATION IN COLORADO

Harry M. Barrett

Colorado history is a microcosm of the history of America. Within the boundaries of the territory which became the Centennial State met the descendants of Puritan and Cavalier and those in whose veins ran the blood of the Catholics, Quakers, Presbyterians, Methodists, Baptists, Lutherans, Free-Thinkers and others who had settled the middle colonies. Hence the history of education in Colorado furnishes a cross section of the educational history of the colonists along the Atlantic coast.

The pioneers of '58 and '59 came to Colorado not to found homes but led by the lure of gold. For the most part they were men unmarried or having families left behind to whom they planned to return when they had struck it rich. Few of the earliest comers expected to remain to found homes in the gold country. Children were few among the early pioneers and the need for education in the mining camps was not acute. Yet most of the hardy men who came to Colorado in the late fifties and still more of the growing numbers who crossed the plains in the early sixties brought with them educational traditions which soon asserted themselves even in a seemingly inhospitable environment. From the first, too, there were a few families with children and the presence of even a few children furnished enough soil for these traditions to germinate.

Educational traditions among Colorado pioneers were as varied as the stock from which they came and these took root and grew side by side. There was the Virginia tradition that education was a family affair and this expressed itself in the private school which was fostered also by the limited number of children and by the centering of attention in the early communities on finding gold, staking claims, and getting out the precious metal. Everybody hoped eventually to strike it for himself, but in the meantime there were ways of making good money by buying and selling and teaming and working by the day in the service of those who had struck it or who had prospects.

The first schools in Colorado, therefore, were private schools, and as Denver was the site where gold had first been found and where the first considerable community sprang up, it was here in the town called then Auraria, west of Cherry Creek and south of the Platte and at the confluence of these streams, that the first school was opened called the Union School on October 3, 1859, "Professor" O. J. Goldrick, schoolmaster.

"The Professor" as he was commonly called, looked the part. He had tramped into Denver one day in silk hat and broadcloth suit, a frock coat, known as a Prince Albert, his kid gloved hand wielding a goad over the backs of the ox-team which he drove. He had come from St. Louis by way of New Mexico whither he had been lured by one Joseph Doyle, a merchant in that section, who offered to take him out on a load of household goods. From New Mexico a friend of Doyle's had beguiled Goldrick to Denver by sending down a small vial of dust as a guarantee of the gold discoveries.

Goldrick was born in Sligo, Ireland, had a B.A. from the University of Dublin, and an M.A. from Columbia University. When he arrived in Denver that day of 1859 he had in a pocket of his broadcloth suit 50 cents. With such professional qualifications he was invited to start a school and consented. With due regard for the amenities appropriate to such an event, Goldrick wrote to John D. Philbrick, then superintendent of schools in Boston, informing him of his intention to open a "Union School" and asking his advice about studies and textbooks. Philbrick replied, concluding his letter: "And now imagine my arm extended with the speed of thought from the cradle of the free school on the Atlantic shores over the Alleghenies, over the Father of Waters to give you a cordial greeting in your Union School on the frontier of civilization at the foot of the Rocky Mountains." The school was opened on October 3, in a rented cabin on Ferry, now Blake street, just west of Cherry Creek. The first day there were thirteen children, including nine whites, two Mexicans and two half-breeds. The enrollment increased, however, and in the following year two other private schools were opened in Denver taught by Miss Lydia Maria King, and Miss Indiana Sopris. After the first Territorial Legislature had passed a law providing for a territorial school system, Goldrick was elected as the first superintendent of Arapahoe County Schools in 1862.

In connection with the greeting from Boston at the opening of the first school in Colorado it is interesting to note that twenty-three years later, in 1882, John D. Philbrick, the author of that greeting, visited the Denver schools, organized and administered since 1874 by Aaron Gove. Mr. Philbrick made a thorough inspection of the schools and made a report which was published by the United States Commissioner of Education, Dr. W. T. Harris, in his biennial report for 1882-83. Mr. Philbrick summed up his account by saying: "I found the Denver school system to be admirable in all respects. Although its origin dates back scarcely more than a decade, its development has been so wisely and energetically conducted that already it belongs to the front rank of city systems. It is pretty safe to say that the creation of a system of schools on so large a scale, of such exceptional merits, and in so brief a space of time, is a phenomenon to which the history of education affords no parallel."

The First School Building

Denver, as the earliest and most considerable settlement, naturally had the first school. This school had no building of its own, however, but met in a one-room log-cabin with a mud roof which happened to be available and reasonably centrally located so that it might be reached from the several parts of the divided Denver and thus merit the name "The Union School". Denver did not for several years erect a building for school purposes, not until 1865, when the Arapahoe school was opened on Arapahoe street between Seventeenth and Eighteenth Streets.

In the meantime the first real schoolhouse built specifically for school purposes had been standing in Boulder since the summer of 1860 when it was built at a cost of some $1,200 through subscription made by citizens of the town. Abner R. Brown, the first schoolmaster in Boulder, had taught at White Plains, New York, and at Muscatine, Iowa. He came through Boulder on a summer morning in 1860. Seeing children on the streets he asked if there was a school there, and learning that there was not he told the people that if he did not make it in the mines at Gold Hill whither he was bound he would return and open a school in Boulder. A short experience in mining decided him to return to the schoolroom. He opened a private school in a two-room cabin while the people took up a subscription and built the first schoolhouse. Into the new building he moved with his pupils in October, 1860. The Boulder school like the Denver Union School was supported by tuition. On the ground where the building stood the Daughters of the American Revolution have erected a marker which bears the legend:

"On this ground was built the first schoolhouse in Colorado in 1860. Erected by Arapahoe Chapter, Daughters of the American Revolution, 1917."

When O. J. Goldrick in 1862, as superintendent of schools for Arapahoe County, organized the first public school in Denver, Mr. Brown came from Boulder to become its first principal with two assistants and 140 pupils. He remained many years in public school work in Colorado and lived to the ripe age of 93, dying in Canyon City in 1922.

The Beginning of Public Schools

The general transition from private to public tax-supported schools in Colorado dates from the establishment by the First Territorial Legislature in 1861 of a school law providing for a Territorial Superintendent of Common Schools, for county superintendents, and for taxes to support the schools. This Legislature made provision also for a permanent school fund, setting aside one hundred feet of each mining lode for the support of the schools. The schools profited little from this fund, however, for the provisions of the law were never adequately carried out, and later the accumulation of some $3,000 from this source was turned over by the Legislature when funds were needed for the establishment of the School of Mines.

The significance of this public school legislation enacted but three years after the first discovery of gold in the territory, is impressive. Demands for the organization of a stable government, for the establishment of courts of law, for an orderly procedure in the determination of mining rights were insistent and engrossing, yet the vision of these Colorado pioneers was not impaired by the pressure of material things. Not only in breadth of view but in practical provisions for the detailed management of a school system at once adequate for immediate requirements and flexible for adjustment to the needs of future years, are evident the sterling qualities of these men and the sound American traditions which they followed.

The first territorial school law, approved November 7, 1861, by Governor William Gilpin, who had been appointed by President Lincoln, provided for the appointment by the Governor of a Territorial Superintendent of Common Schools, who was to serve until his successor should be duly appointed and qualified. He was to receive a salary of $500 a year. Governor Gilpin appointed William J. Curtice, then Territorial Librarian, and the appointment was confirmed by the Council as the law required, the Council being the upper house of the territorial legislature. The duties of the territorial superintendent were: To have general supervision over all district schools of the Territory, see that the school system as early as practicable is put into uniform operation, and to recommend to the several school districts a uniform series of textbooks. He was to file and have available for Governor and Assembly all reports made by county superintendents, whom the law provided should be elected by popular vote in the several counties. He was required to prepare and have printed forms of all records required by this act and transmit them with such instructions in reference to the course of study as he might judge advantageous to the several officials intrusted with their management and care. He was charged with the duty of making further rules and regulations necessary to carry the law into effect according to its intent and spirit which should have the same force and effect as the law itself. He was required to report regularly to the legislature on the first day of its session the condition of the public schools and such other matters as he should deem expedient. County Superintendents were to be chosen at the first election to serve two years.

Superintendent Curtice was succeeded in 1863 by William S. Walker and he in turn by A. W. Arthur. In 1865 a law was passed abolishing the office of Territorial Superintendent and it was provided that the Territorial Treasurer discharge the duties of the office, at a remuneration of $100 a year. The history of eastern state superintendencies, degenerating into the ex-officio practice had been the same as Colorado's territorial experience. It could hardly be expected that a capable superintendent would often be found for $500 a year. Delegating the duties to the

Treasurer saved the Territory $400 a year, but commonly the Treasurer gave scant attention to schools. An exception is to be noted in the case of Columbus Nuckolls, Treasurer in 1867, who made an earnest effort to improve matters. By 1870 with the building of the first railroads more settled conditions prevailed with increase in the number of families in the territory, and education enforced attention. That year the eighth territorial Assembly created the office of Superintendent of Public Instruction, fixing the salary at $1,000, and Governor E. M. McCook appointed to the office William C. Lothrop. He resigned in 1873 and was succeeded by Horace M. Hale then superintendent of schools at Central City, who was followed in 1876 by Joseph Shattuck, of Greeley, as the first State Superintendent of Public Instruction.

The Evolution of the State School System

On November 25, 1875, Horace M. Hale, Territorial Superintendent of Public Instruction, issued a call for a meeting of superintendents, teachers, and friends of public schools in the Denver High School building. The Territory of Colorado was to become the State of Colorado. A Constitutional Convention had been called and education must be provided for in the State Constitution. The call for the educational meeting which expressed the hope that every county should be largely and ably represented, pointed out the imminent necessity for considering questions involving the welfare of the school system of the new state.

One hundred and fifty teachers and friends of education in Colorado met in Denver on December 28, 1875, in response to Superintendent Hale's call and organized the Colorado Teachers Association. Aaron Gove, Superintendent of the Denver Schools, was Chairman of the Committee of Organization which framed the constitution adopted by the Association.

The most important matters considered by the new organization, as anticipated in the call concerned the fundamental law for the establishment of the state school system. The resolution adopted for the guidance of the committee appointed to advise the constitutional convention and a second committee to submit recommendations to the State Legislature made the following provisions:

"The school fund shall be sacredly preserved intact, the

interest on the same, only, to be expended; the sale of such lands as may be given to the State for educational purposes shall be postponed, to the end that the proceeds, in time, may perhaps be sufficient to maintain public schools without taxation; the constitution shall make it the duty of the Legislature to provide for the establishment and maintenance of a uniform system of schools, including elementary, normal, preparatory and university departments, such schools to be free to all residents of the State; to provide for the offices of State and County Superintendents; to provide for the establishment of libraries; to provide for the care and education of the blind, mute and feeble minded; to provide for the establishment of a reform school; to cause all instruction to be imparted through the medium of the English language; to exclude sectarianism, as is set forth as follows in Article VII, Section 3, of the Illinois Constitution: "(Neither the General Assembly nor any county, city, town, township, school district, or other public corporation, shall ever make any appropriation, or pay from any public fund whatever, anything in aid of any church or any academy, seminary, college, university or other literary or scientific institution controlled by any church or sectarian denomination whatever; nor shall any grant or donation of land, money or other personal property ever be made by the State for any church or for any sectarian purpose.)"

A further resolution was passed dealing with the reading of the Bible in the public schools as follows:

"That no law shall be passed requiring the daily reading of the Bible in the public schools nor to exclude it therefrom."

A wholesome and important precedent was the result of action on a proposal to provide for state uniformity of school textbooks. The proposal was defeated and a clause was later included in the Constitution of the State forbidding state adoption of texts, the selection of textbooks being vested by law in the boards of education of the several districts. Experience in other states where state commissions adopt uniform texts for all schools has demonstrated abundantly the wisdom of Colorado in leaving the determination in this matter to the school districts. At numerous sessions of the General Assembly bills providing for state uniformity of texts and even for state printing of schoolbooks have been introduced and have been discovered to be unconstitutional. In

1923 a constitutional amendment providing for state adoption of schoolbooks to be printed by the state was voted upon by the people and was defeated. States which print their own texts, only by permitting school districts to purchase supplementary texts make it possible for the schools in these states to escape the consequences of being limited to an inferior grade of schoolbooks. A similar disadvantage is found to exist where there is state uniformity of texts, although the disadvantage is not so extreme as in the case of the state printing of texts. To the clear vision of these founders of the Colorado Teachers Association and to their sound judgment expressed in the fundamental school law of the commonwealth is due in large measure the standing of the Colorado school system among the state systems of the country in spite of disadvantages in lack of wealth and population and in an archaic state and county school organization, the prevailing type in 1876, which in many states has been changed during the last half century to meet changed conditions through intelligent reconstruction.

Consolidation of School Districts

It happened in Colorado as it happened in the other states that the district system of schools, necessary as it was under pioneer conditions, became a handicap rather then a help as increasing population in the towns brought several districts together in the same municipal corporation. Politically the town might be a unit, while within its boundaries two or more school districts continued to function separately. The need for consolidation of such districts became apparent in many instances long before it took place. Local jealousy and the prospect of eliminating one or more superintendents prolonged the maintenance of separate school establishments with serious economic and educational loss to communities. A conspicuous example was the case of Denver, where seven different school districts each with its own organization were operating close together, several within the corporation limits. By the twentieth amendment to the Constitution of the State the city and county of Denver was established and one of the provisions of this amendment required the consolidation of the seven school districts which was effected in 1903. For several years there were problems of adjustment to be solved and district jealousies to be allayed, but the results in equalization of educational opportunity and in the promotion of educational efficiency have long vindicated the wisdom of consolidation.

In rural districts for many years consolidation was impossible because of distance. With few pupils, small revenue, and limited educational experience the value of the school training furnished was meagre indeed. It was the coming of the automobile which made possible the consolidation of country schools, but it required time to overcome narrow district prejudices and to make clear the advantages of consolidation. The first consolidation of rural schools was effected in 1912 at Appleton, seven miles from Grand Junction. Since that time the movement has spread, slowly at first, accelerated by the demand for a better rural education which grew out of the disillusionments of the World War. There are now in Colorado well over 175 consolidated rural schools housed in modern buildings, graded as well as city schools, and usually including a high school such as could not have been accessible to any of these pupils under the old regime, representing perhaps 800 abandoned one-room box buildings. Thus 35,000 children have been given opportunity for a modern education with the means of preparing for college if they desire and of acquiring an equipment for any future career—opportunities that would have been impossible under the district system.

RECENT EDUCATIONAL LEGISLATION

Colorado has always stood high among the states in education. There may be several reasons for this fact but the most weighty is that Colorado has had good teachers. During the World War the discovery was made in this state as in other states that there was a dearth of good teachers—indeed there was a dearth of even passable teachers. Many teachers had been drawn into the army and many others, both men and women, had been engaged in government work of one kind and another carrying on a multiplicity of activities essential to the prosecution of the war, and in business and industry from which the regular employees had been withdrawn to the training camps. The readjustment following the armistice necessarily took time; some employees whose places had been filled by teachers did not return; business and industry, moreover, had been agreeably surprised by the efficiency shown by teachers as employees. The government, too, had a great deal of "mopping-up" to do after the war and could not at once release emergency employees. There was the further fact that the remuneration tempted many teachers to remain in lucrative positions where they could rather than return to the schoolroom.

In this situation the Governor of Colorado appointed a commission to study the question of teachers' salaries with a view to discovering what if anything could be done to furnish financial inducements to adequately equipped teachers to fill the many vacancies existing in the schools. The report of the commission resulted in the introduction into the General Assembly which convened in 1921 of a minimum teacher's salary bill. After some amendments the bill became a law with the following provisions: A minimum salary of $75 a month for teachers in Colorado, preparation not specified; a minimum annual salary of $1,000 for teachers with two years of training beyond high school; a minimum annual salary of $1,200 for teachers with four years' training beyond high school. The law provided further for an equalization of the tax burden to meet the increased salary minimums by a tax upon all the property of each county to be distributed among the school districts of the county according to the number of teachers in each district.

A logical next step in legislation was the teacher's certification law passed by the General Assembly in 1923 requiring of all candidates taking the teachers' examination specific professional preparation beginning in 1925 and increasing in amount up to 1930.

Reorganization of the Colorado Education Association

Ever since the first meeting of the Colorado Teachers Association in 1875, the enacting of school law for improving education in the state has been due in the main to the organized efforts of this body. The need has long been recognized for a recodification of the body of state school law. In 1916 such a recodification was proposed and was defeated in the General Assembly. Nevertheless at each biennial session of the legislature a program of progressive legislation has been made by the Association, and sometimes, as in 1921 and 1923, the measures advocated by the Association have been enacted into law by the General Assembly.

Often when the legislative program has failed it has been due to a lack of understanding and cooperation by the teachers themselves for the end in view. In order to accomplish a better understanding of educational needs in the state and to enlist wider cooperation by all the teachers of the state the Colorado Education Association in 1925 was reorganized on the basis of local and district units with a representative assembly which should through the local units insure a more general understanding of needs and policies and result in more complete cooperation for the advancement of the cause of education in Colorado. An immediate result of this reorganization was the appointment of a full time secretary, Mr. William B. Mooney, who is charged with the responsibility, under the board of directors of the Association, of organizing and maintaining a continuing and effective educational policy through the coordination of the local units of the organization throughout the state.

Secondary Education

During the territorial period, most of the public schools were ungraded, but graded schools had begun to be organized in the cities. The first institutions of high school grade were private. Two public high schools were established, however, shortly before statehood, and 1876 saw the first high school class in the State graduated from the Boulder public high school. The year following East Denver High School graduated a class of seven. High schools from this time on increased rapidly in numbers and in 1884 on the list of high schools accredited by the University were those in Denver, Pueblo, Leadville, Gunnison, Trinidad, Georgetown, Golden, the Boulder high school then being the preparatory department of the University. In view of the scattered population and the demand of parents outside of the cities for opportunities to prepare their children for college, the school law made provision for the establishment of a Union High School to be supported by any group of contiguous school districts which agree by vote to be taxed for its support. Many counties in the state have at the county seat a high school which may be attended tuition free by any student residing in the county, a county wide tax supporting the school. In many counties there is a county high school system composed of the central high school at the county seat and branch high schools in other towns in the county. Frequently the branch high schools cover but two years of work, upon the completion of which the student may complete his course in the central high school at the county seat. Twenty counties have organized such high schools.

A high school visitor, a member of the faculty of the University of Colorado, now visits annually the high schools of the state. As a result of his visits and his recommendation to the University Senate Committee on High School Relations, the Senate has placed upon the accredited list 170 Colorado high schools. There are 275 four-year high schools in the state. Graduates of high schools upon this list, if they have credit from their respective schools for the completion of the subjects required for entrance, are admitted to the University without examination. The list is also accepted by the other colleges of the state and furnishes a basis for the accrediting of these high schools by the North Central Association of Colleges and Secondary Schools, an accrediting agency for nineteen states. The accredited list of the University includes many private preparatory schools and parochial high schools. In the early years of statehood the East Denver High School acquired an enviable reputation as a fitting school for college among the older colleges and universities outside the state. In recent years not only is this reputation shared by the other accredited high schools of Colorado but the curriculum in these schools has been broadened to provide preparation for entrance into technical and vocational schools and where higher education is impossible to give students a sound foundation for immediate entrance into business and industrial life.

A reorganization of secondary education to include the seventh and eight grades, which, together with the ninth grade form the junior high school, the tenth, eleventh and twelfth grades constituting the senior high school, has taken place in many of the cities of the state both large and small. Although the junior high school can no longer be regarded as an experiment in Colorado, the full advantages of this reorganization in meeting the best possibilities of adolescent education are by no means realized. Complete adjustment of this school to the units in the general scheme of education above and below, with the concomitant adjustment of the older units for a more adequate education for all the children of the public schools, remains as the goal yet to be attained.

Still there has been enough experience with the new organization to encourage the educators of the state in the belief that it involves a real and vital advance in secondary education.

The junior college as a phase of educational reorganization is in 1927 a problem still to be solved. On the one hand are those who believe that the state should establish and maintain in certain cities remote from the existing colleges of the state institutions to provide the first two years of college education. There are others who believe that such junior colleges are desirable, but that, as a phase of secondary education rather than of higher education, they should be locally maintained by cities which need them, with only a moderate subsidy per student to be granted by the state.

STATE INSTITUTIONS OF HIGHER LEARNING

The first institution of higher learning planned during the territorial period was the University of Colorado. In the first territorial legislature, on October 26, 1861, a bill was introduced into the lower House for an act to establish the University of Colorado in the city of Denver. In the committee of the whole to which the bill was referred the words "city of Denver" were stricken out and on October 31 the bill was passed for the establishment of the University of Colorado and the site was fixed at Boulder. On the following day the bill was passed by the Council or upper house, and it was signed by Governor Gilpin on November 7, 1861.

Almost two centuries and a half earlier the first college to be projected in America, the College of William and Mary in Virginia, had been provided for in a bill passed by the House of Burgesses, but the founding of the College was indefinitely postponed because of the disastrous Indian War which followed soon after. When the bill for the founding of the University of Colorado was passed the Civil War was on, and this, with the accompanying financial problems and others incident to the new and sparsely settled territory, prevented action upon the law for the establishment of the institution.

Sixteen years later, on September 5, 1877 the University of Colorado provided for in the Constitution of the State, was opened at Boulder with Joseph Addison Sewell, from Normal, Illinois, as president, and one additional teacher, Justin E. Dow, of Boulder. Forty-four students entered the University and the number increased to seventy-five before the end of the year. Sixty-six names were published in the record for that year, thirty-nine men, and twenty-seven women. President Sewell retired in 1886 and was succeeded by Horace M. Hale, former State Superintendent of Public Instruction. James Hutchins Baker, for seventeen years Principal of East Side High School, Denver, became president in 1892 and served for twenty-two years, being succeeded in 1914 by Livingston Farrand, of Columbia University. During the World War, while President Farrand was serving in France as head of the Anti-Tuberculosis Society, George Norlin, Professor of Greek, was acting president of the University and in 1919 upon President Farrand's resignation Dr. Norlin was elected president.

During the twenty-two years of President Baker's administration the registration at the University increased from fifty-two to nearly 1,300 and since that time it has more than doubled. It is now among the first ten universities in America in point of numbers and it is placed in the A class by university rating agencies. In 1883 the College of Medicine was added; in 1892 it was reorganized, and in 1911 the Denver and Gross Medical Colleges were consolidated with the College of Medicine of the University of Colorado. A gift of $800,000 from the General Education Board in 1921 duplicated by state appropriations caused the transfer of the College of Medicine to Denver where an adequate plant including a psychopathic hospital was erected at Eleventh Avenue and Colorado Boulevard, constituting the most complete plant among medical colleges west of the Mississippi. The colleges of Law and Engineering were established in 1893. In 1904 the Summer Session was established and the attendance at this session has grown until it has been, since 1925, one of the first six in the country. A college of Pharmacy was established in 1911, an Extension Division in 1912, and a School of Business Administration in 1923. The growth of the Graduate School has been especially marked, now showing a registration of 800.

The Colorado School of Mines began as an institution required to meet the instant need of things. Bishop George M. Randall, of the Episcopal Church, had planned a University to be located in Golden to consist of a general college for boys, a divinity school and a school of mines. Jarvis Hall, the boys' college building, was built in 1868 but was blown down in a heavy wind the following year. Matthews Hall, the divinity school, was also built, but with Jarvis Hall was destroyed by fire in 1874. In 1870 the territorial legislature had appropriated $3,872 for a mines building which was completed in 1871 on the same campus with Jarvis Hall and Matthew's Hall. Instruction was begun in assaying and simple chemistry and tests were made of Colorado coals. In 1874 after an appropriation of $5,000 from the legislature the school was transferred by Bishop Randall to the territory. E. J. Mallet the first professor in charge of instruction was succeeded by Gregory Board and he by Milton Moss, a practical chemist, in 1878. Albert C. Hale was placed at the head of the institution in 1880 to be followed by Regis Chauvenet in 1883, who continued as president until 1902 and remained for some time thereafter as professor of chemistry. It was under the Chauvenet regime that the School of Mines acquired a reputation not inferior to that of the other great American School of Mines at Columbia. In the earlier years the courses had been rather rigidly vocational by the necessity of the case and practical efficiency in mining was sought rather than a sound scientific basis for mining engineering. Regis Chauvenet understood both the practical phase and the underlying sciences, and from his day the School of Mines has been indissolubly linked with the development of the mining industry of the state. Charles S. Palmer succeeded President Chauvenet in 1902 and was succeeded in 1903 by President Victor C. Alderson who after several years' service was followed by Presidents Wm. B. Phillips, Wm. G. Haldane, and Howard C. Parmelee. In 1917 Alderson was recalled to the presidency and remained until 1925 when the present incumbent, President M. F. Coolbaugh was elected. The student body of the school has rarely exceeded 500 but the Colorado School of Mines has maintained a reputation high among Schools of Mines both American and foreign.

It was the people of Fort Collins who before 1872 took the initiative in donating 240 acres of land for the establishment there of an Agricultural College. The territorial legislature in 1874 appropriated $1,000 to be used when a like sum should be raised by the citizens of Fort Collins for the erection of buildings. In 1876 the college was chartered and it was opened on September 1, 1879, with President E. E. Edwards in charge. On the resignation of President Edwards, in 1882, Clarence L. Ingersoll was elected president. He was succeeded in 1891 by Alston Ellis who was followed in 1899 by Barton O. Aylesworth. After an administration of ten years he was succeeded by the present president, Charles A. Lory. The Agricultural College has been the beneficiary of national legislation in the two Morrill Acts of 1862 and 1890, by the Hatch Act of 1887 establishing agricultural experiment stations, by the Smith-Lever act of 1914, and it has the administration for Colorado of the Smith-Hughes law of 1917. The services of this institution to the state in agriculture and the mechanic arts have been preeminent and its Home Economics department has been highly efficient.

The first State Normal School of Colorado was opened at Greeley on October 6, 1890, with Thomas J. Gray as president. He was succeeded in 1891 by President Z. X. Snyder whose administration continued to the time of his death in 1915. To President Snyder is due the outstanding character of this institution as a school for the training of teachers. John Grant Crabbe was elected president in 1916 and served until his death in 1925, when George Willard Frazier the present incumbent was elected president. The Normal course was originally a two-years' course and students completing it received a life certificate in Colorado. In 1911, however, the name of the school was changed by the General Assembly to State Teachers College and a four-years' course leading to the B. A. degree was inaugurated. The original two-years' course, however, still gives a teachers' life certificate. A Graduate School and a large and growing summer school are important features of Teachers College.

At Gunnison, on the Western Slope, a State Normal School was established by an act of the Twelfth General Assembly passed in 1899, but the corner stone of the first building was not laid until October 25, 1910, after a building appropriation of $50,000 made by the Seventeenth General Assembly. From the first the school has been under the direction of the board of trustees of the State Teachers College, Dr. Snyder, President of the College being named president, with Charles A. Hollingshead, principal. James Herbert Kelley succeeded Hollingshead as principal, and in 1914 Kelley was elected president, the Normal School being at that time segregated in administration from the Teachers College although still functioning under the same board of trustees. In 1923 the name of the school was changed to Western State College, and a four-year course was inaugurated in addition to the original two-year teachers' training course which gives the teacher's life certificate. In 1919 President Kelley was succeeded by Samuel Quigley who resigned in 1927, Richard Aspinall being elected president.

In 1925 the General Assembly enacted a law establishing a Normal School at Alamosa to be known as the Adams State Normal School. Ira Richardson was elected president.

Another public educational institution was established by the territorial legislature, the Colorado School for Deaf and Blind, at Colorado Springs, which opened on April 8, 1874, J. B. Ralstin, principal. Other principals have been R. H. Kinney, D. C. Dudley, W. K. Argo, and the present superintendent, Thomas S. McAloney. The enrollment for 1874 was twelve.

PRIVATE INSTITUTIONS OF HIGHER LEARNING

In the period from 1861, which marked the incorporation of the University of Colorado by the territorial legislature, to 1877, when the University was opened, two institutions of higher learning on private foundations were established in the state. The University of Denver, under Methodist auspices, beginning as Colorado Seminary, a preparatory school, in 1864, was reorganized as the University of Denver in 1880. The Supreme Court of Colorado certified in a unanimous decision in the University of Denver tax suit, that "this is the pioneer school of higher learning in this state." The first Chancellor of the University of Denver was David H. Moore who was succeeded in 1890 by William F. McDowell under whose administration the site of the University was changed from Fourteenth and Arapahoe Streets, in the city of Denver, to University Park, a suburb later included in the corporate limits of the City and County of Denver. Chancellor McDowell was succeeded by Henry A. Buchtel whose administration, covering a period of twenty-one years, from 1899 to 1920 was marked by the discharge of a heavy indebtedness which had seriously hampered the institution and the establishment of a substantial endowment. Upon the retirement of Chancellor Buchtel, Heber R. Harper was elected Chancellor and served for five years, resigning in 1927. The University consists of a College of Arts and Sciences, a School of Law, a School of Dentistry, a School of Music, a Graduate School, an Extension College and a School of Commerce.

Colorado College, an institution established under the auspices of the Congregational Church, opened at Colorado Springs in 1874 a preparatory department, Jonathan Edwards being the first president. During 1874-75 there were in the College seventy-six students, seventeen of whom were freshmen. President Edwards was succeeded by James G. Daugherty and he by E. P. Tenney. The beginning of the substantial growth and influence of the College, however, dates from the election to the presidency in 1888 of William F. Slocum who remained at the head of the institution for 28 years, until 1916. He was succeeded by Clyde A. Duniway who was succeeded by the present president, Charles C. Mierow in 1925.

The Colorado Woman's College, projected under Baptist auspices in 1887 and chartered the following year, had erected the walls of its original building just east of Denver in 1893, but the institution was not opened to students until September 7, 1909, Jay Porter Treat having been elected president. He was succeeded by John W. Bailey in 1917. James A. White succeeded to the presidency in 1923, and he was followed by the present president, Samuel E. Vaughn in 1926.

The College of the Sacred Heart, Roman Catholic, long known as the Jesuit College, was founded in Morrison in 1884. It was combined with Las Vegas College, Las Vegas, New Mexico, and removed to Denver under the name of The College of the Sacred Heart, in 1887. The institution was empowered to grant degrees in 1889 and the first class of three was graduated in 1890. The name was changed to Regis College in 1921. The president in 1927 is Aloysius A. Breen.

The Iliff School of Theology, Methodist, was opened in 1892 as a department of the University of Denver. Later it was reincorporated as an independent institution which was opened September 14, 1910. The president in 1927 is Elmer Guy Cutshall.

The Saint Thomas Seminary, Roman Catholic, Denver, under the auspices of the Congregation of the Mission, Vicentian Fathers, trains students for the priesthood in the local diocese. The

Seminary was opened in 1908. The president in 1927 is Francis X. McCabe.

Colorado Educators

It has been remarked that the efficiency of education in Colorado is due chiefly to good teachers, and it may be added that the presence of good teachers in the state generally may be credited to wise and efficient leaders. Colorado has been blessed and is still blessed with a large share of educational leaders, richly endowed, thoroughly trained and entirely devoted to the profession. It will not seem invidious, however, to refer briefly to the services of three men who stand out in somewhat distinct fields of education to whom the state owes a debt of appreciation which cannot well be exaggerated.

The first is Aaron Gove, the founder and organizer of the Denver public school system, superintendent of Denver schools thirty years, from 1874 to 1904. Not only did he create and build up a system of schools which was gratefully acknowledged and followed as a pattern throughout the commonwealth and was recognized nationally as among the conspicuously successful city systems of the country, but his was the judgment and foresight which determined the fundamental soundness of the constitutional provisions for the school system of the state.

The second outstanding figure in the history of education in Colorado is Zachariah Xenophon Snyder who came to Colorado as president of the State Normal School at Greeley, and gave to the training of teachers in Colorado the spirit of service and enthusiasm, an influence which is still potent among the students whose lives he touched, and which they pass on to their own students and to the communities they serve.

The third great educational leader is James Hutchins Baker, for over a score of years the great president of the University of Colorado, different from the other two in nearly all external characteristics, stern and forbidding to the multitude, but standing four square to all the winds that blow in his steadfast maintenance of all that goes to make for wholeness and soundness in education.

All that Colorado is or is to be in education rests upon the sure foundations laid by these great schoolmasters.

Chapter 7
COLORADO IN LITERATURE*
Irene Pettit McKeehan

The earliest inhabitants of Colorado—the prehistoric Cliff Dwellers of the Southwest—left, so far as we are aware, no literature, no decipherable records of any kind. In recent years their remains have been the subject of scientific investigation, but the only detailed account of their origin and adventures belongs—despite its title, *The Psychic History of the Cliff Dwellers*—to the field of literature, rather than to that of science. This book, by Emma Frances Jay Bullene, published in Denver in 1905, is of great and astonishing interest to a reader not too scientifically minded. According to the author's own statement, she has been enabled to reconstruct the entire history of the Cliff Dwellers through "psychometry," while holding fragments of pottery or other relics in her hand. "The charm of narrative and minute delineation of home scenes that compose this history have been given in automatic detail, without the slightest mental effort on the part of the writer." By means of this "automatism," the writer has discovered that the Cliff Dwellers were identical with the Mound Builders of the Ohio River valley and that both were descendants of the Vikings.

No Old Norse saga in runic characters having been as yet unearthed in the ruins of Spruce-Tree House or on the headlands of Hoven-Weep, it is the silence surrounding their ancient inhabitants, rather than any knowledge or theories we may have about them, that has inspired modern Colorado poets. In a remarkably successful Swinburnian imitation, "Homes of the Cliff Dwellers" (*Rhymes of the Rockies*, Chicago, 1898), Stanley Wood has caught the tone of haunting pathos appropriate to the subject. The poem is too long to quote entire, but the following stanzas are perhaps the best:

* * * * *

> On the canyon's side, in the ample hollow
> That the keen winds carved in ages past,
> The Castle walls, like the nest of a swallow,
> Have clung and have crumbled to this at last.

---
* When this article was written, another article was contemplated on Colorado Journalism. This fact will explain the omission here of the names of several distinguished men who have contributed to literature only through newspaper work, and also of any reference to the history of periodicals published in the state.

> The ages since man's foot has rested
>   Within these walls, no man may know;
> For here the fierce grey eagle nested
>   Long ago.
>
> No voice of Spring—no Summer glories
>   May wake the warders from their sleep.
> Their graves are made by the sad Dolores,
>   And the barren headlands of Hoven-Weep.
> Their graves are nameless—their race forgotten,
>   Their deeds, their words, their fate, are one
> With the mist, long ages past begotten
>   Of the Sun.

Another poet, Jean Milne Gower, has devoted almost the whole of a charming little book, *Echoes from the Cliff Dwellings* (Denver, 1923), to what she calls "Versicles of the Mesa Verde." One of these, "Challenge," expresses the mystery of the prehistoric Southwest:

> We are the riddle of the ages—
> Lost children of the Mesa—
> Ask nothing of us.
> Ask of the whispering piñon trees;
> They know; perhaps they will tell:
> Ask of the junipers;
> Perhaps they will tell.
> Pharaohs have left their records in
>   sealed chambers,
> But we—we swept our little buff
>   dwellings clean
> And went our way.

Almost as unique in its way as Mrs. Bullene's history is the latest literary production which draws its inspiration from the Cliff Dwellers, *Deric in Mesa Verde* (Putnam's, 1926), by Deric Nusbaum, the twelve-year-old son of the superintendent of Mesa Verde National Park. The book is lively and interesting and attractively illustrated.

The next inhabitants of Colorado, the Indians, were more articulate than the Cliff Dwellers. If they did not write literature, they occasionally talked it, and some white men were willing to listen to them. Hal G. Borland owes a considerable number of his *Rocky Mountain Tipi Tales* (Doubleday, Page, and Co., 1924) to the Ute Indians of Colorado. One of the best of these, "Where Stories Come From," explains how the Bear told All-Alone-Boy the first stories. "But there are many stories that will never be known, for when the Bear died he had not told half the stories he knew." Be that as it may, other collections of Colorado Indian tales exist, as may be seen by reference to a bibliography, *Myths and Legends of Colorado*, compiled by Vera Campbell and published at Greeley by the State Teachers' College, 1924. Some of these myths and legends have been utilized by local poets: by Elijah Clarence Hills in several poems contributed to a compilation called *The Pike's Peak Region in Song and Myth* (Colorado Springs, 1913); by Sara R. Schlesinger in *Legends of Manitou and Other Poems* (Colorado Springs, 1910); by Harriet Louisa Wason in *Legend of the Grand Caverns at Manitou and Other Songs* (Denver, 1899); and by Thomas Nelson Haskell, the founder of Colorado College, in a long poem, *Young Konkaput, King of the Utes* (Denver, 1889). The great fight at Grand Lake, in which a band of Ute Indians was exterminated by the Cheyennes and Arapahoes, has been celebrated several times in verse, notably in two poems, each called "The Legend of Grand Lake," by Joseph L. Westcott, published in *Sons of Colorado*, June, 1906, and by Wilbert E. Eisele, published in *The Trail*, October, 1924. In prose Cy Warman, known at one time as "the Poet of the Rockies," has recounted *Weiga of Temagami and Other Indian Tales* (New York, Caldwell, 1908).

Apart from his own stories, the Indian in Colorado has been the subject of various kinds of literature and near literature, ranging from serious historical studies, like George Bird Grinnell's *The Fighting Cheyennes* (Scribner's, 1915) and Arthur J. Fynn's *The American Indian as a Product of Environment with Special Reference to the Pueblos* (Little, Brown, and Co., 1907) to Hamlin Garland's novel, *The Captain of the Gray-Horse Troop* (Harper's, 1902), the hero of which is an Indian agent engaged in protecting his charges against exploitation by unscrupulous white men. Much of the literary treatment of the Colorado Indian is in what might be called the raw material for literature rather than literature proper. Tucked away in old books and articles containing reminiscences of pioneers and frontiersmen are strange tales of encounters between Indians and white men or picturesque bits about the Indians themselves. Such accounts are found, for example, in "The Personal Memoirs of Captain Charles Christy,.... as Hunter and Trapper for the American Fur Company, and as United States Government Scout," published in *The Trail*, in successive installments from June, 1908, to May, 1909, and in

"Early Days in Fort Lupton, compiled . . . . from the reminiscences and notes of T. L. Monson," also published in *The Trail*, February and March, 1914. "Battle and murder and sudden death" become commonplace in these narratives, but occasionally something decidedly not commonplace makes its appearance. Such, for example, is the story, in T. L. Monson's reminiscences just mentioned, of the group of mysterious Indians with alligators tattooed on their breasts, who visited Fort Lupton in the early days, claiming to be of a superior race and to have made their way clear across the United States from Florida. Their leader was "the chief of all chiefs," and was received as such by the Arapahoes; but the Utes exterminated them in the mountain passes, for their forefathers and the forefathers of the Utes had been enemies years before in a great war to the eastward. The Arapahoes went into mourning for the distinguished strangers and became more than ever hostile to the Utes.

Certain incidents in the warfare between Indians and white men appear and reappear under various guises. The fight at Beecher's Island in the Arickaree or South Fork of the Republican River, between Forsyth's scouts and a mixed band of Arapahoes and Cheyennes, has proved an inspiration to several writers of what purports to be history and reads like melodrama. Colonel Chivington's battle with the Cheyennes at Sand Creek, which may also be referred to as the Chivington or Sand Creek massacre, has given rise to more controversy than literature, but since all the accounts of what happened on that occasion cannot possibly be true, it is obvious that the literary imagination has been at work on the subject. "Sade Smith's Escape, A True Story," published anonymously in *Sons of Colorado*, August, 1906, and "Crossing the Plains in '64, A True Story of the Harrowing Experience of a Woman Still Living," by Major James B. Thompson, in the same magazine, March, 1908, were probably regarded by the editor as two entirely different stories, so markedly unlike are the details. Yet the woman is obviously the same woman, and the incidents recounted occurred on one and the same trip. In the earlier account, a friendly Indian guides the heroine through a herd of buffaloes in order to elude the hostile redskins, who have massacred her companions. In the other, all the Indians are hostile, and the woman's wagon is just on the point of being overtaken by the bloodthirsty savages when cavalry troopers dash up to the rescue. Each is a thrillingly told and convincing story; as literary efforts, it is hard to choose between them, but in the circumstances it is impossible to believe either. One is obviously here in the domain, not of history, but of literature—perhaps, one should say of folklore.

What seems to be an authentic narrative of a very rare sort occurs in an old book published in Philadelphia in 1823: *Manners and Customs of Several Indian Tribes Located West of the Mississippi*, by John Dunn Hunter. The title is a little misleading, for the book is really an autobiography. The author was a white man, captured in infancy by Kickapoo Indians and brought up by them, knowing nothing of his home and parents. Later he lived among the Osages in the valleys of the Kansas, Arkansas, and Platte Rivers and penetrated into the wilds of the Rocky Mountains. His style is somewhat stilted and artificial, but the book as a whole is of unusual interest.

It may be taken as typical of a small group of books dealing at first-hand with explorations and adventures on the plains and among the mountains of Colorado before the gold rush of 1858-9 brought real settlers into the state. Scientific or utilitarian in intention, but intrinsically of great interest are the accounts of the government expeditions under Pike, Long, and Frémont, undertaken respectively in 1806-7, 1819-20, and 1842. If not literature, these may be regarded as the raw material of literature; to the journal of Pike's expedition, for example, Robert Ames Bennet is deeply indebted for the historical facts that add value to his novel, *A Volunteer with Pike* (McClurg, 1909) and Edwin Legrand Sabin for much of his excellent boys' story, *Lost with Lieutenant Pike* (Lippincott, 1919). A less well-known government publication than the accounts of these explorers is *The Prairie Traveler, A Hand-Book for Overland Expeditions*, "published by Authority of the War Department," in 1859, and written by Captain Randolph Barnes Marcy. Whoever wishes to reconstruct in imagination the life of the overland trail before the days of the stage-coach will find this dry, matter-of-fact little manual invaluable and fascinatingly suggestive.

Captain Marcy's other book, *Thirty Years of Army Life on the Border* (Harper's, 1866), is entirely different in character, being a vivid personal narrative of considerable charm. Similar literary qualities are to be discovered in Rufus Sage's *Rocky Mountain Life* (1846), James Hildreth's *Dragoon Campaigns to the Rocky Mountains* (1836), and Thomas J. Farnham's *Travels in the Great Western Prairies, the Anahuac and Rocky Mountains, and in the Oregon Territory* (1843). These books are almost as delightful reading as Parkman's *Oregon Trail*, first published in 1847, a part of which deals, as everyone knows, with eastern Colorado. In this connection, I cannot forbear quoting a passage from Parkman's preface to the 1872 edition:

> I remember that, as we rode by the foot of Pike's Peak, when for a fortnight we met no face of man, my companion remarked, in a tone anything but complacent, that a time would come when those plains would be a grazing country, the buffalo give place to tame cattle, farmhouses be scattered along the water-courses, and wolves, bears, and Indians be numbered among the things that were. We condoled with each other on so melancholy a prospect, but we little thought what the future had in store . . . We knew that, more and more, year after year, the trains of emigrant wagons would creep in slow procession towards barbarous Oregon or wild and distant California; but we did not dream how Commerce and Gold would breed nations along the Pacific, the disenchanting screech of the locomotive break the spell of weird mysterious mountains, woman's rights invade the fastnesses of the Arapahoes, and despairing savagery, assailed in front and rear, vail its scalp-locks and feathers before triumphant commonplace. We were no prophets to foresee all this; and, had we foreseen it, perhaps some perverse regrets might have tempered the ardor of our rejoicing.

Less known than Parkman, but of singular attractiveness, is another early traveler who would certainly have had "perverse regrets" over the intrusion of civilization into the wilds of the West. George Frederick Ruxton, a young English gentleman, educated at Sandhurst Military College, resigned his commission in the British army and, after an unsuccessful attempt to cross the continent of Africa, came to America in 1846. He landed at Vera Cruz, proceeded through Mexico and New Mexico into what is now Colorado, and camped for a time in "Bayou Salade," an old name for South Park, whence he made his way east to civilization. His account of his travels, *Adventures in Mexico and the Rocky Mountains*, was published in London, by John Murray, in 1847. Another book, *Life in the Far West*, first appeared in *Blackwood's Magazine*, in several parts, which were assembled and published in 1849—posthumously, for the young traveler died in St. Louis in 1848 on his way back to the Rocky Mountains. He was, at his death, only twenty-eight. In recent years, after long neglect, his reputation has been growing. He writes well, with a very sensitive appreciation of the beauty and lonely mystery of the mountain wilderness, an eye and a mind quick to note picturesque characters or incidents. A little stream, a branch of the Fountain in El Paso County, has been named in his honor, and one of the younger Colorado poets, Thomas Hornsby Ferril, has celebrated him thus in a poem called *Ruxton Creek:*

> Alone through dusk he sat—
> Safe in Bayou Salade above the Platte,
> Safe from the rumbling dust to Santa Fe,
> Cool in the woven spruce that curtained day,
> While good Panchito browsed along the sage
> Beyond the picket-fire; it was an age
> For picket-fires.
> Broiled beaver-tail was good,
> Better than dripping hump-ribs—cedar-wood
> Was sweet in flapping, snapping, crackling bright—
> Alone, the boy, Bayou Salade, and Night.
>
> And much was in the fire: green Sandhurst, cricket—
> (What would Panchito think of Sandhurst cricket,
> Or Euclid, Covent Garden, polka-dancers?)
> Panchito would not mind Diego's lancers,
> For there was fine hot galloping in Spain,
> Good fun, those civil wars, to come again!
> And more was in the fire: How might he seek
> A trail through Africa to Mozambique,
> Or track from Liverpool to Borneo,
> Or down through Canada to Mexico?
> An idle hand crept through his hunting vest,
> Where Isabella's cross had touched his breast,
> And Drake, and Cook, and Raleigh stood around
> 'Till he was sound asleep upon the ground,
> And stars swept up in royal gallopade,
> And night was purple in Bayou Salade.
>
> Shout, little stream, burst into racing flame,
> For in you burns the spirit of a name;
> Sweep till the seven seas have felt your foam,
> Thunder on every shore. The world is home.

After Francis Parkman and George Frederick Ruxton and the trappers and the "mountain-men," came the pioneers of 1858-9.

> Colorado men are we,
> From the peaks gigantic, from the great sierras and the high plateaus,
> From the mine and from the gully, from the hunting trail we come,
>   Pioneers! O, pioneers!*

---
*Whitman's "Pioneers! O, Pioneers!"

Naturally enough, there were few literary men among the pioneers, and they did not produce much literature. One of them who did write a book almost paid for it with his life. D. C. Oakes died in Denver in 1887; he was known in the early days as "the man who wrote the guide-book." Arriving at Cherry Creek in 1858, he joined Green Russell's party up the Platte River and went prospecting for gold with such promising results that he returned to his home in Glenwood, Iowa, thoroughly convinced of the wealth of the "diggings." Soon after his return he published "a journal containing an account of the explorations of the Green Russell party, which had been kept by Luke Tierney, one of their number," together with "a guide-book of the route to the gold-fields," written by himself.* The book sold in large numbers and was partly responsible for the great rush of emigrants in the spring of '59. It is said that as many as four-fifths of them turned back discouraged by the hardships of the trail and pessimistic reports. Oakes himself returning to Colorado with a steam mill and mining-outfit narrowly escaped lynching at the hands of several of these parties. He was buried in effigy near Julesburg with this inscription on the grave:

>Here *lie* the remains of D. C. Oakes,
>Who was the starter of this damned hoax!

His own account of his adventures on this occasion is lively and entertaining.

Several personal narratives of journeys across the plains in the early days exist either in print or in typewritten manuscripts at the Denver Public Library. Among these are accounts of Emma Shepherd Hill, Frank Crissey Young, Mrs. Clara Viali Colfax Wither, George T. Clarke, and Peter Winne. The most thrilling was published in Chicago in 1860 under the apparently fictitious name of Daniel Blue. It tells the story of a trip to Denver by the Smoky Hill route in 1859. Most of the travelers by this route suffered cruelly from hunger and thirst, and the sole survivor of this particular expedition was rescued by Indians after enduring terrible hardships that culminated in cannibalism. The story would be more effective if told in a less over-colored style.

---

*Article in *The Trail*, Dec., 1909, pp. 7-15, based on D. C. Oakes' own records and claiming to be in his exact words.

Some of the autobiographies of pioneers written and published long after the passing of the frontier make very interesting reading. Among the best of these are Mason Bradford Shelton's *Rocky Mountain Adventures* (Boston, 1920), Sidney Jocknick's *Early Days on the Western Slope of Colorado* (Denver, 1913), Michael Hendrick Fitch's *Ranch Life and Other Sketches* (Pueblo, 1914), Robert McReynolds' *Thirty Years on the Frontier* (Colorado Springs, 1906), Irving Howbert's *Memories of a Lifetime in the Pike's Peak Region* (Putnam's, 1925), and the *Memoirs of Captain Jonathan Shinn*, published in *The Trail*, June to October, 1917. *The Trail*, a magazine printed in Denver and devoted to the interests of the Sons of Colorado, has gathered and preserved much valuable pioneer literature. *The Personal Memoirs of Captain Charles Christy* and T. L. Monson's *Early Days in Ft. Lupton* have already been referred to. Unique in manner, if not in matter, are the contributions of "Vanderwalker of Victor" (*The Trail*, Feb., June, and Nov., 1909, and Aug., 1910), who was a "bull-whacker" on the Santa Fé Trail in 1864. His articles have not gone through the process of literary editing which has taken the flavor out of some of the others. Here is a fair sample of his writing:

> I admit there were occasions when a manipulator of the wild bulls ran out of plain English and used words he hadn't been taught in the primer class, but put any man in his place during a sudden Indian attack while on the road and he trying to work six yoke of irresponsibles into an improvised corral, at the same time trying to do a little execution with an old muzzle-loader, the Indians all the time pouring in basketfuls of arrows into the outfit, making it appear like a traveling feather duster—if there is a man living who wouldn't say 'turkey-red' with the frills to it, why all I've got to say is that the individual has a right to claim his harp at once.

It is difficult to classify the productions of William Gilpin, first governor of Colorado, but he was certainly a pioneer, and his book, *The Central Gold Region*, first published in 1860, republished with additions fourteen years later under the title, *Mission of the North American People* (Lippincott, 1874), is in its entirety one of the most original pieces of work to be noted in this article. Gilpin was an intelligent man, an able governor, and an impressive orator, but some of his ideas were, to say the least, extraordinary. His style deserves the same adjective; he could maneuver battalions of words with the most astonishing success. In a speech delivered at Kansas City, November 15, 1858, he thus describes Colorado:

> Behold, then, the panorama which salutes the vision of one who has surmounted this supreme focal summit of the Cordillera! Infinite in variety of features; each feature intense in the magnitude and the grandeur of its mould; in front, in rear, and on either hand, nature ascending in all her elements to the standard of superlative sublimity! Beneath, the family of Parcs; around, the radiating banks of the primeval mountains; the primary rivers starting to the seas; above, the ethereal canopy, intensely blue, effulgent with the unclouded sun by day, and stars by night; to the east, the undulating plains, expanding one hundred leagues, to dip, like the ocean, beneath the encircling horizon; to the west, the sublime Plateau, chequered by volcanic peaks and mesas, challenged as a labyrinth, by the profound gorges of the streams!

The most comprehensive prose work produced about the pioneers rather than by them is probably Alice Polk Hill's *Tales of the Colorado Pioneers* (Denver, 1884), or, as its later and revised edition is called, *Colorado Pioneers in Picture and Story* (Denver, 1915). The first twenty-one chapters deal largely with Denver, the other forty-five with various localities, strung together on a thread of travel story. The book is full of reminiscences or alleged reminiscences, introduced for the most part as told personally to the writer, but many of the tales are not true and are not intended to be believed; they are full of the kind of humor which consists in obvious exaggeration. Even where the details seem probable, investigation may prove that they have been embellished for literary purposes. As an instance, Mrs. Hill says that the first sermon in Denver was preached in a saloon by the Rev. G. W. Fisher, a Methodist minister, standing in front of the bar; that his text was, "Ho, every one that thirsteth, come ye to the waters, and he that hath no money, come ye, buy and eat; yea, come, buy wine and milk without money and without price"; that "behind him were bottles and glasses in glittering array, and placards adorned the walls reading 'No Trust,' 'Pay as You Go'—'25 cents a drink.'" David Kellogg, writing to *The Trail*, in November, 1912, states that he heard the sermon and verifies the name of the minister, but denies most of the story. The sermon was preached in a Frenchman's cabin; the minister stood on a keg of whiskey; he had no text at all, but began, "Boys, when there's any good to be done, consider me in." The Frenchman did sell liquor in the cabin, but he had no signs and no equipment except two barrels of whiskey and tin cups. Thus does cold reality destroy the picturesqueness of history. If one remembers, however, that Mrs. Hill's book is not history, but literature, it is well worth reading.

Quite accurate from the historical point of view are many of the background details in Edwin Legrand Sabin's stories of pioneer days in Colorado: *Buffalo Bill and the Overland Trail* (Lippincott, 1914), *The Great Pike's Peak Rush* (Crowell, 1917), and *On the Overland Stage* (Crowell, 1918). These are delightful books for boys, frankly fiction, but full of pleasantly presented facts. The author ingeniously introduces into them such real persons as Horace Greeley and "Journalist Richardson," Sam Clemens, and Artemus Ward as passengers on the stage, Wild Bill Hickock, and "Billy" Cody, who in 1860-61 was the youngest rider for the Pony Express.

A good deal of verse, some of it worthy of the name of poetry, has been inspired in Colorado by the pioneers. Most of these are isolated poems, such as "The Pioneer" by Eugene Field, "Ballade of the Pioneers" by Alva Van Riper, "Our Pioneers" by Steuart M. Emery, "Our Brave Pioneers" by C. T. Turner, and "The Fifty-Eighters" by Edward A. Willoughby, himself a "fifty-eighter." A collection of poems could be made dealing with the Santa Fé and other historic trails: of these the best are perhaps "The Old Santa Fé Trail" by Richard E. Leach, "The Dust of the Overland Trail" by James Barton Adams, and "The Old Trail" by Robert McIntyre. Closely allied to these are Ellis Parker Meredith's "First Mate of the Prairie Schooner," celebrating the heroism of the pioneer woman, and Alfred Butters' "Old Bull Whip." The last-named poem has the added interest of having been written by one who himself crossed the plains in 1860 and can truthfully say,

> We remember the time in the great days of old
> When we first started out a-hunting for gold,
> That the merriest sound on the whole long trip
> Was the pop, pop, pop of the old Bull Whip.*

A nameless "Son of Colorado," who in 1863 carried the mail from Buckskin Joe to Sterling City—now no more—produced in "The Mail at Buckskin Joe" (*The Trail*, Oct., 1911) what can

---
*All these poems were published in various numbers of *The Trail*.

scarcely be called a high-class poem, but is a human document of considerable interest. In 1903 Marion Muir Richardson (Ryan) published in Denver a book of poems called *Border Memories*, republished with some additions in 1918 under the title, *Shadows of the Sunset and Other Poems*. In the preface to the second edition the author says, "The childhood of the Great West was my childhood and my first memories of such Americans as have now passed away, the gold miners of a bygone era." The book contains a number of poems dealing with pioneer themes. One of them, "The Gold Seekers," begins vividly:

> The dim stars wheeled above the frontier post,
> The wolf was silent, and the wind was lost;
> The fire roared upward, lighting with its flames
> Four white men's faces and four strong young frames.
> They told how deer were plenty, by the Blue
> In upland forests, till a red man threw
> In from the window ledge a stone that rolled
> Straight to their feet, and it was glittering gold.

Another woman poet, Sarah Elizabeth Howard, was herself a pioneer. Her *Pen Pictures of the Plains* (Denver, 1902) consists of blank verse poems, closely connected in thought, presenting life in the early days of the Greeley colony. In place of the romance and excitement supposed to be characteristic of the West at that time, we have the quiet reality of the wagon-train, the homestead, and the frontier town. The tone of the poems is rather prosaic, but the style is competent, and the book has value because of its fidelity to truth.

Most of the preceding writers treat the pioneer and his adventures with extreme seriousness. Clarence L. Lower's verses are in a lighter vein. His technique is unusually good, and in such a piece as "Dynamite Dan's Narrow Escape; Or, The Tragedy at Blasted Pine" (*Sons of Colorado*, June, 1907), he has achieved the seemingly impossible—a long, humorous poem in impeccable Spenserian stanzas. "Tall yarns" like this seem to constitute his normal subject-matter.

The real "pioneer poet of the Rockies" was Lawrence N. Greenleaf, who was born in 1836 and came to Denver from Boston in 1860. His *King Sham, and Other Atrocities in Verse; including a Humorous History of the Pike's Peak Excitement* (New York, Hurd and Houghton, 1868) is probably the earliest representative of Colorado poetry. It consists largely of humorous verse, full of puns and displaying considerable facility. There is a pleasant eighteenth-century flavor in some of his satiric couplets. A much more serious and ambitious effort was his "Centennial Poem, delivered at the Centennial Celebration in the Centennial State, at Denver, Colorado, July 4, 1876." This includes 290 Alexandrine lines, but has almost nothing in it about Colorado. During his later years Mr. Greenleaf produced a number of interesting poems dealing with genuine pioneer subject-matter, such as "Just Fifty Years Ago," "Early Days in Denver," and "There's A Big Thing in the Mountains." The last-named, built around a favorite phrase of the gold-seekers, expresses well the spirit of the early days:

> When the gold along the valley streams grew 'beautifully less,'
> And the faces of the miners wore a look of sore distress,
> By the fickle smiles of fortune (some with liquid ones!) accursed,
> They were out of their last quarter ere the moon was in her first.
> While their rough and ragged raiment as it fluttered in the gale,
> Showed the verge of bare extremity—"and thereby hangs a tale!"
> With the rocker and the sluice-box they had toiled for many a day,
> But the prospect proved delusive and the diggings wouldn't pay.
> Though most bitter their experience and pitiable their plight,
> There were beating hearts heroic whom no failure could affright.
> While the many to the eastward front, the backward trail pursue,
> To the peaks that seem to beckon turn the faces of the few,
> Over loss and wasted effort who indulge no vain regret—
> There's a big thing in the mountains, and they're bound to strike it yet!

Another pioneer poet, of a slightly later date than Greenleaf, was James Barton Adams (1843-1918), who was born in Iowa, served in the Civil War, and was afterwards a government scout on the plains. His little book of poems, "Breezy Western Verse," was published in 1899 by the *Denver Post*, to whose columns he was a regular contributor. His best-known poem, "The Dust of the Overland Trail," already referred to, is of later date. Nothing could be much better in its way than "The Ruin of Bobtail Bend," in which the author laments the old "wild ways" of an old-time mining camp, ruined by "the moral wave" and "encroachin' piety":

> We could drink our booze in a way profuse an'
>   buck at the faro games,
> An' pound the floor till our hoofs was sore
>   a-swingin' the dance-house dames,
> An' we'd scrap an' fight to our hearts' delight
>   with our other innocent sport,
> With never a fear we would have to square ourselves
>   in the jestice court.
> If a man should scoot down the final chute that
>   leads to the by an' by,

> After leakin' his soul through a pistoled hole,
>   there wasn't no hue an' cry,
> But we'd plant him deep for eternal sleep in
>   respectable sort o' way,
> An' go on a spree to his memory an' forgit the
>   thing in a day.

Among recent poems on the pioneers, the most interesting seem to be Lillian White Spencer's "Pioneer Mother," Thomas Hornsby Ferril's "Canvas Light: A Prairie Song of Farewell," and Margaret Clyde Robertson's "The Woman in the Wagon." The last named appeared in *Poetry Review* (London) in 1925 and won the J. Roberts Foster International Ballad Prize for that year. It gives a grimly serious view of the hardships of woman's life in the covered wagon, in marked contrast to the romantic picture drawn by Mr. Ferril:

> Under canvas noon is amber,
> Less than sunlight, never shade,
> Canvas is the restless cloth
> Where lures are spun and songs are made.
>   * * * * *
> Canvas is the rover's awning,
> Roofs for prairie wagons drawn
> Thin between the sky and peril,
> Dimming twilight, doubting dawn.

Closely connected with the pioneers were the early travelers, who came and went and reported what they saw. Many of their reports were not literature in any proper sense of the term, but manuals of more or less accurate information for prospective miners, ranchers, and tourists. Of the great mass of literary travel narratives, two classes are worth consideration: those in which the travelers themselves were well known and interesting men; and those characterized by some exceptional grace or vigor of presentation.

In the first regular overland stage from Leavenworth to Denver, "Abe Majors's Merchants' Express," traveled three distinguished journalists, Horace Greeley, Albert D. Richardson, and Henry Villard. They arrived in Denver, May 17, 1859, their object being to get for the *New York Tribune* and other eastern papers the real truth about the new gold-fields. After a few days in Denver, they went on to the "Gregory diggings" (Black Hawk), where Greeley himself washed out a pan of dirt "and found several colors." All three men wrote accounts of their adventures. Greeley's appeared first as a series of vivid, personal letters to the *New York Tribune*, afterwards gathered into *An Overland Journey* (N. Y., Saxton, 1860). Richardson's book, *Beyond the Mississippi* (Hartford, Amer. Pub. Co., 1867), includes the record of two later visits to Colorado as well as a good many futher details of "Life and Adventure on the Prairies, Mountains, and Pacific Coast." It is a fascinating narrative, very well written, with curious illustrations. The definitive account of Villard's experiences is to be found in *Memoirs of Henry Villard, Journalist and Financier* (2 vols., Houghton, Mifflin, 1904). He gives a rather appalling picture of Denver's one hotel in 1859:

> This establishment . . . was about 60 feet long and 30 wide. Its four sides consisted of roughly-hewn logs. It had a slanting, skeleton roof, covered with canvas. In the interior were neither floors nor ceilings, nor walls, nor solid partitions to divide the space; but canvas nailed on frames served to set it off for different purposes to the height of seven feet. The front part was occupied by a bar for the sale of strong drinks only, and a dozen gambling tables, at which various games were conducted by experts in the profession . . . Next to the barroom came another space, enclosed by canvas partitions, where the meals were served. Immediately behind it six apartments for sleeping purposes, divided only by the same light material, were set off on each side of a passage . . . . There was no furniture but the gambling and other tables and benches and chairs, made out of rough boards. Bedsteads were provided of the same material, without mattresses or pillows, and also tin wash basins, which the guests themselves filled out of barrels of water standing in the passageway, and emptied, after use, on the dirt floor. Altogether, that hotel was an unique institution, and, of course, without comfort or quiet. In the absence of ceilings and with the thin partitions, a sound in any part of the building was heard all over it.

The next distinguished traveler to visit Colorado was Samuel Bowles, editor of the *Springfield Republican*. His first trip was made in 1865, his second in 1868. They resulted in four books: *Across the Continent* (1865), *The Switzerland of America* (1869), *The Pacific Railroad Open* (1869), and *Our New West* (1869). Only the second is exclusively about Colorado. The material is all interesting in its way, but, on the whole, it is the author's reputation gained in other fields that causes the books to be remembered.

This is not true of Bayard Taylor's *Colorado: A Summer Trip* (Putnam's, 1867). The letters making up the book were originally published in the *New York Tribune*, and record a journey which the author made in the summer of 1866 from Lawrence, Kansas, to Junction City by railroad, thence by stage over the Smoky Hill route to Denver, from there to Golden, Central City, Empire, Idaho Springs, over Berthoud Pass on horseback to Middle Park, Breckenridge, South Park, and back to Denver, to Valmont in Boulder Valley, by stage via Julesburg and the Platte River to Kearney, Nebraska, and by rail from Kearney to Omaha. He gave lectures in all his stopping-places, but does not record their subjects. One of the objects of his journey was to note the possibilities of building a railroad through the mountains, the difficulties of which he entirely underestimates. He is full of a contagious enthusiasm for the mineral wealth of the country, its scenery, and its agricultural resources. With evident amazement he records his discovery "that there is *no* American Desert on this side of the Rocky Mountains." He was much surprised at "the degree of refinement which I have found in the remote mining districts of Colorado. California, after ten years' settlement, retained a portion of the rough, original mining element; but Montana has acted as a social *strainer* to Colorado; or, rather, as a miner's pan, shaking out a vast deal of dirt and leaving the gold behind." Interesting as the book is, the author's evident determination not to over-emphasize the wilder aspects of the country makes it a little tame. Only occasionally do we get such picturesque bits as the following:

> The white wagon-covers of some of these parties contribute to the popular literature of the plains. Many of them are inscribed with the emigrant's name, home, and designation, "accompanied" (as the applicants for autographs say) "with a sentiment." I noticed one which was simply entitled "The Sensible Child." Another had this mysterious sentence, which I will not undertake to explain: "Cold Cuts and Pickled Eel's Feet." "The Red Bull," and "Mind Your Business," were equally suggestive; but the most thrilling wagon-cover was that which met our eyes on crossing the Platte Bridge, and whereon we read: "Hell-Roaring Bill, from Bitter Creek!" In the shade of the cover, between the wheels, Hell-Roaring Bill himself was resting. He looked upon us with a mild, sleepy eye; his face and breast were dyed by the sun to almost the exact color of his hair; his general appearance was peculiar, but not alarming. When we returned this morning, he had departed, and, if all they say of Bitter Creek be true, I think he has done well in changing his residence.

Alexander K. McClure, the afterwards famous publisher, made a journey to the West in 1867-8, and set down his experiences in *Three Thousand Miles through the Rocky Mountains* (Lippincott,

1869). Except as a record of a charming personality, the book is not remarkable. An evidence of the spirit in which he made the trip and also of his very competent English may be derived from the following sentence: "Those who come here overflowing with knowledge, and the grace to dispense it in a patronizing way to the denizens of the plains and mountains, generally go wooling and come home shorn; but those who come as gentlemen, and prove themselves worthy of the title, meet with gentlemen and receive the treatment due."

By the time Charles Kingsley and his daughter Rose came to Colorado in 1874, Denver and Colorado Springs and the neighborhood of the latter city, where he sojourned for about a month, had rather shaken off the crudity of pioneer conditions. Rose Kingsley wrote a book about her travels, *South by West; or, Winter in the Rocky Mountains and Spring in Mexico* (London, 1874), to which her father contributed an appreciative preface. More effective, however, are his brief letters home, printed in *Charles Kingsley, His Letters and Memories of His Life* (edited by his wife, 2 vols., London, 1877). From Glen Eyrie he writes,

> This is a wonderful spot: such crags, pillars, caves—red and grey—a perfect thing in a stage scene; and the Flora, such a jumble —cactus, yucca, poison sumach, and lovely strange flowers, mixed with Douglas's and Menzies' pines, and *eatable* piñon, and those again with our own harebells and roses, and all sorts of English flowers . . . There is a cave opposite my window which must have been full of bears once, and a real eagle's nest close by, full of real young eagles.

He was very ill in this beautiful place, for he had caught a severe cold in San Francisco and had been ordered to Colorado by physicians to recover—if possible. It did not prove possible, and he returned home to die. Either at Glen Eyrie or at Bergun's Park he composed the last poem that he ever wrote, that haunting, tragic *Ballad*, with its rhythm of galloping horses:

> Are you ready for your steeple-chase, Lorraine, Lorraine, Lorree?
>
> * * * * *
>
> You're booked to ride your capping race to-day at Coulterlee,
> You're booked to ride Vindictive, for all the world to see,
> To keep him straight, and keep him first, and win the run for me.

"A singular and charming thing," the great English critic, George Saintsbury, calls it; certainly it has some claim to be considered as the finest poem written within the boundaries of the state.

The story of Eugene Field's hoax in connection with Oscar Wilde's visit to Denver in 1882 is well known. According to one version, as told by Slason Thompson in his *Eugene Field* (Scribner's, 1901, 2 vols., Vol. I, pp. 171 ff.), Field announced Wilde's arrival in Denver a day ahead of time, "secured the finest landau in town and was driven through the streets in a caricature verisimilitude of the poet of the sunflower and the flowing hair." The curious crowd was completely taken in. Wilde, on reaching Denver the next day, saw nothing funny in the incident, but was not annoyed. "His only comment was, 'What a splendid advertisement for my lecture.'" This story has survived largely on account of its connection with Field. Much more worthy of record is Wilde's own account of his experiences at Leadville, set down in his *Impressions of America* (Sunderland, 1906). Oscar Wilde and Leadville! —it would be difficult to conceive of a greater incongruity, yet the two seem to have got along together remarkably well. Leadville, writes Wilde, is

> the richest city in the world. It has also got the reputation of being the roughest, and every man carries a revolver. I was told that if I went there they would be sure to shoot me or my travelling manager. I wrote and told them that nothing they could do to my travelling manager would intimidate me. They are miners —men working in metals, so I lectured to them on the Ethics of Art. I read them passages from the autobiography of Benvenuto Cellini and they seemed much delighted. I was reproved by my hearers for not having brought him with me. I explained that he had been dead for some little time, which elicited the inquiry, "Who shot him?" They afterwards took me to a dancing saloon where I saw the only rational method of art criticism I have ever come across. Over the piano was printed a notice: "Please Do Not Shoot The Pianist. He is Doing His Best."
>
> The mortality among pianists in that place is marvellous. Then they asked me to supper, and having accepted, I had to descend a mine in a rickety bucket in which it was impossible to be graceful. Having got into the heart of the mountain I had supper, the first course being whiskey, the second whiskey, and the third whiskey.
>
> I went to the Theatre to lecture and I was informed that just before I went there two men had been seized for committing a murder, and in that theatre they had been brought on to the stage at eight o'clock in the evening and then and there tried and executed before a crowded audience. But I found these miners very charming and not at all rough.

Charles Kingsley and Oscar Wilde were not by any means our only English visitors. Indeed a favorite pastime of Englishmen up to at least 1890 was to travel to the West and afterwards write it up. They, of course, did not confine themselves to Colorado, but it was in a sense their favorite scene. Many of their books are, frankly, not worth reading. Maurice O'Connor Morris's *Rambles in the Rocky Mountains* (London, 1864) is picturesque, though not exactly kind; Allayne Beaumont Legard's *Colorado* (London, 1872) is amusingly lacking in a sense of humor; Sir Arthur Pendarves Vivian's *Wanderings in the Western Land* (London, 1879) stresses sport and scenery; Samuel Nugent Townshend's *Our Indian Summer in the Far West* (London, 1880) owes its chief interest to the sumptuous illustrations; Lady Duffus Hardy's *Through Cities and Prairie Lands* (N. Y., 1881), is well written, but has little in it about Colorado. Some of these observers were far from accurate; Lady Hardy, for example, writes of Denver, "Ranges of hills and mountains arise on all sides of it." In quite a different class from these superficial travel narratives is the book of another Englishwoman, Isabella Bird Bishop: *A Lady's Life in the Rocky Mountains* (1879). Mrs. Bishop was a real sojourner in the land and records many interesting experiences in an interesting way. She was one of the early enthusiasts over the scenery of Estes Park.

A unique and delightful book is Baron Arnold de Woelmont's *Ma Vie Nomade aux Montagnes Rocheuses* (Paris, 1878). The author was a Belgian nobleman who, in 1876, under the guidance of a picturesque person called Oregon Bill, accompanied two young Englishmen and two young Americans on a hunting, fishing, and exploring trip through the Colorado mountains. He had a pleasantly appreciative attitude toward everything he saw and heard; his memories of Cooper and Mayne Reid, with whom he had spent many "beaux jours" in his childhood, thrilled him with the feeling of living in a story-book when he passed the pipe of peace to an Indian chief. His efforts to transfer Western phrases to his vocabulary and to explain them to his French readers are most amusing. "Joli pays, n'est-ce pas," he exclaims, "où l'on se met si facilement au-dessus de la loi? *Help yourself!*"

Foreigners, of course, have not been the only travelers in Colorado. Charles M. Clark came in 1860, and wrote up his experiences graphically in *A Trip to Pike's Peak and Notes by the Way* (Chicago, 1861). Demas Barnes's *From the Atlantic to the Pacific Overland* (New York, 1866) has an exceptionally picturesque style: "Denver," he writes, "is a square, proud, prompt little place, which, like Pompey's Pillar, is surrounded by immensity." *New Colorado and the Santa Fé Trail* (Harper's, 1880) by Augustus Allen Hayes, Jr., is a lively narrative interspersed with many characteristic Western yarns and not cramped by too much regard for veracity. Ernest Ingersoll's *Knocking round the Rockies* (Harper's, 1883) gives an account of experiences in Colorado and Wyoming in 1874, when the author was attached to the United States Geological and Geographical Survey of the Territories; it is well written and decidedly worth reading. *Seeing the Far West* by John T. Faris (Lippincott, 1920) and *Tales of Lonely Trails* by Zane Grey (Harper's, 1922) are both good travel books, quite unlike in character: the former devotes six chapters to Colorado, the latter only one. Even more recent is Charles Hansen's *My Heart in the Hills* (Dorrance, Philadelphia, 1925), a series of interesting personal essays on camping and climbing in various parts of the State.

It is hard to draw the line between visitors for brief periods and sojourners in the land who become almost or altogether real Coloradoans. The last title might be claimed for Helen Hunt Jackson, whose *Bits of Travel at Home* (Roberts Bros., 1878) deals with her three homes, New England, Colorado, and California. Hamlin Garland's *They of the High Trails* (Harper's, 1916) is hardly a travel book, but a group of sketches portraying vividly the various types of mountain men: the grubstaker, the cow-boss, the remittance man, the lonesome man, the trail tramp, the prospector, the outlaw, the leaser, the forest ranger. Mae Lacy Baggs's *Colorado, the Queen Jewel of the Rockies* (The Page Co., Boston, 1918) is both descriptive and historical; it contains much valuable information and is beautifully illustrated. The author is certainly a Coloradoan, as is also Courtney Ryley Cooper, whose *High Country, The Rockies Yesterday and To-Day* (Little, Brown and Co., 1926) is a very lively and interesting account of the author's experiences on the trail in unfrequented parts of the Rockies, together with valuable advice to campers, automobilists, and hikers. The book contains incidentally many stories of old days in Colorado, pictures of deserted mining-camps, and glimpses of their surviving inhabitants. It suggests the contrast between pioneer times and the present, which is so illuminatingly brought out in Easley S. Jones's "Colorado: Two Generations," originally published in *The Nation*, and later in *These United States* (First Series, Boni and Liveright, 1923). There are few of the states so admirably represented in this compilation.

We have got somewhat off the subject of travel books. Mr. Cooper, for example, deals with life in Colorado as it is lived by the dwellers in the land from the point of view of one of them. We get a similar point of view in *A Tenderfoot in Colorado* by R. B. Townshend (The Bodley Head, London, 1923) and in *A Tenderfoot Bride* by Clarice E. Richards (Doubleday, Page, 1924). Mr. Townshend is an Englishman of good family, a graduate of Cambridge, who came out to Colorado in 1869, and after some wandering "located" a cattle ranch twenty-five miles east of Colorado Springs. Later he went to New Mexico, his adventures in which territory are related in another book, *A Tenderfoot in New Mexico*. In these books we have the real "Wild West," presented in a straightforward, unpretentious, but discerning and dramatic style. Mrs. Richards' adventures belong to a later period, the period of the change from cattle to sheep raising, of the final passing of the open range, and of the coming of the "dry farmer." With considerable literary skill she gives us the personal reminiscences of a rancher's wife on the plains of eastern Colorado. "Bad men," cow-punchers, Mexican herders, blizzards, country dances, horse-breaking, law suits, train robberies, and murders contribute a good deal of action to her pages, but give no impression of exaggeration. This, one feels, is the truth, and it is well told.

From such books as those just described to fiction is but a brief step. Mr. Thomas Fulton Dawson, writing in *The Trail* for February, 1920, claims *John Brent* by Theodore Winthrop as the "original Rocky Mountain romance." This book was published in 1862, shortly after its author's death. It deals with a journey on horseback from California to the Missouri River by two friends, Brent and Wade. A young woman is kidnaped from a Mormon emigrant train near Fort Bridger and is eventually rescued by the two young men at "Luggernel Springs," which is reached through a great canyon known as "Luggernel Alley." The names are, of course, fictitious. Mr. Dawson discusses the claims of various localities in Colorado and Wyoming to be regarded as the originals of "Luggernell," and casts his vote for

Colorado. The discussion, however, convinces one reader at least that Mr. Winthrop, knowing nothing of future state lines and not much in detail about the country itself, allowed his imagination free rein in constructing the background for his story. Colorado can hardly be regarded as the scene of this "original Rocky Mountain romance."

But the book has no right to the title. Reference has already been made to the fact that in 1848 there was published in *Blackwood's Magazine* a series of articles by George Frederick Ruxton, called *Life in the Far West*. After the last of these articles, in the November number, occurs an appreciative sketch of his life, including several quotations from his letters to the editor of *Blackwood's*. In these letters he states that the incidents and characters of *Life in the Far West* are all true to life and based on his own experiences in the mountains. The statement has been accepted at more than its face value, and taken along with the rather misleading title, has been allowed to obscure the fact that the book—for a book it became in 1849—is really a novel. It tells the story of the scout and trapper, La Bonté, son of a St. Louis Frenchman and a Tennessee woman, who, having killed in a duel a young man, a rival of his in love, was obliged to flee into the wilds of the West. He became a "mountain man," married successively and lost two squaws, had many adventures on the plains and in the mountains with Mexicans, Indians, and wild beasts, and eventually made an overland journey to California. On the way back he rescued from an Indian attack a group of emigrants, who had separated themselves from a Mormon party to which they had originally belonged. They turned out to be the family of his old sweetheart, and the story ends with the recognition of the lovers and their union after fifteen years of separation. The plot is rather thin, the love element of comparatively small importance, and the whole tone of the story remarkably realistic and unsentimental. Digressions for "yarns" are abundant; the main interest lies always in the incident at hand rather than in any future outcome. But, with all its defects of construction, the book is a romance of rather superior quality, full of vivid and refreshing action. The conversation is extraordinarily well managed, the dialect of the mountain men being conscientiously and pretty convincingly presented. It may well claim to be the first real "Wild West" novel, and much of its scene is indubitably laid in Colorado.

It is almost superfluous to state that there have been many such novels since, though they did not begin to be produced in any great numbers until the 80's of the last century. The "Wild West" novel or romance may be regarded as a specific literary form, with rules for its composition almost as clearly defined as those for writing French tragedy in the seventeenth century. Of course, there are some variations from the norm, but the following ingredients can be generally recognized: high moral standards, in spite of superficial deviations from conventional behavior, combined with a rigid differentiation of characters into bad and good; a very romantic and chivalrous attitude toward women; abundance of action, which usually includes shooting or actual killing, lynching or near-lynching, other forms of lawlessness and violence and crime or attempted crime, conspiracy of the bad against the good and final victory of the latter; a noble heroine, who may be persecuted and involved in danger and rescued by the hero, or duped by the villain into siding against the hero until the machinations of the evil party are cleared up; a noble hero, who wins out in the end through superior skill, strength, honesty, and courage. On the basis of subject-matter, two main classes of "Wild West" fiction are easily distinguished: ranch stories and mining-camp stories. The railroad, the Forest Service, relations between Indians and white men, and Mexican life are also dealt with, but less commonly. Plots are constructed around disputed titles to ranches or mines or railroad rights of way, around cattle feuds and railroad rivalries, around attempts on the part of crooks to cheat innocent white owners or Indians or the government, around the efforts to identify and punish cattle thieves and highway robbers, or to expose and bring to justice corrupt government officials.

Obviously, this fiction is not all connected with Colorado; in fact, in recent years, considering the entire output, we may regard Wyoming, Texas, and Arizona as the popular settings. Still Colorado is well represented in two ways: by books written by Coloradoans and by books dealing with Colorado life. Mary Hallock Foote, who lived in various places in several western states, was a very prolific writer of fiction. Products of her stay in Colorado are two mining romances, *Led-Horse Claim* (1883), the scene of which is in South Park, and *John Bodewin's Testimony* (1886), which deals with a mining-camp on the western slope of the Park Range. Of the same period are the two novels of Emma Ghent Curtis, a citizen of Denver for many years. The first of these, *The Fate of a Fool* (1888), though it belongs geographically to Southwestern Colorado, has no "Wild West" flavor; the second, *The Administratrix* (1889), is a cattle-feud story, typical, though somewhat less romantic than the average novel of its class. Emma Homan Thayer, who came to Denver from the East in 1882, is chiefly memorable for her beautiful books on wild flowers, but she also wrote fiction: *The English American* (1889); *Petronilla the Sister* (1898); *A Legend of Glenwood Springs* (1900); *Dorothy Scudder's Science* (1901). Of these, only the first is a "Wild West" novel; it relates the adventures of a young Englishman engaged in mining in Colorado and his successful conflict with swindlers and "bad-men." The novels of Frederick Thickstun Clark, for some years a high school teacher in Denver, deal with western localities, though not all with Colorado. He wrote *A Mexican Girl* (1888), *In the Valley of Havilah* (1890), *On Cloud Mountain* (1894), and *The Mistress of the Ranch* (1897). The last-named is a story of a ranch on the Rio Grande, the next to the last a presentation of life in a fictitiously named mining-camp, Donhala City. Dialect is used liberally in both, and the didactic purpose, especially in *On Cloud Mountain*, is a little too evident. Patience Tucker Stapleton (1861-1893), was a brilliant young woman of remarkable versatility, the wife of William Stapleton, editor of the *Rocky Mountain News* and later of the *Denver Republican*. In her short life she produced poems, editorial articles, numerous stories published in various magazines, and four novels: *My Sister's Husband* (1890), *Babe Murphy* (1890), *Kady, A Colorado Romance* (1892), and *My Jean* (1893). *Babe Murphy* and *Kady* are mining-camp stories, full of the usual excitement, but with a good deal of refreshing humor. A conversation in a saloon, reported in *Kady*, may be given as characteristic:

"Terrible tragedy, that," said the blonde.
"Which?" asked the bar-tender.
"Why, the murder of the county commissioners."
"Oh, that? Why there was only five killed," said the bar-tender indifferently.

The work of Mrs. Hattie Horner Louthan, resident of Denver since 1896, is entirely serious. Her first novel, *In Passion's Dragnet* (1903), is, as its name implies, a highly erotic romance, localized in New Orleans. *This Was a Man* (1906) deals with ranch life, mining operations, and labor troubles in the vicinity of Boulder; *A Rocky Mountain Feud* (1910), much the best of the three, is a sheep and cattle story of Routt County, though some scenes are laid in Denver and in Golden. Another Denver citizen, Enoch Anson More, Jr., has produced one rather vigorous mining-camp tale, *Let It Burn* (1892); of his other novels, *A Vision of Empire* (1915) is a story of the French in America, *Out of the Past* (1895) is laid in India, and *A Captain of Men* (1905) in ancient Assyria. *When Cattle Kingdom Fell* (1910) by John Richard Stafford of Colorado Springs is fortunate in its title and is a good representative of what might be called the cowboy-melodrama type; its very exciting events, the background of which is apparently true to fact, are located somewhat vaguely in the neighborhood of the Canadian River and hence not in Colorado. Other noteworthy Western romances by Colorado authors are Mary E. Stickney's *Brown of Lost River* (Appleton, 1900). David Nelson Beach's *Annie Laurie Mine* (Pilgrim Press, 1902), and Elizabeth Egleston Hinman's *Naya* (Rand, McNally, 1910). Mrs. Mary Holland Kinkaid's novels, *Walda* (Harper's, 1903) and *The Man of Yesterday* (Stokes, 1907), though western in locality, are by no means of the "Wild West" type. The former presents the life of a religious co-operative community of German descent "in a Western State," probably Nebraska or Kansas. The latter deals with Indian problems in what is now Oklahoma; the Indian hero is a highly idealized type.

The chief contribution to the romance of the railroad in Colorado fiction was made by Cy Warman (1855-1914). He was a native of Illinois, born on a farm and educated in the common schools; in 1880 he came to Colorado and for some years was in the employ of the Denver and Rio Grande Railroad on the Western slope, as shop-mechanic, fireman, and engineer. He scribbled verses and did newspaper work in his leisure hours. In 1892 he wrote a little song, *Sweet Marie*, which was set to music by Raymond Moore and took possession of the country. This brought him to the notice of S. S. McClure, who started him on his literary career as a writer of light verse and short stories. Most of his work originally appeared in various magazines and was afterwards published in book form by Scribner's or Appleton. His collections of railroad stories, many of them dealing with Colorado localities, are *The Express Messenger* (1897), *Frontier Stories* (1898), *Short Rails* (1900), *The Last Spike* (1906). *Snow on the Headlight* (1899) is a longer tale, having for its subject the great Burlington strike of 1888; *The White Mail* (1899) is a railroad novel of the Western slope. *Tales of an Engineer*, originally published in 1895, and republished along with *Rhymes of the Rail* in 1903, is fact rather than fiction, as is also *The Story of the Railroad* (1898), one of the interesting Appleton series known collectively as *The Story of the West*. *Weiga of Temagami* (1908) is a collection of Algonquin legends. Warman's work, in general, is lively and interesting, though high literary merit could scarcely be claimed for it.

The Helpers (1899), *A Private Chivalry* (1900), *The Grafters* (1904), and *A Fool for Love* (1905) constitute the contribution to fiction of another Coloradoan, Francis Lynde. All these except the first might be called railroad novels, but mining-camps, deflated boom-towns, newspaper business, crime, and politics, especially the last-named activity, add greatly to the interest. The scenes are laid in Denver and in various unnamed Rocky Mountain localities. Frank H. Spearman, who in *The Nerve of Foley* (1900) and *Held for Orders* (1902) produced two series of railroad stories dealing with the territory "from Omaha to the Sierras," has no personal connection with Colorado, but many of his stories have a Colorado setting. More interesting are *The Last Frontier* (1923) by Courtney Ryley Cooper and *Roads of Doubt* (1925) by William MacLeod Raine. The first-named book centers in the building of the Kansas Pacific Railroad—now the Union Pacific—between Kansas City and Denver in 1866; it introduces Wild Bill Hickok and Buffalo Bill as characters and presents in detail the historic fight at Beecher's Island. Mr. Raine's novel, though its details are quite fictitious, celebrates the building of the Moffat Road and makes use of the public-spirited railroad builder, Dave Moffat, as the prototype of one of its chief figures.

The mention of this last book naturally suggests what might be called "the big three" in Colorado "Wild West" fiction: William

MacLeod Raine, Robert Ames Bennet, and Hamlin Garland. Mr. Raine was born in England, but he came to the United States when he was ten years old and has been a citizen of Colorado for twenty years. He began his career as a journalist, and his literary production comprises political and social articles in various periodicals as well as short stories and novelettes in English and American magazines. His first novel, *A Daughter of Raasay*, a Scotch historical romance, appeared in 1902; his second, *Wyoming*, not until six years later. Since then he has published twenty-six novels. Practically all have a "Wild West" setting, but many of them have nothing to do with Colorado; a recent book, *Bonanza* (1926) is a story of the Nevada gold-fields. A quotation from a review of this in *The London Times Literary Supplement* (March 11, 1926) may be cited as a tribute to the author's fidelity to fact in presenting his backgrounds: "In reading Mr. Raine's latest story of the early days in the West one feels that he steers a plot through a number of scenes which might almost be taken direct from the stormy local atmosphere of those times. He is able to reproduce the atmosphere and colour." *Tangled Trails* (1921) is, in Mr. Raine's own words, "set in Denver mostly"; *The Fighting Edge* (1922) belongs to the country "in and around Meeker, though the fact is somewhat camouflaged"; *Ironheart* (1923) is located "somewhere in Colorado"; *Roads of Doubt* (1925), which is of special interest, has already been mentioned.

Robert Ames Bennet has a double claim on Coloradoans, for he is a native son, born in Denver and educated at the Denver public schools. He began his work as a novelist with *Thyra* (1901); his total output includes twenty-six novels. Mr. Bennet does not confine himself so closely as does Mr. Raine to Western life. *Thyra*, the sub-title of which is *A Romance of the Polar Pit*, is an effort of the imagination deserving a place alongside Conan Doyle's *Lost World*; *The Shogun's Daughter* (1910) is, as its name suggests, a tale of Japan; *The Blond Beast* (1918) is a story of the World War. His most ambitious effort, *For the White Christ* (1905), presents a vivid and effective picture of the times of Charlemagne. *A Volunteer with Pike* (1909) has already been mentioned as a historical romance dealing in part with a Colorado locality. Other stories set in Colorado are *Out of the Depths* (1913), which belongs to the Western slope and introduces the Black Cañon of the

Gunnison under the name of Deep Cañon; *Branded* (1924), also connected with the Western slope; *The Two-Gun Man* (1924), characterized in the *London Times Literary Supplement* as "one of the best stories of Western life that this noted author has written," and located, according to Mr. Bennet, in the neighborhood of Platte Cañon and Elk Creek; *The Cattle Baron* (1925), portraying "the Flat Top country in Northwest Colorado"; and *The Rough Rider* (1925), which "starts in Denver, then moves to Cañon City, the Royal Gorge and the mesa on the rim of the gorge." *Out of the Depths* is worth commenting on separately because it is "a romance of reclamation," a phase of Western life not often emphasized in fiction.

Hamlin Garland is, as every one knows, not a Coloradoan, but "A Son of the Middle Border." Frequent excursions and sojourns in the state have, however, left him with an abiding interest in this region, which has resulted in ten books. *Her Mountain Lover* (1901) shifts between Ouray and London and presents an unsophisticated Colorado miner with possession of his heart disputed by an aristocratic Englishwoman and a "little girl" from the mountains; in *Hesper* (1903) an Eastern girl goes to "Sky-Camp"—Cripple Creek—and falls in love with a Westerner; *Witch's Gold* (1906) is another Cripple Creek story, the heroine of which is a health seeker; *Money Magic* (1907)—much the best of the group, a real study of character and hardly in the "Wild West" class, though it contains a few typical scenes—also belongs partly to Cripple Creek, though set principally in Colorado Springs. All these stories involve mining-camp life. *The Captain of the Gray-Horse Troop* (1902) is the most noteworthy Colorado example of the "Wild West" fiction which deals primarily with Indian relations and the attempt to protect the Indians against unscrupulous white men; its location is indefinite, but the "Bear-Tooth Range" is "somewhere in Colorado." The titles of *Cavanagh, Forest Ranger* (1910) and *The Forester's Daughter* (1914) are sufficiently indicative of their subjects. The first, which involves a feud between cattle and sheep men, is a thoroughly readable book. The second contains in its opening chapter one of the best descriptions of Colorado that I have ever read:

> There are two Colorados within the boundaries of the state of that name, distinct, almost irreconcilable. One is a plain (smooth, dry, monotonous), gently declining to the east, a land

of sage-brush, wheat-fields, and alfalfa meadows—a rather commonplace region now, given over to humdrum folk intent on digging a living from the soil; but the other is an army of peaks, a region of storms, a spread of dark and tangled forests. In the one, shallow rivers trickle on their sandy way to the Gulf of Mexico; from the other, the waters rush, uniting to make the mighty stream whose silt-laden floods are slowly filling the Gulf of California.

If you stand on one of the great naked crests which form the dividing wall, the rampart of the plains, you can see the Colorado of tradition to the west, still rolling in wave after wave of stupendous altitudes, each range cutting into the sky with a purple saw-tooth edge. The landscape seems to contain nothing but rocks and towering crags, a treasure-house for those who mine. But this is illusive. Between these purple heights charming valleys wind and meadows lie in which rich grasses grow and cattle feed.

Courtney Ryley Cooper has already been mentioned for his interesting book on the Colorado mountains called *High Country*. He was born in Kansas City, in 1886, but has been a winter resident of Denver and a summer resident of Idaho Springs for some years. He has been a newsboy, a glove salesman, a circus press agent, an actor, a vaudeville dancer, a rodeo and circus manager, an assistant in producing motion picture spectacles, and a contributor of many articles and stories to various periodicals, especially the *Saturday Evening Post*. Having been press agent and secretary to Buffalo Bill, he was naturally called upon to assist Mrs. Cody in preparing the memoirs of her husband, published under the title of *Memories of Buffalo Bill* (Appleton, 1919). His circus experiences have resulted in two entertaining books, *Under the Big Top* (Little, Brown, and Co., 1923) and *Lions 'n' Tigers 'n' Everything* (Ditto, 1924). In addition to his railroad-building story, *The Last Frontier*, previously commented on, he has two other "Wild West" novels to his credit, both with Colorado settings; *The Cross-Cut* (1921) and *The White Desert* (1922). The first of these is a mining romance of recent times; the second deals with a dispute over the ownership of timber-land and a lumber-mill in the mountains. Crime and accusations of crime figure largely in both. *The Eagle's Eye* (1918) purports to be "a true story of the Imperial German Government's spies and intrigues in America .... novelized .... from facts furnished by William J. Flynn, recently retired Chief of the U. S. Secret Service"; though not "Wild West" fiction, it is fully as exciting. His most recent book is *Oklahoma* (1926).

Arthur Chapman, though no longer a Coloradoan, was one for twenty-one years. He is, of course, chiefly known as a writer of verses. His two Western stories, *Mystery Ranch* (1921) and *John Crews* (1926), have no definite connection with Colorado. The hero of the first is an Indian agent; the second is quite out of the ordinary, being the story of a free trader in the neighborhood of Fort Laramie in the early days of the trappers and the fur trade. Zane Grey, who was born in Ohio and lives in California, may perhaps be regarded as the chief writer of "Wild West" novels to-day. Most of his books, however, are about the states to the south and west of Colorado. An exception to this statement is *The Mysterious Rider* (1921), a tale of cattle rustling in the mountains "above Middle Park." Others, not Coloradoans, who have written noteworthy novels with a Colorado setting are William Alexander Hammond, Frank Lewis Nason, and John Harvey Whitson. Hammond (1828-1900) was at one time Surgeon-General of the United States Army, a specialist in nervous diseases and the author of several monographs on that subject. Among his half-dozen novels is *Lal* (Appleton, 1884), the story of a Polish exile who goes to the mountains of Colorado to write a book in solitude and lives through a series of exciting adventures; the heroine, whose name constitutes the title, is an uneducated mountain girl, the supposed daughter of a horse-thief. The book is worth reading. Nason's *To the End of the Trail* (1902) and *The Blue Goose* (1903) are exceptionally realistic and vigorous portrayals of Colorado mining life; the author's professional experience as a mining engineer enabled him apparently to see something besides romance in the working of a mine. Similarly differentiated from the usual "Wild West" romance of ranch life is Whitson's *Justin Wingate, Ranchman* (1905), located in "Paradise Valley" in Southern Colorado and dealing simply and sanely with cattle and irrigation. Mr. Whitson's other book with a Colorado setting, *Barbara, a Woman of the West* (1903), is somewhat hectic by comparison.

Will Irwin's working career as an author has been passed far afield from Colorado, but he was brought up in Denver and hence may be claimed as a product of the state. The plot of his recent novel, *Youth Rides West* (Knopf, 1925), has all the ingredients of the "Wild West" pattern, yet it stands out as definitely superior to most of its kind because of its author's faithful attempt to portray a Colorado mining-camp as it really was in "the Seventies." An English critic notes its exceptional character thus:

> Mr. Will Irwin's *Youth Rides West* has for its setting a period which has inspired a good deal of popular American fiction. The gold rush of the seventies has often fired the imagination of the novelist in proportion to his ignorance of what actually happened; he has discovered adventure and romance where only intense labour, discomfort, danger, and disillusionment were to be found. Mr. Irwin, however, has written a story abounding in colour and excitement which is also singularly convincing as an historical document. He makes no pretence of indulging in fine points of psychology; he has a locality to describe and a simple story to tell. He treats of mining camps, highwaymen, lynching and love as appurtenances of the quest for gold. That Buck Hayden's pursuit of El Dorado should end in the discovery not of gold, but of silver carbonate mines, attests a certain integrity; if the happy ending is a trifle obvious, at least it makes some compromise with the romantic convention on which such tales are usually built.

Exceptional in their subject-matter are three other books: *Beth Norvell, A Romance of the West* (1907) by Randall Parrish; *The Penitentes of San Rafael, A Tale of the San Luis Valley* (1900) by Louis How; and *Windy Creek* (1899) by Helen Stuart Thompson. The scene of *Beth Norvell* is laid in Southern Colorado; the heroine, an actress on the road with a second-rate company, has as her faithful friend a Mexican woman. Crime and conspiracy are thwarted, idealism and love are triumphant, quite as usual. The unusual thing is the friendly and understanding treatment of the Mexicans. Still more remarkable is Mr. How's portrayal of Spanish-American life from the inside, as it were; the incidents in his story are sufficiently exciting to be called romantic, but the whole method is convincingly realistic. The novel deserves more attention than it has received. The same statement may be made of *Windy Creek*. Here romance disappears entirely, and we have a simple, genuine account of life in a rural community on the Colorado plains, with no "bad-men" and no shooting. Local competition of religious sects occupies much attention. A cattle-thief who makes love to a rancher's wife is horse-whipped by her husband, but for his original offense he is arrested, tried, and sentenced to the penitentiary in law-abiding fashion. Though the plot is slight, the characterization is admirable and the style good.

If the books just dealt with are exceptional, those of Andy

Adams, "the cowboy-author," may be called almost unique. He was born in Indiana, reared on a farm, and educated at a country school. While still a youth he went to Texas and for ten years led the life of a cowboy. During the Cripple Creek excitement he came to Colorado, where he has lived ever since. Having lost money in mines, as so many others have done, he turned rather unaccountably to literature and commenced author without training or experience at the age of forty-four. *The Log of a Cowboy* (1903) was so successful that he followed it up in rapid succession with five other books. These all deal with cattle and cowboys. *A Texas Matchmaker* (1904), *Reed Anthony, Cowman* (1907), and *Wells Brothers* (1911) purport to be novels, but the author has no skill in plot-construction and is particularly clumsy at handling women and the love motive. He is at his best when he is telling a yarn based on his own experience, often in large part literally true, but colored and vivified by imagination. He may be compared somewhat diffidently to George Borrow. His best books are, in ascending importance, *Cattle Brands, A Collection of Western Camp-Fire Stories* (1906), thrilling tales of bandits, "bad-men," etc., told in a matter-of-fact fashion in characteristic cowboy lingo, but not overloaded with slang; *The Outlet* (1905), an account of a cattle drive from Texas to North Dakota in 1884; and, above all, *The Log of a Cowboy*, a graphic and picturesque narrative of cowboy life in Texas and of the moving of a great herd of cattle from the mouth of the Rio Grande to the Blackfoot Agency in Montana in 1882. The book is a real Colorado classic and deserves to be better known.

It would hardly be feasible to mention every novel or romance which has part of its setting in Colorado. Lillian Bell's *Interference of Patricia* (1903) is a story of Denver finance and society, full of rather artificially startling comments on the climate and the social life of the city, the latter of which is represented as somewhat peculiar. "Even Denver draws the line somewhere," the author remarks. In Kipling's *Naulahka* (1891) the scene opens in Topaz, Colorado, and the hero's persistent devotion to his home town even in distant India is characteristic and delightful. *The Song of the Lark* (1915) by Willa Cather presents for the background of its heroine's youth a small town in Colorado, which is not intrinsically different either in the book or in reality from small towns in Nebraska. This collection of instances might be increased, but with no particular profit. Suffice it to say that the survey of fiction dealing with Colorado has revealed one great and significant gap. Ranch life of the past has been portrayed in detail often enough; ranch life of the present has been touched on; mining-camps of a bygone era have had numerous romantic and some realistic chroniclers. What remains to be done is to picture the life, to draw the characters, of the decayed mining-camp of the present, the sleepy, little mountain village, with its tumble-down, deserted buildings, its memories of the past, its stranded old men and women, its isolated youth, its winter seclusion, its brief period of activity, perhaps, due to the summer people. Such villages as Gold Hill, Ward, Central City cry aloud *to-day* for observant interpreters.

Probably a large proportion of the readers of "Wild West" romances are adolescents. But there is a group of writers who address themselves directly to boys and who may be taken up separately. The most important of these is Edwin Legrand Sabin, born in Illinois and now living in California, but for some years a citizen of Denver. Four of his best books, *Lost with Lieutenant Pike*, *Buffalo Bill and the Overland Trail*, *The Great Pike's Peak Rush*, and *On the Overland Stage*, have been already noted. Merely to name all his boys' books with a Colorado setting would take more space than we can afford. Typical are *Scarface Ranch* (1914), a cattle story of Western Colorado; *The Circle K* (1911), which belongs to the sheep country "about where Colorado and Utah join"; *Treasure Mountain or The Young Prospectors* (1913) and *Old Four-Toes or Hunters of the Peaks* (1912), sufficiently explained by their sub-titles; and *With Carson and Fremont* (1912), a boys' historical romance. *Kit Carson Days* (McClurg, 1914), which is not fiction, but biography with detailed social and geographical background, is a valuable book, well written and fully documented. Sidford Frederick Hamp, a native of England, but for many years a resident of Colorado Springs, has written a number of Western stories for boys, some of them originally published in *St. Nicholas* and the *Youth's Companion*. His best book is *Dale and Fraser, Sheepmen* (1906), which deals not only with sheep, but also with wolves, mountain lions, range-fires, Mexican herders and padres, difficulties of water supply, and hidden treasure. John Harbottle, who belongs to Greeley and is a graduate of the State Teachers' College there, in addition to a number of short stories, has produced *The Luck of Laramie Ranch* (1913) and *Finding His Stride* (1915). The latter recounts the success of a young mining engineer in the construction of a great irrigation project. Everett McNeil, like Mr. Sabin, is a prolific writer of boys' books, whose work cannot be taken up in detail. *The Hermit of the Culebra Mountains* (1904), *The Lost Treasure Cave* (1905), and *With Kit Carson in the Rockies* (1909) have a Colorado background. These are lively and entertaining stories which any boy might enjoy. The second of the three named contains a delightful incident of some Indians stealing a box of Roman candles, thinking them to be big cigars, and starting to smoke them with astonishing results. George Alfred Henty, the English purveyor of boys' books, who apparently hit upon every possible locality and period for the subjects of his juvenile romances, naturally enough lighted on Colorado; *In the Heart of the Rockies* (Blackie, London, n. d.) has nothing of much interest in it except the writer's ignorance of the country which he is writing about and especially of the native speech of its inhabitants.

Girls' books dealing with the West are rare. Mabel Earle, a Coloradoan, has written *New Fortunes: How Molly and her Brothers Came to Boulder Gulch* (Barnes, 1903) and Susan Coolidge (Sarah Chauncey Woolsey), not a Coloradoan, has produced *Clover* (Little, Brown and Co., 1909), a story of a girl who sojourned in the Rocky Mountains for the health of her brother. Charlotte M. Vaile (Mrs. Joel F. Vaile, 1854-1902) published a number of girls' stories: *The Orcutt Girls* (1896), *Sue Orcutt* (1897), *The M. M. C.* (1898), *Wheat and Huckleberries* (1899), *Two and One* (1901), *The Truth about Santa Claus* (1903). Of these, only *The M. M. C.*, which has for its sub-title *A Story of the Great Rockies*, deals with Colorado life; the heroine is a young school teacher in a mining-camp called Silvercrest.

A considerable number of Colorado authors have written fiction, which, though some of it may have to do with Colorado localities, is not at all western in its character. A recent writer of considerable importance, born in Kentucky, but resident in Denver from 1922 until his death in December, 1926, is George Looms. His novels include *Stubble* (1922), *John-No-Brawn* (1923), and *The Caraways* (1925), all published by Doubleday, Page, and Company. The first of these is a realistic and very interesting story of Kentucky life. The last is a tragic, rather melodramatic tale, unidentified as to locality. *John-No-Brawn* recounts the adventures of a young Kentuckian who contracts tuberculosis during the World War, spends some time at a Government Hospital in Denver—no attempt being made to disguise its identity,—and finally "takes the cure" in a mountain cabin under the care of his wife. The book is a grim study of invalid psychology and of hospital life. Less realistic, perhaps, but having a similar realistic purpose is *The Cage* (Appleton, 1907), by Charlotte Teller; this is a story of the West Side in Chicago, dealing largely with labor troubles and mission work. Its realism is somewhat spoiled by the rather melodramatic love story of its hero, a Polish exile and labor agitator. The obvious social criticism in *The Cage* naturally connects it with a group of what might be called propaganda novels. Isaac N. Stevens, a citizen of Colorado since 1880, has published three such novels: *The Liberators* (1908), *An American Suffragette* (1911), and *What Is Love?* (1918). The second, the heroine of which is a woman lawyer in New York City, has more merit as fiction than either of the others. The first, which has for its sub-title, *A Story of Future American Politics*, exists mainly for the advocacy of a mild form of socialism or, at least, of the nationalization of basic industries. In the third, which is highly idealistic, the plot has a tendency to disappear entirely. Two other socialistic novels by Coloradoans, with prophecies of future events that time has already falsified, are *Waiting for the Signal* by Henry O. Morris and *John Harvey, A Tale of the Twentieth Century* by Anon Moore, the penname of James M. Galloway; both these books were published in Chicago in 1897, and both deal in part with Colorado scenes. Sidney C. Tapp, a Georgian by birth, now lives in Kansas City, but his only venture in fiction, *The Struggle* (New York, 1906), was published during his residence in Denver; it has a good deal of plot, but is largely devoted to propaganda against the trusts.

By some stretch of the term, all the preceding writers may be classed as realists. The work of George Leonard Knapp, long a resident of Pueblo and Denver, though now living in Chicago, is decidedly romantic. *The Scales of Justice* (Lippincott, 1910) is a novel of crime and the underworld; *The Face of Air* (Lane, 1912) is a mystery story of the sea, very well done; *The Quest of the Golden Cities* (Dodd, Mead and Co., 1924) is a historical romance of the days of Coronado. Ellis Parker Meredith, now Mrs. Henry H. Clement of Washington, D. C., belongs by birth to the West, though not to Colorado. She was born in Bozeman, Montana, and in 1889 began her career as a newspaper woman on the *Rocky Mountain News*. A very important incident in this career was her active work for woman suffrage in Colorado. In 1901 she published her first work of fiction, *The Master-Knot of Human Note* (Little, Brown). One hesitates to call it a novel, for it is rather a fantasy dealing with a man and a woman marooned together in a cabin in the Rocky Mountains by a cataclysm that submerges all the rest of the land. *Heart of My Heart* (McClure, 1904), her second book, has for its sub-title *A Romance of Motherhood*. The scene begins in Colorado, but is transferred to New England; the plot interest is secondary. *Under the Harrow* (Little, Brown, 1907), which is more truly a novel, deals with theatrical and literary life in New York. Louise Lyndon Sibley belongs more to Massachusetts than to Colorado: her novel, *A Lighthouse Village* (Houghton, Mifflin, 1901) has a New England setting. *The Skein of Life* (Lippincott, 1897) by William Ricard Mackay and *Art Thou the Man?* (Dodd, Mead, 1905) by Guy Robert La Coste, who wrote under the pseudonym of Guy Berton, have no particular local color, though the scene of the latter is laid in Denver. Mrs. John Ellsworth Graham's book, *A Toltec Savior* (Dillingham, 1901), is sufficiently described by its sub-title, *A Historical Romance of Ancient Mexico*. A more recent and very promising writer is Marianne Gauss, author of *Danae* (Harper, 1925). The heroine is a woman lawyer, who marries a man to save him from her adverse testimony in a bribery case; the book is a love story with some emphasis on character study, but, though located in Colorado, it makes no effort at securing local color.

Several of the novelists dealt with in the preceding paragraphs have also written and published short stories. Among other Colorado short-story writers may be named Mary Talbot Campbell, William Carey Campbell, Charles Newman Crewdson, Paul DeLaney, Alma Martin Estabrook Ellerbe, William Chester Estabrook, Lewis B. France, Anna Fuller, Thomas Crawford

Galbreath, Helen Green, Clarence L. Lower, Christine Whiting Parmenter, Elia Wilkinson Peattie, Caroline Hosmer Rhone, Clara Sherwood Rollins, and Mrs. Wilson Woodrow. Joe Mills has not only contributed a number of short stories to various periodicals, but has also published *The Comeback* (Sears, 1925), an outdoor adventure story of some length and considerable interest. His most recent book, *A Mountain Boyhood* (Sears, 1926), an interesting portrayal of life in the Colorado mountains, is not fiction, but autobiography. A beautiful little book, difficult to classify otherwise than as a short story, though technically it is not one at all, is *The Faith of the Little Shepherd* (Sears, 1926) by Grace Adele Catherwood—Mrs. J. O. Billig—of Boulder. *The Great Divide*, a magazine published in Denver from 1889 to 1893, transferred to Chicago in 1894, and rapidly degenerating after the transfer, contained, especially during its Denver career, a good many stories by Colorado authors, including James McCarthy (Fitz-Mac), Lelah Palmer Morath, Lute H. Johnson, Emma Ghent Curtis, and Mary G. Crocker. Some idea of the kind of stories favored by this magazine may be indicated by the captions under two pictures in a single issue: "There Lay Mattie Bound Hand and Foot," and "In the Middle of the Road Stood a Masked Man with a Knife Uplifted over the Heart of the Girl he Loved."

"Lute H." (Lucius Henry) Johnson, in addition to writing short stories for *The Great Divide* and other magazines, deserves special mention as one of the very few Coloradoans who have written for the stage. Three of his plays, *Magnolia Plantation*, *Coming Home*, and *Sheep*, have been successfully produced. The last-named was put on by Walker Whiteside at the Broadway Theater in March, 1924, was afterwards well received in several western and eastern cities, including Washington, and favorably reviewed by leading critics. It is a real Western drama. Mr. Johnson's new musical comedy, *Tom*, the music for which was written by Robert Hayes, of Cheyenne Wells, is now* in the hands of a New York producer.

Outstanding among the story writers, not only of Colorado, but of the United States at large, is Wilbur Daniel Steele, who, though he was born in North Carolina and now lives in Massachusetts, spent his boyhood and youth and received his education

---
*December, 1926.

in Denver. In 1921 the O. Henry Award Committee gave him a special prize for maintaining over a period of three years the highest level of distinction among American short story writers. In 1925 he won first place in the fourth competition held by *Harper's Magazine* with a story, published in that magazine in September, 1925, "The Man Who Saw Through Heaven." This is unquestionably a masterpiece. James Finch Royster's *American Short Stories* (Scott, Foresman and Co., 1925) draws on the work of thirteen authors, Mr. Steele being the only one who is represented by two selections, "Down on their Knees," and "Footfalls." Both of these deal with the Portuguese immigrants on Cape Cod. Mr. Steele seldom writes about Colorado, but "Brother's Keeper," in *Harper's* for December, 1925, has its scene in a Colorado plains town. Its chief figure is a pioneer citizen, loyal to the town that he has helped to create and horrified at the degeneracy of the present-day youth and at the demoralizing influence of the modern picture-show. Like all Mr. Steele's work, it is characterized by masterly technique and real intelligence. One of the refreshing things about his stories is that they always contain ideas.

Miscellaneous writers of fiction whose connection with Colorado is very slight or whose contribution to literature is very limited are Ralph Henry Barbour, Winifred Black Bonfils, James W. Coulter, Vivian Cory, Paul Lawrence Dunbar, Edward W. Gilliam, George Barr McCutcheon, Webb Rockefeller Miller, Meredith Nicholson, George I. Putnam, Harry Perry Robinson, Julia A. Sabine, Charles E. Schuyler, Eugene Walter, and Marguerite Zearing.

Verner Z. Reed (1863-1919) deserves more notice. Most of his stories were contributed to *The Great Divide*, but were afterwards collected and republished in three volumes, *La-to-Kah* (1897), *Tales of the Sunland* (1897), and *Adobeland Stories* (1899). These all deal with Indians or Mexicans. From 1889 to 1891, Mr. Reed was one of the editorial writers for the *Commonwealth Magazine*, a Denver publication which deserved a longer life. He also contributed a number of essays and travel sketches to various other magazines, among them the *Atlantic Monthly*. *The Soul of Paris and Other Essays* (John Lane, 1913) contains some of these contributions. All these literary productions Mr. Reed found time for in the midst of a busy life occupied with mining, banking, manufacturing, and irrigation enterprises. He is representative of a small group of intelligent men who are difficult to classify except as Colorado men of letters. Among the most distinguished members of this group are two presidents of the University of Colorado, James Hutchins Baker (1848-1925) and George Norlin. President Baker's essays and addresses on various educational subjects have been gathered into a series of volumes: *Education and Life* (1900), *American Problems* (1907), *Educational Aims and Civic Needs* (1913), *American University Progress and College Reform* (1916), *After the War—What?* (1918), *Of Himself and Other Things* (1922). Most of President Norlin's publications have been in the field of classical scholarship, but his recent book, *Integrity in Education and Other Papers* (Macmillan, 1926), is an example of "humane letters" in the most liberal sense of that phrase. It applies to problems of modern life a truly Hellenic clarity of vision and expression. Eugene Parsons, who is still living and working, has been a man of multifarious activities and especially serviceable to the cause of literature in Colorado. No one can write on the subject without being heavily indebted to him. It is impossible to enumerate all the contributions which he has made to various magazines, but it is imperative here to mention his series of articles on "Colorado Poets and Poetry" in *The Trail* (1921-22), and three of his books, *The Making of Colorado* (1908), *A Guidebook to Colorado* (1911), and *The History of Colorado* (1920). Chauncey Thomas, editor of *Outdoor Life* and of *The Trail*, who has been connected in times past with several other magazines and newspapers, is a native Coloradoan, having been born in Denver in 1872. His widely scattered contributions deal with sport, outdoor life, and frontier history.

It is evident that we have passed in the last paragraph from the field of fiction to that of miscellaneous prose. Owing to the fact that the latter, save for travel narratives already dealt with, is devoted largely to scientific and historical subject-matter, most of it falls outside the scope of this article. Some few examples, however, are primarily of literary interest. A readable and unusual autobiography is that of Joseph Ray Buchanan, published under the title of *The Story of a Labor Agitator* (New York, Outlook Co., 1903). The author was in Colorado in 1878-87, first as a printer, afterwards as editor of the *Denver Labor Inquirer;* the latter part of his career belonged to Chicago. He recounts the history from the inside of various strikes and labor troubles in a personal and rather graphic fashion. Even more unusual is the *Life of Tom Horn, Government Scout and Interpreter, Written by Himself* (Denver, 1904). Tom Horn was hanged for murder in the Wyoming Rustler War in 1903 and is buried in Boulder. In the book, which was written while the author was under sentence of death, he claims to be completely innocent. It is a human document of rare interest, written in a straightforward, unpretentious, and thoroughly adequate style.

Charles Lee Bryson's *Tan and Teckle* (Revell, 1908) and *Woodsy Neighbors of Tan and Teckle* (Revell, 1911) are literary presentations of nature-study for children. But, of course, the great exponent of nature-study in Colorado literature is Enos Mills (1870-1922). Though not a Coloradoan by birth, his entire manhood was identified with the state and especially with Long's Peak and Estes Park, in the neighborhood of which he made his home. He may well be called the founder of the Rocky Mountain National Park, for to him is due the inception of the campaign for its establishment, eventually successful in 1915. His literary work began with contributions to various magazines and culminated in a series of books of great interest and popularity: *Wild Life in the Rockies* (1909), *The Spell of the Rockies* (1911), *In Beaver World* (1913), *The Rocky Mountain Wonderland* (1915), *The Adventures of a Nature Guide* (1920), and *Waiting in the Wilderness* (1921). All these are based on the first-hand experiences of the author, a close observer in intimate contact with nature. They are less scientific than the essays of John Burroughs and John Muir, but their literary appeal is of a similar character. Of all recent Colorado authors, Mr. Mills' name is perhaps the most widely known.

Of earlier literary residents of Colorado, the most famous are probably Eugene Field and Helen Hunt Jackson. Neither one was so fundamentally a Coloradoan as Mr. Mills. Eugene Field, in fact, spent only about two years in the state. He came to Denver from Missouri in 1880, when just past thirty, as managing editor of the *Denver Tribune* at the munificent salary of forty dollars a week. In addition to directing the staff of the paper, he wrote dramatic and musical criticisms, and numerous verses and paragraphs under such headings as the "Nonpareil Column" and "Odd Gossip" or "Odds and Ends." He seems to have been the original newspaper columnist. His most famous contribution to the *Denver Tribune* was the so-called *Tribune Primer*, a series of alleged primer lessons, collected and published separately under that title; this was Field's first book and is now rare and valuable. Among his poems which appeared originally in the *Tribune*, the best is probably "The Wanderer" (June 22, 1883):

> Upon a mountain's height, far from the sea,
>   I found a shell,
> And to my curious ear this lonely thing
> Ever a song of ocean seemed to sing—
>   Ever a tale of ocean seemed to tell.
>
> How came this shell upon the mountain height?
>   Ah, who can say
> Whether there dropped by some too careless hand—
> Whether there cast when oceans swept the land
>   Ere the Eternal had ordained the Day.
>
> Strange, was it not? Far from its native sea,
>   One song it sang—
> Sang of the mighty mysteries of the tide—
> Sang of the awful, vast profound and wide—
>   Softly with echoes of the ocean rang.
>
> And, as the shell upon the mountain's height
>   Sings of the sea,
> So do I ever, leagues and leagues away—
> So do I ever, wandering where I may,
>   Sing, O my home—sing, O my home, of thee.

Field, whose hoaxes and practical jokes were famous in his day, attributed these verses to the pen of Helena Modjeska, the Polish actress and exile, whom he much admired, and it was long before she succeeded in convincing the public that she was not their author. In *A Little Book of Western Verse* (1889) appear a number of Field's poems inspired by life in the "Blue Horizon Camp," which has been identified with Gold Hill. The best-known of these is "Casey's Table d'Hôte," celebrating the old hotel in that village, now transformed into the Blue Bird Lodge. In 1883, Eugene Field left Denver for Chicago, where he spent the rest of his life.

    Helen Hunt Jackson's maiden name was Helen Maria Fiske. She was born in Amherst, Massachusetts, in 1831. Before she came to Colorado as a health-seeker in 1873, she had already published a volume of verse, and the first series of *Bits of Travel*, which deals with European countries. In 1875 she married her second husband, William B. Jackson, in Colorado Springs, where she made her home for the rest of her life. Her second series of *Bits of Travel* has already been mentioned as containing some delightful descriptive sketches of Colorado; one of the most interesting and attractive is "The Procession of Flowers in Colorado." Among her books of fiction, only two have a Colorado setting: *Nellie's Silver Mine* (Roberts, 1878) and *Zeph* (Roberts, 1885), a posthumously published story, which she left unfinished, with the conclusion in outline. Her most famous novel, *Ramona* (Roberts, 1884), has its scene in southern California, where she spent a good deal of time during the latter part of her life and where she died in 1885. Of her poems, first published in complete form after her death (Roberts, 1886), a number were inspired by Colorado scenes and experiences. The most famous is "Cheyenne Mountain," a sonnet to the peak on which she was afterwards buried.

> By easy slope to west as if it had
>   No thought, when first its soaring was begun,
>   Except to look devoutly to the sun,
> It rises and has risen, until glad,
> With light as with a garment it is clad,
>   Each dawn, before the tardy plains have won
>   One ray; and after day has long been done
> For us, the light doth cling reluctant, sad
>   To leave its brow. Beloved mountain, I
>   Thy worshipper, as thou the sun's, each morn
>   My dawn, before the dawn, receive from thee;
>   And think, as thy rose-tinted peak I see,
>   That thou wert great when Homer was not born,
>   And ere thou change all human songs shall die!

Both Eugene Field and Helen Hunt Jackson, in spite of the importance of their prose, are commonly classified as poets. Colorado poetry has received considerably more attention than any other phase of Colorado literature. In a preceding paragraph of this article reference was made to Eugene Parsons's discussion of "Colorado Poets and Poetry" in *The Trail*. Even more complete is the information given in *Evenings with Colorado Poets*, edited by Francis S. Kinder and F. Clarence Spencer. The first edition was published in Denver in 1894 and contains selections representing forty-six authors; the third edition (1926) omits twenty-four of these and adds forty new names belonging to the period since 1900.

Very refreshing is the improvement in quality manifested by the more recent poetry. In addition to the poems themselves, each book gives biographical sketches of the poets included. Since this information is so detailed and so easily accessible, it would hardly be worth while to repeat all or any considerable part of it here. No effort, therefore, will be made in this article to cover comprehensively the field of Colorado poetry. Certain omissions in the previous surveys of the field will be filled in. Otherwise, the treatment will be very informal, stressing particularly interesting subject-matter and dealing briefly with a few of the outstanding figures among the poets. Whether or not an individual author is represented in the following discussion depends, not so much on the relative excellence of his work, as on the nature of the subjects that he has treated.

In dealing with poetry produced in Colorado about the Cliff-Dwellers, the Indians, and the pioneers, mention has already been made of the names of Steuart M. Emery, Thomas Nelson Haskell, Elijah Clarence Hills, Richard E. Leach, Clarence L. Lower, Robert McIntyre, Ellis Parker Meredith, Margaret Clyde Robertson, Sara R. Schlesinger, Lillian White Spencer, C. T. Turner, Alva Van Riper, Harriet Louisa Wason, and Edward A. Willoughby; quotations have been given from James Barton Adams, Alfred Butters, Thomas Hornsby Ferril, Jean Milne Gower, Lawrence N. Greenleaf, Marion Muir Richardson, and Stanley Wood.

Closely allied to the Indian and the pioneer as subjects for poetry are the miners and the cowboy. The miner, except in connection with real pioneer poetry, has been somewhat neglected, save for Arthur Chapman's poem, "The Dead Prospector" (*Out Where the West Begins*, Houghton, Mifflin, 1917, p. 6). The cowboy is well represented. Arthur G. Clark's *Poems by a Cowboy* (Denver, 1901) were produced by a young man under twenty; they are surprisingly free from local color. Not so John M. Kuykendall's "Veteran Cowboy's Ruminations" (*The Trail*, Jan., 1910), the second stanza of which is typical:

> Didn't have no dandy riders with their fancy-bosom shirts,
> Didn't have no love-knot ribbons tied by girls upon our quirts,
> Didn't pack no looking-glasses in our saddle bags, to see
> If the wind an' our complexion seemed inclined fur to agree.
> Didn't wear no chaparejos trimmed with fringes an' with beads
> Fur to keep our tailor breeches from the brushes an' the weeds,
> An' you bet you never saw us, it's as true as preachin', boss,
> With a hundred dollar saddle on a twenty dollar hoss.

"Cowboy Love Lyrics—Outclassed," by Robert V. Carr (*The Trail*, Sept., 1912) and "The Cowboy's Valentine" by Addie Cropsey Hudson (*The Land Where the Coyboy Grows*, 1915, p. 10) picture the cowboy in love. Mrs. Hudson's poem, though not very Western in flavor, is charming:

> Can cowboy's love compete with those
> Who write so grandly? Ah, who knows!
> Is love to great men more divine
> Than love that stirs this heart of mine?
> The circles of the lariat
> Frame pictures of a face, and yet
> A rope of pearls were far more fit
> To frame the face I see in it.
> A name goes rippling through my mind
> With love, I love, entwined, combined;
> Ah, would that I owned many herds
> Of golden-edged and learnéd words,
> And then, one-thousandth part I'd tell
> Of love that in my heart doth dwell.

In "The Longhorns," a poem originally published in the *Denver Post* (copied in *The Trail*, Aug., 1911), Walter Juan Davis laments the passing of "the cussed critters" that gave "us old-timers" so much trouble "in the days of long ago." A similar lament is given a more literary expression in Arthur Chapman's "Cow-Puncher's Elegy" (*Out Where the West Begins*, pp. 17, 18):

> Where have gone those trails historic, where the
>   herders sought the mart?
>   Where have gone the saucy cow-towns, where the
>   gunman played his part?
> Where has gone the Cattle Kingdom, with its armed,
>   heroic strife?
>   Each has vanished like a bubble that has lived
>   its little life.
>   Oh, the spurs we set a-jingling
>   And the blood that went a-tingling
> When we rode forth in the morning, chaps-clad
>   knights in cavalcade;
>   And the mem'ries that come trooping,
>   And the spirits, sad and drooping,
> When the cowman looks about him at the havoc time
>   has made.

This theme of the passing of the old-time West recurs again and again in Colorado poetry. The second stanza of A. J. Fynn's "Land where the Columbines Grow," adopted by the legislature in 1915 as the State Song, presents a different phase of the same idea:

> The bison is gone from the upland,
> > The deer from the cañon has fled,
> The home of the wolf is deserted,
> > The antelope moans for his dead,
> The war-whoop re-echoes no longer,
> > The Indian's only a name,
> And the nymphs of the grove in their
> > loneliness rove,
> But the columbine blooms just the same.

"The Land where the Columbines Grow" is, of course, Colorado. The poem is not by any means the only one inspired by the state itself, nor is it the only claimant to the title of "State Song." Maude McFerran Price's "Colorado" and Clem Yore's "Colorado" are both regarded by some authorities as officially entitled to that name. The earliest poem called "Colorado" is probably that by Ned Farrell, printed in 1868 in his very prosaic and practical handbook, *Colorado: The Rocky Mountain Gem*. It begins,

> All hail to Colorado!
> That Rocky Mountain gem!
> That glistens on the summit
> Of Columbia's diadem.

Numerous similar poems, though many of them are better as poetry, have been produced since: among them may be mentioned those by James Arthur Edgerton, John Girdler, Sophronia Maria Westcott Talbot, Hattie Horner Louthan, Anna Pritchard, J. Ernest Whitney, J. D. Dillenback, and Lillian White Spencer. Mrs. Virginia Donaghe McClurg's sonnet on "Colorado" catches well the spirit of the State:

> O "Colored Land"! beneath a turquoise sky,—
> > Sun-kissed from dazzling peaks to opal plains,
> > What pulses throb within thy silver veins!
> What forces strove in thee for mastery!
> The Manitou here dwelt in days gone by
> > In crystal springs, to cleanse all mortal stains;
> > Here the swart Spaniard strove for golden gains;
> Lone hunters saw thy virgin purity.
> Now plenty's garners gild the quiet fields,
> > And marts are swayed by olive-sceptered peace;
> To mighty multitudes her wealth she yields,
> > As shifting seasons pass and years increase;
> For fair "Columbia," bending toward the West,
> Now wears this crimson rose upon her breast.

"Out Where the West Begins," Arthur Chapman's famous poem, is, as everyone knows, primarily in celebration of Colorado, though it may be claimed that the locality "where the skies are a trifle bluer" includes more than one state. The poem gives title to what is undoubtedly the most popular book of poetry produced in Colorado. It is almost entirely devoted to subject-matter characteristic of the West. So is *Cactus Center* (Houghton, Mifflin, 1921), the author's second book of verse, which is largely in dialect.

Naturally a favorite theme of Colorado poets has been the magnificent scenery of the state. A collection of what might be called "scenery poems" was published in Chicago in 1898 under the title, *Rhymes of the Rockies;* the best of these is probably "Homes of the Cliff Dwellers" by Stanley Wood, already quoted, and another poem by the same author, "Cheyenne Canyon." A second collection, *The Pike's Peak Region in Song and Myth*, put together by Elijah Clarence Hills in 1913, illustrates the importance of that locality in the poetic history of the state. One of the principal contributors to this compilation, J. Ernest Whitney (1858-1893), resident for the last four years of his life in Colorado Springs, published in 1891 a book entitled *Pictures and Poems of the Pike's Peak Region*. Among these poems is a sonnet on "Pike's Peak":

> Lone, hoary monarch of the Titan peaks,
>   Offspring of heaven and earth in planet jars,
>   Bare-bodied savage, grim with unhealed scars,
> To thy wild band thy voice in thunder speaks;
> Thy sword-stroke is the avalanche that wreaks
>   Quick vengeance on thy kneeling victim. Wars
>   Come but to yield thee homage, and the stars
> Visit thee nightly, yet thy long gaze seeks
>   Unsatisfied the playmate of thy prime—
> O longing like to mine!—that goddess bright,
> The ocean stream. O deep embrace! that time
>   Forgets not, ere stern gods beyond thy sight
> Her dungeons sunk. Thy memory that! thy hope
> This ocean-seeking stream that cheers thy slope.

There are many other poems on Pike's Peak. One of them, Katherine Lee Chambers' "Prospective View from Pike's Peak," won the Western Eisteddfod Prize in 1897. Another, by an unknown "Western poet," quoted in Augustus Allen Hayes's *New Colorado and the Santa Fe Trail* (Harper's, 1880, p. 52), illustrates a flippant attitude almost unique among these "scenery poems";

I'm looking at your lofty head
  Away up in the air,
Eight thousand feet above the plain
  Where grows the prickly-pear.
A great big thing with ice on,
  You seem to be up there.

Away above the timber-line
  You lift your frosty head,
Where lightnings are engendered,
  And thunderstorms are bred;
But you'd be a bigger tract of land
  If you were thin out-spread.

Other Colorado poets besides Mr. Whitney have published books almost entirely devoted to "scenery poems." Among the most significant of these are *Songs of the Rockies* by Charles Edwin Hewes (1914), dealing with the Estes Park Region; *Wedding Bells, A Colorado Idyll*, by William E. Pabor (1900), comprised of a series of poems put together as the itinerary of a bridal journey; and *Mountain Idylls and Other Poems* by Alfred Castner King (Revell, 1901), the blind poet of Ouray. Harriet Louisa Wason (1839-1904), who came to the San Juan country in the gold-rush of 1873 and lived afterwards for many years at Del Norte, might have been included among the pioneer poets, except that her poetry has none of the pioneer flavor; her three books, *Letters from Colorado* (Boston, 1887), *Legend of the Grand Caverns at Manitou and Other Songs* (Denver, 1899), and *A Tale of the Santa Rita Mountains* (Denver, 1904), deal principally with scenery and legends. In this group of books should be mentioned, with special commendation, Jean Milne Gower's *Echoes from the Cliff Dwellings* already referred to and another collection of her scenery and nature poems, *Kaleidoscope, Little Pictures of Colorado* (Denver, 1923). An interesting collection might be made of poems about the rivers of the state, to include Dr. McKendree DeMotte's "Bride of the Silver San Juan," (Denver, 1912); Marion Muir Richardson's "Colorado River" (*Commonwealth*, Nov., 1889); William E. Pabor's haunting verses with the musical name, "Rio de las Animas Perdidas," originally published in the *Great Divide* (Kinder and Spencer, 1926, p. 42): A. J. Fynn's "Rio Grande River" (*The Trail*, Oct., 1924), and Lillian White Spencer's "Rio Grande del Norte" (Kinder and Spencer, 1926, p. 232). It is not often that a city can be celebrated in a "scenery poem," yet this is surely a proper title to apply to Martha Coleman Sherman's "Denver" (*The Trail*, Aug., 1915), which begins thus:

> In a hollow of the mountains, like a jewel in
> a ring;
> Under skies of deepest azure, where the mountain
> finches sing;
> Where the summer loves to linger, as a bird
> upon her nest;
> Filled with pride and joy is Denver—Queen of
> All the Golden West.

Perhaps, if one were to choose a single poem to interpret the inner significance, rather than merely to paint a picture, of Colorado scenery, one would choose Lillian White Spencer's sonnet, "Wild-cat Ledge," which won the Contemporary Verse Sonnet Prize in 1923:

> The Platte, long wandering but caught at last
> In old Missouri's arms, tells there a tale . . .
> The prairies hear: like seekers of a grail
> They hurry on the quest and, cleaving fast,
> Wide windy golden harvest seas are cast
> On green shores of Nebraska where the trail
> Is one with Kansas, and leads up to pale
> Virginity, inviolate and vast.
>
> They near and fling rich flowered robes away—
> In scant grass vesture pilgrim plains are torn
> And bruised yet stumble forward. Tiptoe, they,
> Unheeding spite of stone and thrust of thorn,
> Pause on a cliff and Colorado thrills
> With their exultant cry: "The hills! The hills!"

The plains, introduced as an exultant symbol in the sonnet just quoted, generally carry a more somber message to Colorado poets. Mary Sylvester Paden's "Dusk in the Desert" (Kinder and Spencer, 1926, p. 49), Marion Muir Richardson's "Eastern Plain" (*Border Memories*, 1903), and Pearl Riggs Crouch's "Thirst" (quoted, Kinder and Spencer, 1926, p. 11, from *Contemporary Verse*) are fairly cheerful; but Jean Milne Gower's "Dry Farms" (K. and S., p. 133) is pretty grim, and Mrs. Nellie Burget Miller's "Drought" (*In Earthen Bowls*, Appleton, 1924, p. 31) is poignant with tragedy:

> The sun drops red through a curtain of dust,
> White scars seam the alkali plain,
> No sound or motion—save over there
> A tumble-weed starts on its endless quest
> For God knows what—or where.
> The brown grass clings to the fields like rust,

> But deep in my heart is the sound of rain—
> The stealthy moccasined feet of the rain—
> Pat, pat on the sun-baked crust;
> Like dear remembered dreams of love
> In sleepless nights of pain.

Edith Colby Banfield (1870-1903), the niece of Helen Hunt Jackson, spent the last years of her short life in Colorado Springs. In her posthumously published volume, *The Place of My Desire* (1904), there are several poems appreciative of Colorado, but her best verses express the homesickness of

> a lover of New England ways,
> Of country roadsides and familiar flowers, ...
> The quiet East and all its wooded scenes.

"Sailor Blood" voices a vigorous protest against Colorado scenery:

> The mountains rise to a barren sky,
> And the level plains are parched and dry;
> Like a stagnant sea they mock my gaze
> With their limitless horizon haze;
> They have no breath, they mock at me,
> Whose soul cries out for the living sea.
>
> I am scourged of the dust that sweeps the plains,
> And the great dry winds that bring no rains;
> I am scourged of the dust, I am choked and blind,
> And the health of waters I can not find,
> And my sailor blood makes wild in me
> For the wet of the storm, and the salt of the sea!
>
> Child of the sea, how can I bear
> The wide still plains, and the desert air?
> Sands of the sea I hear by night
> In dreams that have not sound nor sight,
> And my heart doth yearn and strain by day
> For the throb two thousand miles away.

A very curious contrast and parallel to Miss Banfield's poem may be found in Dorothy Stott Shaw's "On the Fossil Ridge" (K. and S., p. 229, quoted from *American Poetry*); it may also be compared with Eugene Field's "Wanderer":

> I am hill-born and have not sailed the sea;
>   Only the granite crag and sandstone spire
> Out of the dawn and moonlight call to me—
>   Pearly, or tipped with fire.
> I am hill-born and have not sailed the sea;
>   Yet, in the sudden peace of early dark,
> I have seen ghosts sweeping in mystery
>   Over the mesa stark.

> Ghosts of green waves, endless and fathomless,
>   Hushing a drowning western world to sleep;
> And our one peak taking the cool caress—
>   An island in the deep.
> This sandstone slab, that sheer, sky-lifting crest
>   Sink to a slender reef of palm trees, where
> A grim sea monster takes his uncouth rest
>   Under a tropic air.
>
> I have heard mighty thunder on the rock
>   And the wet rage of water on the sand—
> Water that dipped no pink sail with its shock,
>   And brought no ships to land.
>
> I am hill-born and have not sailed the sea;
>   Only the crag and cliff have known me well;
> Here at my feet the sea has come to me—
>   I gather here a shell!

Nature in Colorado is not confined to what the guide-books call scenery, and poets of the state have found inspiration in those commoner aspects of the external world that have stimulated poetic activity elsewhere. There are many such nature poems in *Winter Dandelions* (Boston, 1924), an accomplished little volume of verse by Martha Coleman Sherman, whose "Denver" has been already referred to. Sam Brown, Jr., published in 1890 *May-Day Dreams*, etc., and in 1904 *Happy Days, Carolings of Colorado*, etc. He was born in Colorado near Littleton, in 1860, camped and prospected in the San Juan country, in the valleys of the Grand and the Gunnison, and elsewhere in the state. He finally settled down on the banks of the Platte. In spite of these facts, his poems show little or no local color. They deal with the ordinary features of nature, and are saved from conventionality only by an occasionally striking lyrical effect, illustrated by "Angling in the Platte" (*Happy Days*, p. 28):

> On a log beside the Platte,
> With my tackle and my basket,
> Sitting where I long have sat,
> I am fishing! Should you ask it?
>
> Idling,—dreaming time away!
> Thinking many happy thoughts to-day.
> Fleeting moments never heeding,
> While the hungry fishes feeding,
> Still I watch and still I wait;
> Let the minnows steal my bait!
> Mine—mine is the pleasure and repose—
> That the never-fretting, catch-forgetting,
>   gladness-netting angler only knows.

It is a far cry from such an idyllic scene to "The Snowstorm" (Kinder and Spencer, p. 112), as portrayed by Pearl Riggs Crouch, but both pictures are characteristic of Colorado:

> Across the plain the wind whines through the sage,
>   And boots the tumbleweeds with veering whim;
> The day is dimming through the merging mists
>   And huddled herds head south against the rim.
>
> On flurried wing the snowbirds, wheeling low,
>   In shrill, staccato chorus whir away;
> In vagrant gusts the snowflakes eddy by,
>   And closer swirls the circling wall of gray.
>
> Unleashed, the north wind swings his whistling whip—
>   The air is blinded by a whirling veil;
> And riding through the maelstrom, madly-free,
>   Exultant shriek the demons of the gale!

Other interesting nature poems in *Evenings with Colorado Poets* (1926) are Emma Playter Seabury's "Old Winter in Colorado," Delphine Harris Coy's "Lost Cabin," Mrs. McClurg's "Colorado Anemones," Mrs. Spencer's "Spring Song of Aspens," and Addie Cropsey Hudson's justly famous "Indian Pink."

A theme which has naturally attracted several Colorado poets is the timber-line tree in its struggle for life against heavy odds. Generally it is interpreted in terms of the conflict of the human soul, as in Mrs. Miller's "At Timberline" (*In Earthen Bowls*, p. 29), Surville J. DeLan's "Timber-Line" (*Crude Ore from the Rocky Mountains*, 1889), and Anna Spencer Twitchell's "To a Mountain Pine" (Kinder and Spencer, p. 247). Quite different is the conception of Joseph Henry Ayres in "The Cedar of the Timberline" (*Outdoor Life*, Feb., 1923), which concludes thus:

> Serene it stands until the very last,
>   Upon the snow-capped mountain peak sublime;
> It stands as landmark of receding past,
>   Defying storm—a sentinel of time!

Trees, very unlike those at timber-line, are connected with human life in a very dissimilar way by John Girdler, whose "Old, Old Trees" was originally published in *The Christian Nation:*

> In boyhood's days I loved the mellow earth
> Between my toes; wild berries on the hill;
> The call of birds; the madly sudden birth
> Of flowers in spring; a plunge in waters chill—
> All these I loved, but more than all of these
> I loved the evening voices of the trees.

> I used to wonder what an old man dreams
> Who sits and smiles and looks so far away,
> But now I know he splashes through the streams,
> Counts bird eggs, chases butterflies at play;
> But, better still, the quiet evening breeze
> Bring him God's message in the whispering trees.

As the preceding poems illustrate the wide range of possibilities in dealing with trees, so the following show how unlike may be the treatment of night effects in poetry. The first is by Howard V. Sutherland, and is called "Approaching Night" (*Out of the North*, FitzGerald, 1913):

> The lower'd skies are grey; the trees are bare.
>   A week ago they gleam'd in splendid rows
> Of gold and crimson; now in gaunt despair
>   They stand like gosts above new-fallen snows.
>
> The world seems even greyer than the skies.
>   'Twas yesterday the homeward-honking geese
> Fled as from death. They know too well what lies
>   Behind this sinister, foreboding peace!

It is an entirely different kind of night that is portrayed with exquisite subtlety in Jean Milne Gower's "Little Red Foxes" (*Echoes from the Cliff Dwellings*):

> Baying to the moon are the little red foxes,
> All silvered with moonbeams like powdered spruce.
> And up above, the owl hoots dismally—
> It seems so foolish to that wise one
> That little red foxes should bay to the moon.

From moonlight into darkness and from peaceful Colorado to war-shaken France we pass in Robert Donaldson's "Night Road" (*Turmoil*, Houghton, Mifflin, 1919):

> A pitch-black road, and rain;
> Mud underfoot;
> No lights;
> The crunch of wheels;
> The jangle of a chain;
> The noisy bumping of a camion train.
>
> Dim forms;
> The shuffling steps of men;
> The slush of mud;
> A vivid lightning flash,
> A rocket's flare,
> A shell's slow droning through the air.
>
> Black dank woods;
> An endless wagon line;
> A spurt of fire,
> A crash—then blackness;
> Endless rain;
> The noisy bumping of a camion train.

Robert Donaldson, the author of the preceding verses, is, without much question, Colorado's leading representative in the field of war poetry. He was born in Denver in 1896, attended the East Denver High School and Stanford University, and was in service in France from 1917 to 1919. His first volume, *En Repos and Elsewhere Over There* (Houghton, Mifflin, 1918), was published in collaboration with Lansing Warren, a Californian, whose contributions were mostly in a light tone. Mr. Donaldson's second volume, *Turmoil*, is altogether serious and shows considerable promise. Eugene Dimon Preston, another son of Colorado who served in France, died in 1926. A memorial volume published by American Legion Post Number Five of Colorado Springs contains a number of poems by him, including some very competent ones on war experiences which are reprinted in *Evenings with Colorado Poets*. L. C. McCollum's *Rhymes of a Lost Battalion Doughboy* (1921) would perhaps hardly claim to be real poetry.

In "The End of the Quest" (Kinder and Spencer, pp. 227, 228), Dorothy Stott Shaw welcomes back the young "Knights of Nowadays," who fought in the World War, and ends with:

> Welcome to the high hills and the wide, wide valleys,
> Welcome to the still nights when the sounds of
> triumph cease;
> Some found the Grail again,
> Some found only Faith again,
> But all brought home a guerdon—the deep cup
> of peace!
> And a long thought of Galahad,
> Galahad, Galahad,
> Galahad comes not again.
>
> He bore the Grail in clean young hands,
> He loved it with his clear young eyes,
> He followed it all shiningly
> Into Paradise!

Two Colorado Galahads who came not again were Charles N. Bliss of Boulder and Forbes Rickard, Jr., of Denver. Poems by the former are published in a volume called *The Cliff Dwellers* (Boulder, 1922). *Songs with Tears*, by Forbes Rickard, Jr. (Portland, Me., 1919) is a slender little book containing four short essays, some letters, and sixteen poems, only one of which, the "Class Poem," read at the commencement exercises of Bowdoin College in 1917, touches on a war theme. He was killed in action in July of the next year, aged twenty-two. Reading his "Class

Poem" one is filled with unutterable regret for such "inheritors of unfulfilled renown." It ends thus:

> Deep-brooding pines, beneath whose aging peace
> The sunlit faces flash, and turning go—
> Remember us, who take a swift release
> And in far lands defend the best we know.
> Deserted halls, that echoed to the sound
> Of these our voices seeking after truth—
> Forget the carelessness you often found;
> Remember still the strivings of our youth
> That mixes dreams with laughter, songs with tears,
> Pure gold with dross, and never will confess
> The deepest of its loyalties and fears
> Till suddenly it renders all—no less.

Forbes Rickard, Jr. is not represented in *Evenings with Colorado Poets*. Several other Coloradoans who have published volumes of verses and are not included in this anthology deserve mention here. Probably the earliest such volume produced and printed within the state was T. O. Bigney's *Colorado Tales and Legends of the Earlier Days* (Pueblo, 1875); the astonishing figure of speech with which the author begins his "Indian Legend of Middle Park" may give an idea of his quality as a poet:

> The thorax and the pelvic space
> Of the grand old Rocky range
> Are the vasty, ever-beauteous parks—
> Features fair and strange;
> Peculiar to this giant chain
> Which holds the continent's vast brain!

Thomas Brewer Peacock of Denver wrote the Columbian Prize Poem, "Columbian Ode," read at the Chicago World's Fair in 1893. He had previously published (Putnam's, 1889) *Poems of the Plains and Songs of the Solitudes, together with The Rhyme of the Border War*, the last-named being a long romantic narrative in the manner of Sir Walter Scott. Lyman H. Sproull, who wrote, according to his own statement "amid the life of a mining camp, ... in a little placer cabin which he calls home" at Cripple Creek, reflects very little of that life in his four books: *Lines by Lamplight*, *Hours at Home* (1895), *Camp and Cottage* (1896), and *Snowy Summits* (1898). Jean Hooper Page (1869-1912) was at one time a feature writer on the *Denver Post*; her book of verse, *Through Field and Fallow* (Neely, 1897), contains nothing characteristic of Western life. On the contrary, there is a good deal of local flavor in Bernard L. Rice's *View from Pike's Peak and Other*

Poems (Denver, 1898), Albert Fletcher Bridges' *Poems* (Colorado Springs, 1898), and Harry Ellard's *Ranch Tales of the Rockies* (Canon City, 1899). Meditative, didactic, and sentimental are most of the poems in Arthur W. Barnes's *Buttercups and Clover*, published under the pen-name of Arthur Ward (Denver, 1902), in Mary E. Steele's *Stray Bits of Song in Prose and Verse* (Philadelphia, 1902), and in Emma Tolman East's *Rhymes of an Idle Hour* (Denver, 1903). George Salmon Phelps (1847-1904) won first prize in a poetry competition conducted by *The Great Divide* in 1891 for a poem on "Pike's Peak." He also wrote "Palmer Lake," "The Royal Gorge," and "Mount of the Holy Cross." With an "Ode on McKinley" he won first place at the National Eisteddfod (Welsh poetic competition), Scranton, Pennsylvania, 1902. His *Cloud City Chimes* was published in Denver, 1903. Henry Pelham Holmes Bromwell (1823-1903) was a teacher, editor, lawyer, and Congressman, who spent the last thirty years of his long life in Colorado. His rather large poetic contribution consists entirely of booklets published in Denver after his death by his daughter: *The Song of the Wahbeek* (1909), *On Buena Vista's Field and Other Early Poems* (1918), *The Two Processions* (1918), *Translations* from poems by various German authors (1919), *Further Light and Other Poems* (1920). The last-named contains some tributes to Lincoln, whom he had known personally. The booklets taken together reveal a cultivated, but not strikingly original, mind. Two volumes of verse mainly religious in tone are *Jacob and Other Poems* (1907) by Caroline M. Butterfield and *Quatrains of Christ* (New York, 1907) by George Creel, widely known as a newspaper man. *Mountain Idylls* by Alfred Castner King, the blind poet of Ouray, has already been mentioned; a second volume of his, *The Passing of the Storm* (Revell, 1907), deals largely, like the first, with Colorado scenes. The same may be said of Lelah Palmer Morath's *At the Foot of Pike's Peak* (Colorado Springs, 1905), Lottie Schoolcraft Felter's *Landscapes and Waterscapes* (Canon City, 1908), George L. McDermott's *Mountain Breezes* (Denver, 1911), Leila Peabody's *Little Book of Verse* (Boston, 1912), Amanda Blocker Byrd's *Reveries of a Homesteader* (Denver, 1916), and Susie Kerin's *Poems of Sunny Colorado* (Denver, 1922). Mrs. Alice Carry Verner's *Handful of Autumn Leaves* (New York, 1911) is rather superior in quality to most of these volumes; the first and last stanzas of her "Lang Syne" are worth quoting:

> Long, long ago, when life was full of sweetness,
>   One radiant summer with no winter cold,
> When every day was happy to completeness,
>   It did not seem we ever could grow old;
>
>   *   *   *   *   *
>
> Then, time with slow and hesitating finger
>   Told off his rosary of days; now, fast,
> Like pearls from loosened cords, they will
>   not linger,
> But glide into the ocean of the past.

Two women writers who have contributed a good many poems to Denver newspapers are Almira Louisa Corey Frink (1836-1903) and Alice McHarg Ferril. The latter is the wife of William C. Ferril, editor of the *Rocky Mountain Herald*, and the mother of Thomas Hornsby Ferril. One of her most attractive lyrics, "Instead of a Peacock," appeared in the *Rocky Mountain Herald* in June, 1926; it consists of eight stanzas and begins thus:

> I used to long with all my heart
>   A peacock to possess,—
> To perch upon my latticed gate,
>   My garden wall to bless.
>
>   *   *   *   *   *
>
> O these were visions entertained
>   For half my life it seems,
> But Providence vouchsafed me not
>   The peacock of my dreams.
>
> But He has lately sent to me
>   A yellow-bird instead,
> Who knows there is a woodsy nook
>   Within my bracken bed.

An almost unique contribution to Colorado literature is to be found in the verse plays written for the Cactus Club of Denver by James Grafton Rogers and printed for them in 1920. The first, *The Fire of Romance*, produced September 6, 1919, is an effective evocation of spirits representing the past history of Colorado: Coronado, Fray Marcos, Pike, James, and George Jackson, the discoverer of gold. The second, *The Goldenrod Lode*, played in the outdoor theater of the club, September 4, 1920, presents the story of a miner, a crooked sheriff, a forest fire, and other features justifying its sub-title, *A Frontier Drama;* some of the effects in this play are singularly picturesque and poetic.

Poets represented in *Evenings with Colorado Poets* who have not been named in this article and who deserve special attention are Katherine Prescott Bemis, Emma Ghent Curtis, Charles Julian Downey, James Arthur Edgerton, Margaret Harvey, Heloise M. B. Hawkins, George Sanford Holmes, Elisabeth Kuskulis, Harry McGuire, Elizabeth Dimon Preston, and Milton S. Rose.

Mrs. Nellie Burget Miller and Howard Vigne Sutherland may be singled out for special mention for their literary versatility. Mrs. Miller is recognized as the poet-laureate of Colorado. In addition to her book of poems, *In Earthen Bowls* (Appleton, 1924), she has published *The Garden Year Book* (1916), *The Land Where the Good Dreams Grow, A Dance Fantasy* (Colorado Springs, 1921), *The Flame of God* (Dutton, 1924), a prose devotional work, and *The Living Drama* (Century Co., 1924), a very valuable book for students of drama.

Howard Vigne Sutherland, if he really belonged to the state, would require a good deal of space, but only seven of his fifty-eight years were spent in Colorado, where he sojourned in passing from South Africa *via* South America and the Klondike to California and Pennsylvania. He has tried his hand at prose tales, problem plays, Klondike ballads, lyrics of various sorts, and blank verse. To his Colorado period belong in prose, *The Promise of Life* (Rand, McNally, 1914), in rhyme *Out of the North* (FitzGerald, 1913) and *The Girl Beneath the Cherry-trees* (FitzGerald, 1914), in blank verse three series of *Idylls of Greece* (Sherman, French and Co., 1908; FitzGerald, 1910 and 1914), and *The Woman Who Could; a Play with a Purpose* (FitzGerald, 1911). The *Idylls of Greece* are serene, classical narratives in marble-like blank verse, exquisitely accomplished in the manner of Walter Savage Landor. "Prokris and Kephalos" in the First Series begins:

>A little love makes life endurable;
>Much love would make us gods. And knowing this
>I bide within the shadow with my harp
>And sing of love, and lovers who beheld
>Long years ago the beauties ye ignore
>The while ye seek, with strain'd and tired eyes,
>The Stairs of Silence, winding ever down.
>And though no more my notes may reach the skies

> Like his of old who charm'd the surging seas
> And made the thrushes listen, yet perhaps
> Men's hearts may gain some comfort from the strain
> And bless the singer though the stars be mute.
> I sing the Past, and singing am content
> If one look up.

Damon Runyon resembles Mr. Sutherland in his wandering propensities, though he did not start so far away or travel so widely. He is a native-born Coloradoan, who served in the Spanish-American War, did newspaper work in Denver, acted as press correspondent in Mexico, Germany, and France, and now lives in New York City. His verses, contributed to a great number of magazines, have been republished in two volumes, *The Tents of Trouble* (1911) and *Rhymes of the Firing Line*, by Desmond FitzGerald of New York. Many of them record his experiences in the Philippines. It has been well said that he belongs to "the school of Kipling and Service."

Thomas Hornsby Ferril, from whose work two passages have already been quoted, was born in Denver in 1896, was educated at the East High School in that city and at Colorado College, served in the war, and has since been engaged in newspaper work in Denver. Verses of his have appeared in many of the leading periodicals. In 1926 he was accorded first place in the annual competition of the Yale University Press for the *Yale Series of Younger Poets*, and his volume, *High Passage* (Yale University Press, 1927) is the result. The title poem is in celebration of the flight westward of the first bees, high above the rivers and the plains and the traveling emigrants.

Edna Davis Romig, who belongs to the faculty of the University of Colorado, is well represented in *Evenings with Colorado Poets* by eleven poems of superior quality, most of which were previously published in various magazines. "High Heart," which first appeared in *The Mesa*, was selected for Braithwaite's *Anthology of Magazine Verse for 1926*:

> High heart, high heart, I triumph in your laughter;
> No spirit prouder and none one-half so gay.
> I pause to mark your swift and fine adventure—
> No hero rides more gallantly away.
> High heart, high heart, you will keep your secret,
> No craven word of yours will ever tell:
> They needed not a bludgeon for your breaking;
> A finer blow had answered just as well.

The recent publication by Jamie Sexton Holme (Mrs. Peter Haynes Holme) of *Star Gatherer* (Harold Vinal, 1926) is an event of unusual importance in Colorado literary history. The author is a native of Mississippi, but a resident of Denver. Forty short poems make up the book, poems full of a singing music, technically competent, and displaying a rare imagination. The quaint and tender whimsicality of "Stay-At-Home" recurs in several other songs:

> If life should ever come to be
> At all a thing of certainty—
> If I had years and years to spend,
> Before the years seemed like to end—
>
> I'd visit Sicily and France,
> And all the countries of Romance,
> I'd have a castle in Touraine,
> And lie on sunny shores of Spain.
>
> If I had years to throw away,
> I'd see the temples of Cathay,
> And sail before a lazy breeze
> In yellow junks on China seas.
>
> I'd bow the knee at Hindu shrines,
> And warm myself with Eastern wines.
> I'd ride a camel in Algiers,
> If I had years and years and years!
>
> But since the years seem swift and few,
> I think that this is what I'll do—
> I'll have my own low roof above,
> To shelter me and those I love.
>
> I'll cling quite close to friendly hands,
> That are not found in foreign lands,
> And those with time to spare, may roam,
> But I shall be a stay-at-home.
>
> I shall have far enough to go. . . .
> It's not as if the years were slow!

Mrs. Holme's power to express poignant emotion with an arresting simplicity and concreteness is illustrated in "After":

> All is said and done now, our time of love is over—
> We have kissed and said farewell, you and I—
> But I cannot hear a lark sing in the clover,
> I cannot hear a meadow-lark, and keep my eyes dry.
>
> I will find a new love, the old one forsaking—
> I will shed no tears for what was so sweet—
> But I cannot keep my wilful heart from breaking
> When I see a young moon above a field of wheat.

Tragic seriousness and playfulness are very close together and inimitably expressed in "Joy":

> Joy is but a tight-rope
> You may walk upon.
> Out of mist and cobwebs
> All its strands are spun.
>
> Balance back and forward,
> Run a step or two.
> Sway in time to music
> Any tune will do!
>
> Never look behind you
> Till the rope is crossed.
> Never look before you,
> Else you may be lost.
>
> Never look beneath you,
> Lest a step you miss.
> Joy is but a tight-rope
> Over an abyss!

There are not many poets of the state who can be classed with Mrs. Holme. One, who may challenge comparison with her, is not included in *Evenings with Colorado Poets*.* Lucile DuPré, who lived during the latter part of her life in Denver, was a gifted violinist, whose career was thwarted by disease. After her death, *The Poems of Lucile DuPré* (Boston, 1923) were published with an appreciative introduction by Katherine Lee Bates. The poems had not been prepared for publication by their author, and some few of them show slight crudities, which might easily have been removed by revision. On the whole, however, they are real poetry, mystical, musical, and intense. So little known is this rare poet even among Coloradoans and so many are her eminently quotable verses, that it is difficult to choose those most worthy of reproduction here. "Rhymes," unquestionably one of her happiest inspirations, is lighter in tone than most of them:

> Ho, dancing Rhymes in airy dress
> Of fancy's flying phantasies,
> How many times your fleeting chimes
> Ring out to fling us happiness!
>
> Bright elves astride these whirling words,
> Ye ride gay-bridled humming birds
> With double wings—a sweet surprise—
> Or are your steeds twin butterflies?

---

* The omission is due to the fact that the editors could not secure from the owner of the copyright permission to reprint Miss DuPré's poems.

> Float by! We neither know your name,
> Nor why you go nor whence you came,
> Yet some of you are caught—unwise
> Sky visitors, shy butterflies!

More typical is the sustained, spiritual intensity and magnificent phrasing of her "Sonnet on Courage":

> As when against the ocean's wrath one rows
> Singing through gulfs of death, so valiantly
> Each one's deific will from chaos grows
> To strength immortal, ruling sea and sky.
> Little he reaps who in the sea-field sows;
> We will sow thoughts as stars, flinging them high,
> Death disregarding; God within each knows
> The harvest-time of peace and victory;
> Failure and triumph, life and death proclaim
> This faith divine—We sons of God aspire
> Freely to keep inviolate His flame—
> This moaning ocean shall be Hermes' Lyre!
> Shepherd of stars and men we chant thy name
> Among a myriad swinging worlds of fire.

On such a note of beauty we may well end our survey of poetry produced in Colorado and by Coloradoans. To attempt to treat adequately or even to catalogue poems inspired by Colorado scenes in men and women who have no connection with the state would be too long and arduous a task to enter upon here. Two examples only will be given: Katherine Lee Bates's well-known hymn, *America the Beautiful*, "came singing into the mind of this passionate patriot in the summer of 1893, as she stood on Pike's Peak, surrounded by 'purple mountain mysteries,' with the 'spacious skies' overhead, and the 'fruited plain' at her feet" (Marion Pelton Guild in *The Chautauquan*, January, 1912); and Walt Whitman's "Spirit that Form'd this Scene" was written in Platte Cañon. It seems in its way to sum up, if not the effect of Colorado literature, at least its hope, its intention, its underlying idea:

> Spirit that form'd this scene,
> These tumbled rock-piles grim and red,
> These reckless heaven-ambitious peaks,
> These gorges, turbulent-clear streams, this
>   naked freshness,
> These formless wild arrays, for reasons of
>   their own,
> I know thee, savage spirit—we have
>   communed together,
> Mine too such wild arrays, for reasons of
>   their own;

Was't charged against my chants they had
    forgotten art?
To fuse within themselves its rules precise
    and delicatesse?
The lyrist's measured beat, the wrought-out
    temple's grace—column and polish'd arch forgot?
But thou that revelest here—spirit that form'd
    this scene,
They have remembered thee.